Daily Wisdom
for Women

2016 Devotional Collection

© 2015 by Barbour Publishing, Inc.

Print ISBNs 978-1-63409-314-9, 978-1-63409-705-5

eBook Editions:
Adobe Digital Edition (.epub) 978-1-63409-611-9
Kindle and MobiPocket Edition (.prc) 978-1-63409-612-6

Published by Barbour Books, an imprint of Barbour Publishing, Inc., P.O. Box 719, Uhrichsville, Ohio 44683, www.barbourbooks.com.

Our mission is to publish and distribute inspirational products offering exceptional value and biblical encouragement to the masses.

 Member of the
Evangelical Christian
Publishers Association

Printed in China.

Daily Wisdom
for Women

2016 Devotional Collection

BARBOUR BOOKS
An Imprint of Barbour Publishing, Inc.

A NEW BEGINNING

*In the beginning God created the heavens and the earth. The earth
was without form, and void; and darkness was on the face of the deep.
And the Spirit of God was hovering over the face of the waters.*
GENESIS 1:1–2 NKJV

Every year in January, many people make resolutions hoping to achieve
new milestones in their lives. There's nothing wrong with this practice,
but too many of us attempt to start over fresh while still carrying last
year's baggage. If we harbor resentment and attitudes from past failures
and unrealized goals, we are in for more disappointment.

Before God created the earth, it didn't have shape or life to it. He
started out with a dark, formless place. As His Spirit hovered over the
waters, He created a planet full of life and substance. When He finished,
a beautiful creation hung in the universe. Now it could be inhabited by
life and bring glory to God.

As we begin a new year, God's Spirit, who dwells within us, can
start with a blank page and create a new environment. If we allow Him
to take charge, He can bring new energy and sparkle to the coming
months. With God's help, let's lay aside all the disappointments, pain,
and misgivings of the past year and start over fresh. Let Him set the
goals that will bring glory to Him through the life we live in this new
year.

*Father, create in us a new beginning. Help us to forget the failures
of the past and allow You to write a new resolution for our lives.*

SPEAK WORDS OF LIFE

The tongue can bring death or life;
those who love to talk will reap the consequences.
PROVERBS 18:21 NLT

During a conversation with her mom, Laura expressed her frustration with appointments and doctors. The irritation she felt could be heard in the words she spoke. Instead of dropping the matter, she continued grumbling and complaining.

As she prepared dinner that evening, Laura thought about what she had said and realized she had complained and grumbled for no reason. She realized her words might cause her mom some anxious moments and have a negative effect on her decisions. Laura regretted her hastily spoken words and critical attitude. She had grumbled when she should have let the situation pass. She called her mom and apologized. Her mom didn't seem to be upset about their conversation, but Laura's earlier words could not be changed.

Words are powerful and once spoken can never be erased. The words we speak affect other people for either good or bad and, according to the writer of Proverbs, can bring death or life. The apostle James tells us in his writings that the tongue can start a big fire if we aren't careful. If we're one of those people who loves to talk and we allow ourselves to criticize or complain, we will reap unpleasant consequences. We should strive to speak life-giving words to those around us.

Father, use my tongue to speak words of
life to others and bring glory to Your name.

A New Heart

"I will give you a new heart and put a new spirit within you;
I will take the heart of stone out of your flesh and give you a heart
of flesh. I will put My Spirit within you and cause you to walk in
My statutes, and you will keep My judgments and do them."
Ezekiel 36:26–27 nkjv

Sue accompanied her husband, Bill, to a follow-up appointment with the cardiologist following a heart procedure a few months earlier. The nurse checked his blood pressure and took an EKG; then the doctor came in for a visit. After talking with them for a few minutes, he said, "Everything looks great, perfect in fact. It doesn't mean the AFib won't come back, but let's continue with the medication you're taking. It's good for your heart and will help protect you." They left the doctor's office feeling good about Bill's condition.

Before we met Christ, each of us had serious heart problems. In short, we needed a heart transplant. Our hearts were sinful, self-centered, and full of carnal desires. God saw our need and provided the necessary operation. He promised us a new heart and a new spirit. He removed the heart of stone and gave us a heart of flesh, one that would respond to His touch. He placed His Spirit within us to teach us to follow His statutes. As we do, He will give us the good report we need to hear from the Great Physician who performed the surgery.

Father, give me a heart of flesh touched by
Your Spirit and receptive to Your voice.

God Makes Us Beautiful

For the LORD takes pleasure in his people;
he will beautify the humble with salvation.
PSALM 149:4 NKJV

Standing in front of a magazine rack can be depressing if you believe everything on the covers. Women in skimpy clothes with long, flowing locks and perfect figures adorn most magazines. The article titles are just as daunting: "How to Have the Body of Your Dreams in 30 Days," "What Men Really Want in a Woman," and "Lose 10 Pounds in a Week." Their information on how to be beautiful and be the perfect woman tempts a lot of women into buying the latest issue, thinking it will solve their problems.

The world's definition of beauty is a far cry from God's. We were created in His image; made in His likeness. There's nothing wrong with trying to lose weight, buying a new dress, or getting our hair cut. We all want to look and feel our best—but not by the world's standard. Trying to measure up to others leads to disappointment and low self-esteem.

As God's children, we are made beautiful through Him. It's not a physical beauty like the world lauds. It's an inner loveliness that comes through knowing Christ. We take on a beauty the world can't understand or achieve. To those who know us and love us, we are beautiful women because of God's Spirit within us, radiating a beauty beyond human imagination.

Lord, give me an inner beauty through Your
Spirit that I might bring You glory and honor. Amen.

Making Good Decisions

*Trust in the Lord with all your heart, and lean not on
your own understanding; in all your ways acknowledge
Him, and He shall direct your paths. Do not be wise in
your own eyes; fear the Lord and depart from evil.*
Proverbs 3:5–7 NKJV

Everyone goes through tough times, and having to make important decisions during those dark days only adds to the pain and frustration. Marilyn wanted to do the right thing in regard to a failing relationship, but she worried she would make a mistake she'd regret. She went to an older Christian friend for advice. He listened and talked with her, but in the end, he said, "You need to make a decision, but only you can do it. No one can make it for you."

Marilyn knew her friend was right. She began praying earnestly about the situation, relying on God for wisdom and courage. Some days were still hard and she didn't know which direction to take, but she continued to trust God and wait for His help. When the resolution came, Marilyn knew God had intervened and worked things out for the best.

When we learn to trust the Lord and not our own limited understanding, He will direct our paths. The secret is to trust Him with all our hearts and acknowledge Him. God is personal for each of us. He wants to be included in our decisions and our daily lives. No matter what we face, He knows how to resolve it. Whatever you need, trust Him.

*Father, give me Your wisdom and understanding.
Help me rely on You and not myself.*

KNOWING WHAT TO SAY

*"The Lord GOD has given Me the tongue of the learned,
that I should know how to speak a word in season to
him who is weary. He awakens Me morning by
morning, He awakens My ear to hear as the learned."*
ISAIAH 50:4 NKJV

Sometimes it's hard to know what to say to a friend or loved one when tragedy strikes their family. We all know the usual trite lines like "Everything will turn out for the best," or "I'm sorry for your loss." Even though these aren't bad words, they do little to comfort someone in pain.

We are limited in our ability to comfort. We can sympathize with others, but unless we have experienced what they are going through, we cannot feel the depth of their pain or how it is affecting them. It's in these times that we need God's Spirit to help us be a comforter.

Isaiah writes that the Lord gave him a tongue so he would know how to speak the right word to someone who was weary. We can apply this scripture to our own lives and ask God to give us the right word to speak to the one needing comfort. If we allow Him, God will awaken our ears to hear His voice every day. Then we can speak God's words and bring a measure of comfort to a hurting individual. When we give His word to someone, it will be the right one.

*Lord, open my ears to hear Your message of
hope and speak it to someone in need.*

GOD HAS A PLAN

"For I know the plans I have for you,"
declares the LORD, "plans to prosper you and not to
harm you, plans to give you hope and a future."
JEREMIAH 29:11 NIV

Bill and Sue decided to sell their home and move to a smaller city. They agreed they would not get in a hurry. They wanted God's will for their future home. Sue prayed about the things she wanted in their new home—an older house with wood floors and moldings, room to create a home office, and space for her book collection.

They met with a real estate agent, but neither Sue nor Bill felt God leading them to buy any of the properties they viewed. Two years passed as they continued watching the market for a house. They hoped for a quick sale of their home, but no one showed any interest for months; then a young couple made an offer. Around the same time, Bill and Sue found two houses they liked, but after an inspection learned the first one had too many problems. They made an offer on their second choice. After they closed and moved in, Sue was walking through the home one day when she stopped in the middle of a room and looked around. Everything she had asked God for was in the home they had purchased. Peace settled over her as she realized God had known the location of the right house and when it would become available and had directed them according to His plan.

Father, help me realize You always have a
plan for me and it will be for my best.

Get Up and Try Again

But may the God of all grace, who called us to His
eternal glory by Christ Jesus, after you have suffered a
while, perfect, establish, strengthen, and settle you.
1 Peter 5:10 NKJV

Have you ever fallen down in your Christian walk? It doesn't mean you are no longer a Christian, but you stumbled over something in your path that caused you to lose your footing. Perhaps you didn't see the obstacle in time. It's painful to fall, and sometimes it's hard to get up and continue on. While you're lying on the ground spiritually, Satan uses this opportunity to taunt you and accuse you. "You're not really a Christian. If you were, you wouldn't have fallen. You wouldn't have made a mistake. God doesn't need people like you. He's tired of fooling with you. Why don't you just give up?"

Sound familiar? Not only does it sound familiar, but if you're not careful, you will begin to believe it. The shame and remorse you feel because of your shortcomings only add to the lie Satan has just whispered in your ear. Don't listen to any more of his lies. God is a God of grace. The key is to stand up from the place where you have fallen and allow God to restore you, strengthen you, and establish you. He is faithful to His people.

Lord, forgive my shortcomings and extend grace once more
to Your servant. Give me strength to continue the race.

HOLD YOUR TEMPER

A hot-tempered person stirs up conflict,
but the one who is patient calms a quarrel.
PROVERBS 15:18 NIV

For the third time in a week, Jane called her Internet provider hoping for a solution to her problem. Internet service had been sporadic for several days and she hoped to reach someone who could give her some answers.

The person on the other end of the line sounded young and inexperienced, but Jane decided to give her a chance. As they discussed the problem, the technician tried several ideas to get the service working again, but to no avail. She finally offered a solution that would require Jane to pay a fee of one hundred fifty dollars. Jane felt angry the company would require a large fee in light of the fact she was already paying a monthly fee and not receiving good service. The longer they talked, the more stressed and upset she became. In spite of the frustration she voiced to the other person, the girl remained polite and helpful.

Jane felt like giving the service technician a piece of her mind, but knew it wouldn't solve anything. With God's help, she remained calm in spite of the stress she felt. They ended the call by wishing each other a good day despite the failure to resolve the situation. Even though Jane still didn't have an answer to her problem, she was glad she had not spoken in haste and made the situation worse.

Lord, keep me calm in the face of anger and trouble.
Help me not to quarrel even when I feel justified in doing so.

Dressed to the Nines

*Put on all of God's armor so that you will be
able to stand firm against all strategies of the devil.*
Ephesians 6:11 nlt

Have you ever left your house feeling as though you had forgotten
something and weren't completely ready to face the world? Maybe you
left home without putting on the belt that matches the dress you're
wearing or traveled to an out-of-town conference without the proper
shoes. It may have been something as simple as forgetting to put on
your watch or lipstick. Whatever the case may be, you feel underdressed
and incomplete because of the missing item. You feel as if everyone is
looking at you, which makes you feel self-conscious and keeps you from
being your best on those days.

Paul wrote to the Ephesians, and to us, that it's important to put
on the whole armor of God. This is our spiritual wardrobe. He lists the
various pieces we should wear every day in order to stand against the
devil and his tricks. We cannot afford to forget even one item. Why?
Because the missing piece makes us vulnerable in that area. The enemy
knows to attack us there. Each day, we must equip ourselves with
the armor God has given us, from the breastplate of righteousness to
the sword of the Spirit. Before you start your day, be sure you're fully
dressed. Don't allow the devil to keep you from feeling confident and
being at your best for God.

*Lord, help me to realize the importance of wearing the armor
You have provided and to never leave home without it.*

COMING OF AGE

*Brothers and sisters, I could not address you as
people who live by the Spirit but as people who
are still worldly—mere infants in Christ.*
1 CORINTHIANS 3:1 NIV

In Japan, the second Monday of January is known as Coming of Age Day. Special ceremonies are held in honor of those reaching a certain age. These ceremonies recognize both the expanded rights and increased responsibilities of new adults. All young adults who turned or will turn twenty between April 2 of the previous year and April 1 of the current year and who maintain a residence in the area are invited to attend.

As Christians, we don't have a "coming of age" ceremony or celebration, but there comes a time in our lives when we need to accept the responsibility of a mature Christian no matter what our age. Paul told the church in Corinth he couldn't address them as people who lived by the Spirit because they had not taken on this maturity. He had to treat them as infants, feeding them milk to sustain them. An infant doesn't have any responsibilities; she's dependent on others to take care of her. As we grow in Christ, we need to accept responsibility for ourselves and begin to come of age no matter how old we are so that we can become a viable part of the kingdom of God.

*Lord, help me to grow up in You, to come of age
and be a mature Christian who brings glory to Your name.*

Let God Fight for You

*"O our God, will You not judge them? For we have no power
against this great multitude that is coming against us;
nor do we know what to do, but our eyes are upon You."*
2 Chronicles 20:12 nkjv

Sue was called as a witness in a robbery. Never having been involved in anything of this nature, she felt fearful of what might happen when she saw the young man who had robbed her. He was only fifteen, but he had an adult accomplice who had recently been released from prison. Would the perpetrator recognize her, and would he or his accomplice take revenge on her for testifying against him? She wanted to be brave, but fear threatened to paralyze her. She knew her strength came from God and prayed for His help.

When she was sworn in, Sue took her place on the witness stand. The adult was being tried for his part in the crime, but the juvenile needed to be identified. The judge turned to Sue and said, "We're going to bring in a young man. If he's the one who robbed you, all you have to do is shake your head yes or no." When it was over, she felt great relief and knew God had been with her in the courtroom that day.

No matter who or what we face in life, God will be with us. He supplies the power and strength we don't have. If we allow Him to fight for us, we will have victory.

*Father, help us to keep our eyes on You,
knowing the battle is Yours.*

MAKING IT TO THE TOP

*I once thought these things were valuable, but now I consider
them worthless because of what Christ has done. . . . I press on
to reach the end of the race and receive the heavenly prize
for which God, through Christ Jesus, is calling us.*
PHILIPPIANS 3:7, 14 NLT

The world believes who you know can take you far in life. You need the
right contacts with clout to make it to the top. You need to run with the
right crowd to be successful. You may even be expected to do unethical
or immoral things to move up in the company. Women are sometimes
asked to have affairs with their superiors. You may be asked to lie for
your boss, dress a certain way, or flirt with potential customers. This
lifestyle is degrading and results in unhappiness and tragedy for many.

God's Word teaches a different example. Knowing Christ is the best
decision we can make as we go through life. He will never ask us to do
anything immoral but will give us a pure heart and teach us to respect
ourselves and others. It may mean we don't run with the popular,
successful crowd. We may get passed over for a promotion or a raise,
but knowing Christ gives us hope for the future. As we press toward
the mark for a higher calling in Him, we find peace and wisdom in our
daily lives.

*Father, show me the path I should walk and give me wisdom
to take each step, knowing You will walk beside me.*

THE GIFT OF PEACE

*"Peace I leave with you; my peace I give you. I do not give to
you as the world gives. Do not let your hearts be
troubled and do not be afraid."*
JOHN 14:27 NIV

. . . .

Watching the news every day is enough to make anyone uneasy and
restless, especially if the news stories are happening nearby. People
disappear every day, children are abused, and cities are torn apart by
rioting and looting. There seems to be no end to the evil that abounds
in every city and town across our country. How can anyone live in peace
under those circumstances?

As Christians, we can have peace even in the face of all the tragedy
happening around us. Jesus made a promise to His disciples and to us as
well. He was going back to the Father, but He was giving us a priceless
gift. He gave us His peace. The world can never give us the peace that
Jesus gives. It's a peace that we, the recipients, can't even understand. It's
too wonderful for our minds to grasp, but we know it comes from Him.

Whatever is happening in your world, Christ can give you peace.
None of the problems you're facing are too big for Him, whether it's
trouble in the city where you live or pain in your own home. He is
saying to you, "don't let your heart be troubled about these things, and
don't be afraid."

. . . .

*Jesus, I ask for Your peace to fill my heart and mind.
Help me not to be afraid of the problems I'm facing.*

Dwelling on the Important Things

Set your mind on things above,
not on things on the earth.
COLOSSIANS 3:2 NKJV

Andrea spent the morning cooking and baking, getting ready for a family get-together at her sister's house. She worked hard on each of her dishes, especially the pie, then loaded the food into the car and drove to her sister's. Delicious food covered the kitchen counter and Andrea added her contributions to the bounty. When it came time for dessert, Andrea sliced into the pie she had spent time carefully putting together. To her dismay, the filling had not set like it should have. Disappointment clouded her day. In spite of the good time she had visiting with everyone, she felt her time and money had been wasted on the pie.

Sometimes we worry about little things and forget to look at the big picture. If all we see are the things that go wrong or the trouble around us, we have missed what's important. Instead of focusing on spending time with her family, Andrea fretted about how long it had taken her to fix the pie and how much she had spent on the ingredients.

As Christians, we can focus on our problems and the little things that frustrate us, or we can keep our minds on heavenly things and know we have hope beyond what troubles us here. Christ is bigger than anything we may have to endure here on earth.

Lord, help us to keep our minds fixed on You so that the problems
we face are seen through Your grace in our lives.

RENEWING THE MIND

Don't copy the behavior and customs of this world, but let God transform you into a new person by changing the way you think. Then you will learn to know God's will for you, which is good and pleasing and perfect.
ROMANS 12:2 NLT

. . . .

We are surrounded by technology that introduces us to new ideas all the time. No matter what your choice of electronic device, you have the world at your disposal. Sometimes the information isn't acceptable for Christians. We may not have asked for these bits of information, but they invade our world every day. No matter where we turn, evil is present on all sides. Paul wrote to the Roman church telling them not to be conformed to the world around them, but to allow God to transform them and renew their minds. Can we as twenty-first-century Christians do the same? Yes, we can.

1. Don't allow yourself to view or read everything that comes across the screen in front of you. If it appears suggestive or impure, it probably is.
2. Take time to read your Bible every day. Don't let the cyber world be your only source of information. Hear what God has to say to you personally.
3. Ask God to renew your mind and show you what is profitable for you as a Christian.
4. Don't accept something just because everyone else does it even if it's "politically correct." Choose today to be transformed by the renewing of your mind.

. . . .

Father, help me not to conform to the world's ideas. Renew my mind and help me to know Your acceptable will for my life.

FOR SUCH A TIME AS THIS

*"And who knows but that you have come to your
royal position for such a time as this?"*
ESTHER 4:14 NIV

Women often find themselves in positions they wish they could change.
A young Jewish woman named Esther was taken along with several
other women to be a part of King Xerxes' harem. She had no choice in
the matter. Whatever her plans had been for the future, they were now
lost to her. But instead of grumbling and complaining, she acted in such
a way she won the favor of those over her. Eventually, she was brought
before the king and pleased him so much he made her queen.

There came a day when all Jews in the region were in danger for
their lives. Esther had never revealed her nationality. Now she stood
to lose all because of it. She could have taken a chance, hoping no one
would find out she was a Jew, but her uncle Mordecai said maybe this
was the reason she was in her position as queen—to save her people
from death. Esther went before the king, asking for the safety of the
Jews. The king granted her request and an entire nation was saved.

We may not always know why we're in a certain place or position,
but God knows. It may involve being a virtuous wife, mother, or
employee, but it could also involve interceding for a lost soul or
encouraging someone who has lost all hope and given up on life.

*Lord, help me to see beyond my own needs
and discover Your bigger plan for my life.*

STAND BY YOUR MAN

*Her husband can trust her, and she will greatly enrich his life.
She brings him good, not harm, all the days of her life.*
PROVERBS 31:11–12 NLT

Dr. Martin Luther King Jr. was a pastor and influential civil rights leader and was awarded the Nobel Peace Prize for his work. On April 4, 1968, he was assassinated, leaving behind a wife and four children. Coretta Scott King could have given herself to grief and bitterness after the death of her husband. Instead, she picked up the torch and moved forward, standing by her husband even after he was gone.

Mrs. King concentrated her energy on fulfilling her husband's work by building the Martin Luther King, Jr. Center for Nonviolent Social Change. She led the campaign to establish Dr. King's birthday as a national holiday. An award was established in her name for black authors and illustrators of books for children and young adults that demonstrate an appreciation of African American culture and universal human values. The award commemorates the life and work of Dr. King. Coretta brought him good, not harm, and enriched his legacy.

You may not have a husband whose name is known around the world, but as a Christian woman, with God's help, you can greatly enrich his life on a daily basis. What a wonderful gift, to be a woman he trusts who will bring him good and not harm all the days of his life.

*Lord, help me to be the kind of wife who
greatly enriches my husband's life.*

GOD KNOWS YOU

You have searched me, LORD, and you know me. You know when I sit and when I rise; you perceive my thoughts from afar. You discern my going out and my lying down; you are familiar with all my ways.
PSALM 139:1–3 NIV

Mary had a million things she wanted to do and only so much time to get them done. She had a self-imposed schedule for meeting deadlines and taking care of her obligations. Unfortunately, her body didn't cooperate. She awoke on a Monday morning feeling terrible. A cold virus had taken charge, leaving her weak and achy. Mary didn't have the energy she needed to get her to-do list done. Fretting about it didn't solve anything. The work would still get done, but not on Mary's planned schedule.

A famous line by Robert Burns reminds us, "The best-laid schemes of mice and men often go awry." The world around us blames it on Mondays, bad luck, or Murphy's Law, but the fact remains that all of us encounter bad days. We don't know what lies ahead for us or what each day holds, but we still make plans to fill our calendars. As Christians, we can rest assured that God is in control of our lives. He knows all about us. While we sleep, He's watching over us. He's familiar with all our ways. When our plans go awry, He knows it. When unspeakable tragedy happens, He's there for us. We need to leave our time in His hands.

Father, help us place our schedules in Your hands, knowing You aren't controlled by a calendar or clock.

THE LORD MADE THIS DAY

This is the day the LORD has made;
we will rejoice and be glad in it.
PSALM 118:24 NKJV

Renee hated dark, overcast days without any sunshine. She felt lethargic and depressed on those days. She avoided looking out the windows too much on cloudy, cold days, the gray sky a constant reminder the sun was hiding from her. After the colorful, cheerful celebration of Christmas, the dull drabness of January seemed to last forever. She felt like curling up somewhere and sleeping until winter passed. She could hardly wait for spring to arrive, but wishing didn't take away her dismal feelings or change the seasons.

As Christians, we don't have to feel depressed because it's a dark, wintry day. We can rejoice because we know God made this day and is in charge in spite of the gray skies overhead. If we only had sunshine in our lives, how would we know the way God can work to make each day a blessing even when there are gray skies overhead?

Sometimes even when the sun is shining, our world looks cloudy because of some unpleasant task or trial. Christians aren't exempt from the dark, but we don't have to live there. Each day can be brightened by God's presence in our lives reminding us that He made the day and we can be glad about it.

Lord, help me to see past gray skies
and find the light of Your love in my life.

Such as I Have

> *Then Peter said, "Silver and gold I do not have, but what I do have I give you: In the name of Jesus Christ of Nazareth, rise up and walk."*
> Acts 3:6 NKJV

Have you ever been asked to fill a position for which you felt unqualified? Your first thought is to say no. Surely there is someone better qualified than you for the job. Satan doesn't make your decision any easier. He whispers negative thoughts into your ears. "You can't do that; you're not good at it." "Everyone's looking at you and thinking what a bad job you're doing." "You're making a mess of this. Let someone else do it." All of his thoughts are lies, of course. Maybe you aren't as experienced as the last person who had the job, but you're the one God chose. You may not have the abilities or talents of others, but you have something God can use.

When Peter and John approached the lame man at the gate of the temple, Peter didn't hesitate to tell him they didn't have any silver or gold for him. But he had something the man could use. He said, "What I do have I give you." God is looking for those who are willing to give what they do have. He knew before He called you what you could do, and He also has the ability to qualify you to do whatsoever He requires. Give God whatever You have and allow Him to use it.

> *Lord, use me and whatever I have for Your glory.*
> *Help me to surrender all I have to You willingly.*

Only One God

But for us, there is one God, the Father, by whom all things were created,
and for whom we live. And there is one Lord, Jesus Christ,
through whom all things were created,
and through whom we live.
1 Corinthians 8:6 nlt

A coworker told Sue she had decided there were many ways to God. Sue knew the Bible teaches there is only one God and one way to Him. She liked and admired the woman who had spoken to her, but she was thankful she knew what God's Word says. Many voices express themselves in our world, each believing they know the right way, each wanting to convert others to their way of thinking. It's important to know the truth and to listen to the right voice.

The voices may be saying, "If you want to fit in, you need to change," "You must be more tolerant," or "That isn't politically correct." Some of these voices may sound good and we may be tempted to agree. Be careful that your good intentions don't set a trap for you. The voice of error can sound pretty good sometimes.

As Christians, we need to follow God's voice even when it makes us look politically incorrect. We can do this only by reading and knowing God's Word. Only then can we know the difference between the voice of truth and the voice of error. There is only one God, and we must know Him intimately to be able to distinguish between the voices.

Father, draw me close to You so I will always
recognize Your voice and know the truth.

MINDING YOUR OWN BUSINESS

*Make it your goal to live a quiet life, minding your own business
and working with your hands, just as we instructed you before.*
1 THESSALONIANS 4:11 NLT

In the 1960s there was a popular TV sitcom that had as one of its
characters a nosy lady named Gladys Kravitz. She spent her time
peering out her windows at all the neighbors to see what they were
doing. Any little incident had her shrieking for her husband, Abner, to
come and see what was happening.

It's easy to judge the Gladys Kravitzes of the world and think we're
above those acts. We might not feel that eavesdropping on a coworker
or family member is wrong. We're only concerned for them. Wanting to
hear the latest gossip doesn't mean we're nosy, does it? Snooping on our
neighbors is okay; we're a part of the neighborhood watch, after all.

Paul wrote to the members of the Thessalonian church that they
should live a quiet life and mind their own business. In this day of cell
phones and computers, we can know everything that's going on and
pass it to someone else in a matter of seconds. If we are attempting to
live by God's Word, we must be careful about our texts and emails. It's
tempting to pass on that juicy tidbit about someone else, but it can be
hurtful to others and destroy our testimony for Christ. Paul's advice to
the Thessalonians is good advice for us also.

*Lord, help me to mind my own business
and live a quiet life according to Your Word.*

WE HAVE HOPE IN CHRIST

And if our hope in Christ is only for this life,
we are more to be pitied than anyone in the world.
1 CORINTHIANS 15:19 NLT

Karen's heart was broken by the unexpected loss of her husband. Ken had been the focus of her world and they had shared a close relationship. She kept wringing her hands and asking, "What am I going to do?" With her husband gone, Karen felt she had nothing to live for. She loved her children and grandchildren and spent time with them, but they couldn't fill the void left by Ken's absence. She was without hope, a woman to be pitied.

Losing anyone we love can be a devastating experience, but as Christians, we know there is still life in Christ. Our families are important to us, but Christ must be the main focus of our lives. He has promised us eternal life if we're faithful to Him and endure until the end.

If our hope is built on our life here on earth, we will be miserable when trouble strikes. We will have nothing to stand on. An old hymn says, "On Christ the solid rock I stand, all other ground is sinking sand." Life as we know it here will someday pass away, but eternal life in Christ gives us hope for the future. "My hope is built on nothing less than Jesus' blood and righteousness."

Jesus, help me place complete trust in You,
for You are the way to life and hope for the future.

KEEP YOUR EYES ON JESUS

I keep my eyes always on the LORD.
With him at my right hand, I will not be shaken.
PSALM 16:8 NIV

A recent news story told of a young man in a truck who took his eyes off the road to text on his phone. He didn't realize the traffic ahead of him had stopped. He ran over the top of the car in front of him and crushed to death a woman and her mother who were sitting in the backseat. Charges were filed against him. Chances are he will serve prison time for the accident. Had he kept his eyes on the road in front of him, two people would still be alive today.

The young man on his phone may have thought the text message was of extreme importance, but he probably realizes now that nothing was more important than watching the road ahead. As Christians, we must keep our eyes always on the Lord. Taking our eyes off Christ and looking at the world around us can result in spiritual death for us and others as well. When we have Christ at our side, He will alert us to those obstacles that could cause us to get distracted in our Christian walk. Nothing is more important than keeping our eyes on the Lord. As we do so, life's priorities fall into place and we aren't apt to have a spiritual wreck.

Jesus, keep me alert to the path ahead and help me walk
in Your footsteps, knowing they will guide me to safety.

Living Water

*The woman said to him, "Sir, give me this water so that I won't
get thirsty and have to keep coming here to draw water."*
John 4:15 niv

- -

The Samaritan woman who came to draw water from Jacob's well didn't
know she would meet Someone who would change her life drastically.
Her life had been filled with relationships that didn't work. She may
have felt worthless and used. That day may have started out like every
other day in her life, but when she approached the well, Jesus was
waiting. He asked her for a drink. When she questioned His reason, He
in turn offered her water—living water. If she drank of it, she would
never thirst again. She was all for never having to come to the well again
to draw water, not realizing Jesus was offering her spiritual life, not a
physical refreshment. As they talked, she found living water that gave
her a new lease on life.

Some days life can seem like one endless task after another; it
exhibits a sameness that makes us weary. We thirst for something better,
or maybe just different. Maybe it's time for a trip to the well. As we
come to Christ in prayer, seeking a much-needed drink, we will find
Him waiting at the well, offering the same living water to each of us
that He offered to the Samaritan woman. Are there any among us who
don't need times of spiritual refreshing in our lives? Grab a bucket and
go to the well. Jesus is waiting.

- -

*Jesus, help me to drink from Your well of living
water so I will never thirst again.*

RESTORING THE BROKEN PIECES

*And the vessel that he made of clay was marred in the hand
of the potter; so he made it again into another vessel,
as it seemed good to the potter to make.*
JEREMIAH 18:4 NKJV

Marcia enjoys restoring old furniture, giving it new life. She strips away the old finish that is scratched and ugly, sands the wood to a beautiful sheen, and covers it with a coat of new varnish or paint. Sometimes she replaces old, worn fabric with a new piece of cloth. When she's finished, she has a "new" piece of furniture. But it doesn't happen overnight. It takes patient, loving care to get it just right. If you were to visit her home, you would find it full of beautiful furniture, lovingly restored by Marcia.

Jeremiah went to the potter's house and saw the potter at work on a vessel of clay. While the potter was working on the piece, it became marred. The potter didn't toss the clay away but kept working, fashioning it into another vessel. God wants to restore lives scratched and marred by sin just as Marcia restores furniture and the potter molded clay into usable vessels. No matter what has stained or disfigured our lives, God can mold us into the person He wants us to be. To become a usable vessel, we must allow the Potter to knead and work the clay. Even if we fall off the Potter's wheel by our own choice, He can pick us up and remold us into a new creation.

*Father, help me to stay on the Potter's wheel
until You are finished with me.*

BE STILL

*Be still, and know that I am God; I will be exalted
among the nations, I will be exalted in the earth!*
PSALM 46:10 NKJV

Vanessa stepped outside into the blistering August heat to take out the garbage. She couldn't wait to get back inside where it was cool. When she tried to open the door, it was locked. Panic seized her for a moment, but she realized there was nothing she could do about it. She lived miles from town and her husband wouldn't be home from work for a while. She looked around for a place to get out of the sun and spotted a large shade tree. She sat down under the tree and looked around. For the first time in a long time, she noticed the beauty of God's creation that surrounded her home. God's blessings were apparent everywhere she looked. By the time her husband arrived home, she felt rested and refreshed in spite of the heat. She realized God had probably been trying to get her attention for some time. She just hadn't been listening. It had taken getting locked out of her house to make her stop and listen.

Has God been trying to get your attention lately? If you're rushing around, buried in responsibilities and tasks you feel are important, what will it take for God to make you stop and listen to His voice? What will it take for you to "be still" and acknowledge Him?

*Father, help me to slow down
so I can hear You speaking to me.*

SPEAK GENTLY

A soft answer turns away wrath, but a harsh word stirs up anger.
The tongue of the wise uses knowledge rightly, but the mouth
of fools pours forth foolishness.
PROVERBS 15:1–2 NKJV

Karen knew better than to question Don about the discussion they'd had the day before. She knew her words had made him angry. She hated confrontation but wanted to clear the air between them. When he didn't answer her, she became frustrated and the tone of her voice changed from friendly to annoyed. Don instantly became defensive and spoke in a loud, angry tone. As a result, the unsettled atmosphere in their home continued.

How many arguments could be avoided if we could learn to speak to others in gentle tones? It's not always easy to do so when others answer with harsh words that stir up resentment or hurt our feelings. The writer of Proverbs tells us that those who are wise use knowledge in the right way. In other words, we need to choose our words carefully and think before we speak. When we're angry, we say foolish things we regret later.

One of the ways we can give soft answers and use knowledge rightly is to pray before we decide to have a discussion with someone who will not welcome our conversation. If we know ahead of time we will be confronted with a difficult situation, we can ask God to guard our speech and give us soft answers.

Father, give me wisdom to know how to give soft
answers and speak wisely to those around me.

Five Minutes of Glory

And whatever you do in word or deed, do all in the name of
the Lord Jesus, giving thanks to God the Father through Him.
Colossians 3:17 nkjv

A local writers' group gives members a chance to share with the rest of the group their writing successes. They call this time "five minutes of glory." The author is allowed to stand in front of the group for five minutes to share what they've published recently. They are allowed to hold up a copy of the published work and share any information about the piece that they'd like. This five minutes is intended as a means of encouragement for those seeking publication or just beginning to write. It is not meant as a bragging session.

Sometimes as Christians, we forget to share "five minutes of glory" with others by telling them what God has done for us personally. We should never take credit for the blessings that come our way or do good deeds with the purpose of impressing others. Our time of sharing with others should give God full credit and serve as encouragement for others who may need a good word.

The next time God does something for you—either a blessing from Him or an ability He has given you to accomplish a task—share "five minutes of glory" with someone else. Just be sure all the glory goes to God.

Father, all glory be to You for the things
You have accomplished in my life.

WATCH WHERE YOU'RE GOING

Your word is a lamp for my feet, a light on my path.
PSALM 119:105 NIV

Vickie had her mind on her husband who was in the hospital and didn't notice the concrete parking space barrier. She hung the toe of her shoe on it. Without warning, she fell forward, landing on her left knee. She stood and examined her wounds. Her hand was scraped and her knee hurt, but nothing life threatening. She went on to the hospital to visit Sonny even though she could tell her knee was swollen. Later, the evidence of her fall showed in ugly black and blue bruises. She placed ice on her knee and kept it elevated as much as possible. The injury wasn't serious, just painful.

Sometimes we hang our toe on obstacles in our Christian walk. We may stumble around spiritually and even fall sometimes, but we don't have to remain on the ground. We can pick ourselves up and begin walking again. It may be painful at first, and we may even sustain a few scrapes and bruises and feel swollen from our fall, but God offers us healing. All we have to do is reach for His Word. God has given us a lamp through His Word, which shines light on our path as we walk day by day. Turn on the lamp by reading your Bible daily.

Father, open my understanding as I read Your Word,
that I may see clearly the path I need to travel.

QUIET TIME

He says, "Be still, and know that I am God."
PSALM 46:10 NIV

. . . .

As you were growing up, how many times were you told to sit or stand still? And honestly, they were "tells" even if the adult added a "please." It may have seemed like you were merely being asked to be quiet, or not fidget, or not bump into another child, or not kick the seat in front of you. Could we as children have misread these dictates to be still? Were we actually being told to calm ourselves so that we might hear or learn something important rather than just as a control of our outward behavior?

Our earthly parents told us to be still just as our heavenly Father has instructed us to be still. When we calm ourselves physically and mentally, we are better able to focus our minds and listen with our hearts. We become open to hearing the Lord's direction for our lives. We allow ourselves to feel the peace that comes with the presence of the Holy Spirit within us.

Quiet time is a precious commodity. With mobile electronic devices, it seems we are constantly communicating via phone, text, or social media. Consider making time to put the electronics down and give yourself the gift of being still.

. . . .

Lord, in all the busyness I call my life, please help me to heed
Your command to be still. I know You are my God
and will direct me when I make quiet time
to focus on You. Amen.

WITH CHILDLIKE FAITH

So in Christ Jesus you are all children of God through faith,
for all of you who were baptized into Christ
have clothed yourselves with Christ.
GALATIANS 3:26–27 NIV

It's Groundhog Day. Children young and old will check to see if Punxsutawney Phil sees his shadow today. According to folklore, if it's cloudy when Phil emerges from his burrow, then we'll enjoy an early spring; if it's sunny, the groundhog will pop back into his burrow after seeing his shadow, which predicts six more weeks of winter.

On the second of February, can a groundhog's behavior actually predict the weather for the following six weeks? It can if we have childlike faith in the folklore. In reality, more people enjoy the activities surrounding Groundhog Day than actually believe its weather prediction.

As Christians, we choose to give our childlike faith to Jesus. The Bible tells us we become clothed in Christ when we choose to be baptized in Christ. We become children of God when we make the commitment of baptism based on our faith in Christ Jesus. Through our faith, we choose to believe the predictions that God has revealed through the prophecies in His Word. We know that God's Word will never fail us, unlike the predictions that come from the folklore of common man.

Lord, I am choosing to place my faith in You. I am committing to
follow You and read Your Word daily. Accept my childlike
faith and clothe me with Your grace. Amen.

Mind and Heart

*Accept instruction from his mouth
and lay up his words in your heart.*
Job 22:22 niv

. . . .

Although they were sisters, Alice knew she and Sally were as different as day and night. Alice liked to be organized and methodical. She always kept a to-do list and tried to have an overall plan to reach goals. Alice was comfortable evaluating opportunities, determining requirements, and translating everything into a written plan. If something changed, Alice tried to be flexible and revise her plan as needed.

Sally, on the other hand, appeared to make a plan only when all else failed. To Alice, it seemed like Sally put off making a decision until the decision literally made itself. Alice loved her "big sis," but she couldn't understand how Sally had survived, let alone successfully balanced marriage, motherhood, and a career.

At a family reunion, their aunt put things in perspective for Alice. She said, "I am so pleased that you and Sally have both become the women that God intended. It's remarkable how similar you are. It's wonderful to see you both use your minds to listen for God's direction and then act from your heart. It's as evident as the noses on your lovely faces that your hearts for Jesus rule your lives."

. . . .

*Lord, thank You for making each of Your children different and unique.
Help me listen to You with my mind and then follow
the path directed by my Christian heart. Amen.*

Obey and Serve with Your Heart

*And now, Israel, what does the LORD your God ask of you but
to fear the LORD your God, to walk in obedience to him, to love him,
to serve the LORD your God with all your heart and with all your soul.*
Deuteronomy 10:12 NIV

One morning Bonnie felt compelled to share muffins with her neighbor,
Richard. As a widow, Bonnie wasn't comfortable taking her freshly
baked muffins to the divorced man. She didn't want a neighborly
gesture to be mistaken for romantic interest.

When she still felt the need at 3:00 p.m., Bonnie gave in and
walked to Richard's with a plate of muffins. She left Richard's glad she
had obeyed her heart. It seemed like he appreciated her neighborly visit
even more than her gift.

As Bonnie walked home, she greeted Marge, an elderly neighbor
out for exercise. Moments after they passed, Bonnie heard a loud
thud. Turning, she saw that Marge had fallen and had been knocked
unconscious when her head hit the pavement. As she hurried to Marge's
side, Bonnie called 911. Before finishing the call, Richard had joined
her with a blanket. While Bonnie stayed with Marge, Richard went to
get Marge's husband.

As Bonnie watched for the ambulance with Marge, she realized
the reason she had felt compelled to take muffins to Richard. The Lord
needed both her and Richard to be together at this time to help Marge.

*Lord, thank You for being patient when I need extra urging to do Your will.
I want to obey when You ask me to be Your servant. Amen.*

He Will Give You the Words

"Alas, Sovereign LORD," I said, "I do not know how to speak; I am too young." But the LORD said to me, "Do not say, 'I am too young.' You must go to everyone I send you to and say whatever I command you."
Jeremiah 1:6–7 NIV

Marianne was asked to give the message for an upcoming Sunday worship service when the pastor would be on a retreat. At first she hesitated, then nicely said no. She remembered mentioning that she wasn't trained in the ministry and really didn't believe she had enough public speaking experience. Somehow, the lay leader didn't hear her. He just said, "Well, I believe you'll have a worthy message."

That evening, as Marianne considered her predicament, she took it to the Lord in prayer. She repeated her reasons for not being capable of preparing and giving the requested sermon. Her devotional reading the following morning was about how God told a young Jeremiah that he would one day be a prophet to nations. Could this be the answer to her prayer? Like Jeremiah responding that he was too young, Marianne had responded by saying she lacked training and experience. Marianne knew that, like Jeremiah, if she trusted the Lord, He would give her the message she needed to deliver.

God, I trust You to show me the words You need me to share and with whom. As I go through each day, I want to obey Your will and speak as You direct. Amen.

IF YOU DON'T HAVE ANYTHING NICE TO SAY. . .

*Then the LORD reached out his hand and touched my mouth and said to me,
"I have put my words in your mouth. See, today I appoint you over
nations and kingdoms to uproot and tear down, to destroy
and overthrow, to build and to plant."*
JEREMIAH 1:9–10 NIV

Suzy felt blessed to have grown up with her maternal grandmother
living with her family. Being a godly woman, Grandma had reinforced
life lessons with the teachings found in the Bible.

As an adult working in the competitive business world, Suzy
struggled with Grandma's adage, "If you don't have anything nice to
say, don't say anything." Suzy believed this principle had always served
her well. But as a manager, she felt conflicted when she had to deliver
unpopular directions or feedback. Suzy contented herself by conducting
herself professionally and fairly, even when she had to say things people
didn't want to hear.

God didn't tell the prophet Jeremiah that He would put only
nice words into his mouth. He told Jeremiah that as he interacted
with others, he would have to tear down and destroy as well as build
and plant. Sometimes progress requires leaders to say difficult things.
As a Christian woman, Suzy can speak nicely while being an effective
leader—even when she has to deliver messages that aren't nice.

*God, thank You for the wisdom I find in the scriptures. Help me use
that wisdom to speak nicely, especially when my job
requires me to be tough. Amen.*

A TIME FOR EVERYTHING

*There is a time for everything. . .a time to search and a time
to give up, a time to keep and a time to throw away.*
ECCLESIASTES 3:1, 6 NIV

Learning to tell time when we were children wasn't easy. Understanding
the clock face and the function of the little hand pointing to the hour
was simple. But it was confusing to learn that it's ten minutes after the
hour when the big hand is on the 2 or that it's a quarter till the hour
when the big hand is on the 9. At least now with digital clocks when it's
ten past the hour the digital display shows 10.

Eventually we all learned the essential lesson of telling time and
understanding that time passes. As the Bible tells us, there is a time for
everything in life. There are times when we need to search for answers
and times to give up and surrender to the Lord. There is a time for us to
hold fast to ideas and things, and a time to let go and throw away goals
from our past.

Sometimes we cling to old priorities that actually drag us down. If
we find that certain items or relationships are pulling us away from our
Christian walk, we need to consider giving those up and letting go, for
our own good.

*Lord, thank You for giving me time for everything in my life. Help me to
trust Your guidance when facing the need to give up or let go. Amen.*

PRAISE TO BE RAISED

*My God, I cry out by day, but you do not answer, by night,
but I find no rest. . . . To you they cried out and were saved;
in you they trusted and were not put to shame.*
PSALM 22:2, 5 NIV

Life isn't easy. We've heard many platitudes meant to encourage us. *Being a complainer is not attractive. You need to find the silver lining in every cloud. If life gives you lemons, make lemonade. Smile even when it hurts.*

Most of us try to begin our day by thanking God for our blessings before we face our challenges. But when we feel despair, is it acceptable to complain, or do we need to bury those emotions? The Bible recounts times when people cried out to the Lord, times when they voiced their complaints. In Psalm 22 we're told that Christ poured out His soul to His heavenly Father throughout His sufferings. If we follow Christ's example, we can take our complaints to God in prayer as long as we, like Christ, also acknowledge our love for and trust in God.

If we just complain to others, we won't solve our problems. If we praise God and trust Him to stand with us during our trials, He will raise us up to handle our problems. Maybe we need to replace those old platitudes with this one: Complain and remain, or praise to be raised.

Lord, thank You for listening to my complaints and saving me from my sins. Even during my struggles I will praise You as my God and Savior. Amen.

He Will Fill You Up

*I am the LORD your God, who brought you up out of Egypt.
Open wide your mouth and I will fill it.*
Psalm 81:10 niv

Beth didn't understand why her best friend, Nicole, got up each Sunday for Bible study and church. As an adult, Beth felt free to make her choice to skip the organized religion thing.

Life was good. Beth and Nicole had jobs at the same bank. Beth's car was almost paid for and she had just purchased her first home. Then came the announcement that their bank had been bought by a larger one with a branch down the street. Beth and Nicole would lose their jobs when their location closed.

Beth railed to Nicole about how unfair it was that they were being eliminated. She feared she might lose her house. Nicole let Beth vent her financial worries until she started to blame God.

Nicole told Beth that God would never forsake them. He wanted to help them with their problems and fill their souls with His blessings. Nicole encouraged Beth to attend church with her on Sunday and open herself to the Lord's blessings.

The following day Beth said, "Nicole, I've been so foolish. I thought I could handle things without attending church. I want what you have. I want to feel the peace that comes from knowing my happiness is found in my relationship with God and not in my earthly possessions."

Lord, thank You for knowing what blessings I truly need. Help me to hunger for You more than I hunger for earthly things. Amen.

THE PUSH TO FINISH

*Being confident of this, that he who began a good work in you
will carry it on to completion until the day of Christ Jesus.*
PHILIPPIANS 1:6 NIV

Emma was a procrastinator. If she could put something off until tomorrow, she would. Emma did well at work, where her supervisor set progressive due dates. Emma worked well under the pressure of deadlines.

Emma's personal life always included unfinished projects. Scrapbook supplies waited in the box until the week before a photo album was to become a birthday gift. A baby quilt, begun when she learned her sister was pregnant, sat waiting for the binding until the night before the shower. The projects started with love and joy became last-minute pressure cookers as she hustled to finish.

Emma's husband told her that she created too much stress for herself. He suggested that she might be happier purchasing gifts rather than trying to create more personal treasures.

After considering her husband's thoughts, Emma concluded that she truly did want to have these creative projects in her life. She agreed that procrastination took away from her overall pleasure of doing projects. However, she did follow through and she did complete things by the time they were needed. Emma told her husband, "Just as God has promised to complete the good work He has begun in me, He gives me the grace to finish the good works that I begin."

*Lord, thank You for continuing the good works You have begun in
my life. Help me to follow Your example and finish each
of the good works that I begin. Amen.*

FORGIVE AS CHRIST FORGIVES US

*Anyone you forgive, I also forgive. And what I have forgiven—
if there was anything to forgive—I have forgiven in
the sight of Christ for your sake.*
2 CORINTHIANS 2:10 NIV

Hannah admitted to Pastor Susan that she harbors resentment toward her brother, John. Now that her parents had passed away, Hannah knew it was time to improve their relationship.

Hannah shared her belief that their mom had favored John. She always seemed to make excuses for him. John was painfully shy. He didn't do as many chores as Hannah because his required more skill. Then, as adults, John's job was so important that Hannah should fit her holiday plans to his.

Pastor Susan drew three circles on a paper and labeled one each for Hannah, Mom, and John. She then drew a line between Hannah and Mom and between John and Mom. Pointing to her diagram, she said, "It seems your relationship problems with John center on your mom. Is it possible that you need to begin by forgiving her for the favoritism you perceived toward John?"

Pastor Susan told Hannah that most of us need to forgive our parents for behavior that has hurt our feelings. Parents do the best they can, but they aren't infallible. When a parent falls short of a child's expectation, the child will need to forgive that parent just as our parents and our heavenly Father forgive us.

*Lord, thank You for giving me loving parents. Help me to forgive them
for the times their best did not meet my expectations. Amen.*

LEADING OUR COUNTRY WITH PRAYER

*"Yet, LORD my God, give attention to your servant's prayer
and his plea for mercy. Hear the cry and the prayer that
your servant is praying in your presence."*
2 CHRONICLES 6:19 NIV

Today, as we remember Abraham Lincoln's birthday, we are reminded of the far-reaching impact one leader can have on a country and on history. What can we learn from Lincoln about the importance of God in our lives?

In the Handbill Replying to Charges of Infidelity, dated July 31, 1846, Abraham Lincoln stated: "That I am not a member of any Christian Church, is true; but I have never denied the truth of the Scriptures; and I have never spoken with intentional disrespect of religion in general, or any denomination of Christians in particular." Then in a conversation with Noah Brooks he said, "I have been driven many times upon my knees by the overwhelming conviction that I had nowhere else to go. My own wisdom and that of all about me seemed insufficient for that day."

This great leader knew he couldn't handle everything alone or with just the help of those designated to assist him. Abraham Lincoln realized the truth of scripture and the need to take problems to God in prayer.

During worship we often pray for our president and our leaders. Many also pray individually for them. Today, let's give thanks for leaders like Abraham Lincoln who pray for us and our country.

*Lord, thank You for Your promise to hear the prayers of Your servants.
Bless our leaders with wisdom for the positions they hold. Amen.*

DON'T STUMBLE OVER YOUR PRIDE

Pride goes before destruction,
a haughty spirit before a fall.
PROVERBS 16:18 NIV

When we praise a child, we often express our pride in them. The excitement of seeing a toddler do new activities is often accompanied by little claps, big smiles, and joyous comments like "I'm so proud of you." We encourage children to be proud of their accomplishments and to build on their successes. Since God cautions us about the failure that can follow pride, should we encourage it in children?

Secondary education now utilizes group projects that don't focus on building competitive pride. Based on one completed project, each group member receives the same grade. Students learn the value of teamwork and the success that comes from working together. The group project encourages each student to value the output from the team as much as their individual contribution.

News reporters love to reveal the problems that follow celebrities who become overly prideful. When they become too focused on themselves and their accomplishments, they often lose those who support and love them. Pride also seems to stand in the way of good sense and the ability to heed warnings of danger. Without prudent caution, people make poor choices that lead to failures.

The Bible even tells us in 1 Timothy 3:6 that the devil lost his position in heaven due to pride. We certainly don't want to stumble over our pride and share his fate. We need to see our value as part of God's team.

Lord, help me understand that I am here to serve You. I want to humble myself so that my accomplishments reflect Your goodness and grace. Amen.

LOVE ONE ANOTHER

Greet one another with a kiss of love.
Peace to all of you who are in Christ.
1 PETER 5:14 NIV

Our capacity for love is unlimited. If we ever wonder how much love one person can shower on others, we need only to consider the love between a parent and a child. There is scientific evidence that when a baby is born a hormonal process occurs for both parents that ensures parental love for the new life. If it were truly just a matter of some unseen chemical that causes parents to offer unconditional-love-for-life, how then can we experience that same type of love for an adopted child or a grandchild? How does it happen that we have dear friends we love even though we don't always "like" them?

How? Love is a choice. We choose to give and receive love. As Christians, we must heed God's command to love one another. In 1 Peter we read that we are to greet one another with love.

As when you were a child and shared valentines with your friends, think today of those you love as God loves you. Reach out and show them your love. It can be as simple as a call, text, or email saying, "I love you." Today is a good day to ensure that your loved ones *know* that you love them, unconditionally.

Lord, thank You for all those You have given me to love.
Help me to show Your love as You have commanded. Amen.

Our Nation's Leaders

For lack of guidance a nation falls,
but victory is won through many advisers.
Proverbs 11:14 NIV

. . . .

Annika laid out the plan for her family's "presidential history" themed vacation. She described each stop she and her husband, Joseph, had selected. When their kids began to complain about the long drive to Mount Rushmore in South Dakota, Joseph interrupted. He reinforced how important it is to learn by traveling to historic sites.

Eleven-year-old Lily asked why they couldn't go to historic Florida and visit theme parks. Thirteen-year-old Bryce asked why they couldn't do an environmentally sound "staycation" at the water park a short forty-five-minute drive away.

With Joseph's nod of encouragement, Annika told the kids how awesome it was when Grandma and Grandpa took her and her siblings to see Mount Rushmore. Annika explained that reading about past presidents or seeing the current president on TV wouldn't give them the same perspective. She said, "When you stand below the sixty-foot granite sculptures of Presidents Washington, Jefferson, Lincoln, and Roosevelt, you'll get a feel for the solid foundation our presidents have laid for our great nation. The United States has progressed for over two hundred years based on amazing leaders."

Joseph added, "Even scripture tells us the importance of guidance for a nation to succeed. Your mom and I believe we'll all benefit from this trip, even though it will mean many hours on the road."

. . . .

Lord, thank You for those who have answered the call to lead our
nation. Please guide and protect our president as he
makes decisions for the good of all. Amen.

HE LIFTS YOU UP

*Humble yourselves, therefore, under God's mighty hand,
that he may lift you up in due time.*
1 PETER 5:6 NIV

Nancy's homework for Bible study was to list actions of a humble person and identify two humble people. Her dictionary app showed descriptive terms like *not proud or arrogant*, *modest*, and *courteously respectful*. Those made sense, but what really caught Nancy's attention was the definition of the verb *humble*: "to destroy the independence, power, or will of a person."

Nancy jotted, "Actions: surrender my will to God, give God the power to direct my path, and follow God's will in life." She then thought about people who displayed humble actions. Her son-in-law, Jason, met the criteria. Although he was a medical doctor, he only used his title at his practice. He routinely volunteered his skills for youth athletic programs and disaster relief.

Next, she thought of Mildred. In her eighties with limited mobility, Mildred still handled hospitality outreach for their church. She called visitors who signed the friendship folder at worship, and she placed regular calls to shut-ins. With both, she would ask if there was anything the church could do and was careful to listen to what was said and sometimes to what wasn't said.

The final section of Nancy's worksheet left space for "Conclusions." Nancy wrote, "Humble people serve others with the unique abilities that God has given them. God rewards a humble person in a way that helps them continue to prosper and serve."

*Lord, I want to humble myself to Your will. Thank You for
lifting me up as I serve others. Amen.*

PRAY FROM YOUR HEART

*My heart is not proud, LORD, my eyes are not haughty; I do not concern
myself with great matters or things too wonderful for me. But I have
calmed and quieted myself, I am like a weaned child with
its mother; like a weaned child I am content.*
PSALM 131:1–2 NIV

Josephine was busy. Between her job, family, and church activities, she
barely found time for herself. She did feel good that after six weeks she
was still meeting her New Year's resolution to read her daily devotional.
She wasn't as pleased with her goal of quieting herself for her daily
prayer time. She talked with the Lord each day, but she hadn't found
quality quiet time for prayer and reflection. Yes, she was quiet during
her hurried prayers at bedtime, but she was so tired by the end of the
day, she didn't think of that as quality time.

Josephine loved the image of Jesus praying in the garden surrounded
only by the beauty of nature. Honestly, though, sitting quietly made her
feel antsy. She was the kind of person who had to be busy. Her method of
enjoying nature was taking a thirty-minute brisk walk.

Josephine decided to leave her headphones at home and try praying
during her daily walk. She was amazed at the satisfaction she derived
from sharing this time with the Lord. Brisk walking raised Josephine's
heart rate, but it also lowered her defenses and opened her heart for
personal reflection.

*Lord, I want to share my heart with You when I pray.
Help me find the quiet time that will content my soul. Amen.*

LISTEN FOR HIS WHISPER

*After the earthquake came a fire, but the LORD was not
in the fire. And after the fire came a gentle whisper.*
1 KINGS 19:12 NIV

In 1996 at the Brookfield Zoo in Illinois, a three-year-old boy climbed a wall and fell eighteen feet into the gorilla enclosure. Sounds of panic came from spectators. Screams escalated as Binti Jua, an eight-year-old female gorilla, walked to the boy. Spectators reported feeling panic as they feared the gorilla would maul the child.

Instead, Binti Jua carefully picked the boy up and carried him to the zookeeper's gate. She appeared to console him as she stayed by his side offering protection from other gorillas. Zoo personnel were able to safely retrieve the boy, who made a full recovery.

Often when tragedy occurs people ask, "Where was God? How could He allow this to happen?" When a wild animal like Binti Jua displays compassion for an injured child, it's easy to see where God was in the incident. He didn't make the boy climb the wall or prevent his fall. God was not in the spectators' screams of horror. But after the tragic event came God's gentle whisper. He guided the safe rescue of the boy using one of His creatures, a gorilla.

When the storms of our lives occur, don't ask God how He could have let it happen. Instead, praise Him for the ways His gentle whisper provides us with His aid.

*Lord, thank You for being with me when I face tragic events in my life.
I appreciate the gentle whisper of Your support after each storm. Amen.*

If at First You Don't Hear. . .

*The LORD came and stood there, calling as at the other times, "Samuel!
Samuel!" Then Samuel said, "Speak, for your servant is listening."*
1 SAMUEL 3:10 NIV

. . . .

Have you heard the anecdote about the man who wouldn't leave his
home when asked to evacuate as a flood approached? When a van
stopped for him, he said, "I'm a good Christian; God will take care
of me." As the waters rose, the man went to a second-floor window.
When a boat stopped for him, he again declined help. Eventually, he
took refuge on the roof as the floodwater filled his home. A helicopter
lowered a ladder to him, but he again refused to evacuate. He knew
the Lord would save him. Unfortunately, the man drowned. In heaven
he said to God, "I lived a Christian life; why didn't You save me?" God
replied, "My son, I tried three times, but you refused My help."

Do we listen and respond when we hear something new or unfamiliar?
Do we heed timely warnings of danger? Do we accept Christian help from
others? If we at least try to listen for God and respond the best we know
how to do, He will reach out to us more than once. Just as He did when he
called to Samuel in the temple, God will keep trying to reach those who are
listening for Him.

. . . .

*Lord, thank You for patiently offering Your help to me. Help me to
listen and hear, that I might respond as I should. Amen.*

HEAR GOD'S WORDS

Naaman's servants went to him and said, "My father, if the prophet had told you to do some great thing, would you not have done it? How much more, then, when he tells you, 'Wash and be cleansed'!"
2 KINGS 5:13 NIV

Janet was in awe when someone at church would report that the Lord had talked to them. Janet didn't think the Lord had ever talked directly to her.

She decided to privately ask how people knew the Lord had talked to them. Andrew told Janet he heard the Lord tell him this girlfriend would become his wife. How? When both his sister and his best friend told him, "She's the one," he just knew. Lucia said, "The Lord told me to attend this church." How? The third time her roommate invited her to attend, she just knew. Rose told Janet that the Lord told her she should relocate. How? One evening Rose told her daughter that she still hadn't decided where to move. Her daughter responded, "I think you have." After Rose repeated that she hadn't yet decided, her daughter repeated her opinion that Rose had. The following morning Rose just knew the Lord had spoken to her.

As with the story of Naaman, we need to listen to those who care about us. God can use those who serve Him to deliver His messages. God may use a servant who appears to us as a family member or friend.

Lord, thank You for talking to me. Help me to know when Your message is coming through one of Your servants. Amen.

THIRSTING FOR MILK

*In fact, though by this time you ought to be teachers, you need someone
to teach you the elementary truths of God's word all
over again. You need milk, not solid food!*
HEBREWS 5:12 NIV

Lila was a new Christian. She had made the choice to become a
Christian as a mature adult and was now eager to learn more through
Bible study. She asked the pastor which Sunday school class she should
join. When he suggested the women's class, Lila told him she would
rather go to something for beginners. The pastor told her the church
didn't have a beginners' class. He assured Lila that she would be
comfortable in any group.

Lila was skeptical but took the offered text for the women's class.
The first Sunday Lila attended, the leader asked everyone to introduce
themselves. Of the eight women in the class, three called themselves
cradle-to-grave Christians, two had been Christians over twenty years,
and three had made their decision over forty years ago.

When it was Lila's turn, she told the ladies that as a new Christian
she didn't think she had enough background to fit in. The leader laughed
as she opened her Bible to Hebrews 5:12. After reading the scripture
aloud, she said, "Lila, we are all still growing in our Christian walk. We
will never reach a point where we have all of the answers and, being new,
you can probably provide insights and ask questions that would never
have occurred to us. So let's grow together."

*Lord, thank You for quenching my thirst with the milk contained in the
Bible. Help me to thirst for the knowledge that only You can provide. Amen.*

I CANNOT TELL A LIE

My lips will not say anything wicked,
and my tongue will not utter lies.
JOB 27:4 NIV

We've all heard the George Washington anecdote written by Parson Weems. At age six, when questioned by his father about a dead cherry tree, George Washington replied that he couldn't tell a lie. To this day, knowing that he couldn't lie to his angry father gives Americans great respect for our first president.

His father's response to George is not as commonly known. He reportedly held out his arms to his son and told him that he was glad George had killed his tree. His father told George that hearing him take honest responsibility for his actions was worth more than a thousand trees that blossom in silver and produce fruits of gold.

Just as George Washington honored his father by responding truthfully about his actions, God expects His children to be honest. In Job 27:4 God gives us two expectations for honesty. We are told that we should not say anything wicked and we should not utter lies. This scripture ensures that we know being deceitful—concealing or distorting the truth to mislead or cheat—is just as bad as lying. Even when it's hard, God wants us, like George Washington was, to be truthful in all ways.

Lord, thank You for giving clear expectations on the need
to be truthful. Help me to be honest with others. Amen.

OBEY WITHOUT DELAY

I will hasten and not delay to obey your commands.
PSALM 119:60 NIV

Belinda felt compelled to personally deliver the shawl her church was praying over. The hand-crocheted shawl was intended for her friend Cheryl, who was now in hospice care near her family over one thousand miles away. After worship, Belinda asked the pastor if there was a plan for getting the shawl to Cheryl. When she learned there wasn't a plan, Belinda knew what she needed to do. Amazingly, there was a reasonably priced round-trip flight available that very day.

By making the impromptu trip and taking the shawl, Belinda was able to personally share the love and prayers of their church with her dear friend Cheryl and her family. Soon after Belinda returned home, she received a call from Cheryl's husband. He told her that Cheryl had gone home to be with the Lord, wrapped securely in the prayer shawl. When she heard the peace in his voice, Belinda understood why the Lord had needed her to immediately make the trip to Cheryl's bedside.

Often we rationalize why we can't do something we feel called to do. We tell ourselves we don't have enough time, money, or skill. As Christians, we need to use our talents to determine how to accomplish the tasks our Lord asks us to accept. We need to be prompt "can do" Christians, like Belinda.

Lord, thank You for using me to meet the needs of others.
Help me listen for Your commands and for the urgency needed. Amen.

Consider the Source

The heart of the discerning acquires knowledge,
for the ears of the wise seek it out.
Proverbs 18:15 niv

Joy asked her eight-year-old daughter why she had tried to climb the tree that she fell from. Lily looked up from the cast on her broken arm and tearfully admitted that the neighbor boy had told her to climb the tree, so she thought it would be okay. Joy explained to Lily the importance of considering the source of information before making a decision. Although the neighbor boy was two years older, Lily would have been wise to double check with an adult. Lily was suffering the consequences of being gullible.

Like Lily, we need to consider the source of information. In the current age of twenty-four-hour news coverage, the same story is reported over and over. It's easy to believe that it must be true when we hear or read a story repeatedly. However, we need to listen with care to what is actually said. People can stretch or omit parts of the truth to sensationalize or distort a story. Discerning listeners use their minds and available resources to verify information before they accept its truth. At a minimum, an Internet search engine can be used for research.

We don't need to doubt the Word of God; we need to doubt the words of man. We need to take time to consider the source of information and wisely seek its confirmation.

Lord, thank You for giving us the ability to wisely discern true knowledge and not be gullible to false information. Amen.

PEACE WITHIN

A heart at peace gives life to the body, but envy rots the bones.
PROVERBS 14:30 NIV

Valerie carried a chip on her shoulder. Born to an unwed teen mother, she grew up knowing money was always in short supply. Valerie acted out her anger issues, causing school performance problems and brushes with law enforcement. Valerie had it in for the goody-two-shoes girls from wealthy families. She escalated her pranks until she was caught stealing.

During her interview with the high school disciplinary officer, Valerie said that it wasn't fair that her victim had so many more opportunities because she was born into money. She told the officer that it made her sick to be in class with the lucky goody-two-shoes girl.

"Valerie," the officer said, "you aren't using that term correctly." She went on to describe the old British fable titled "Goody Two-Shoes." Goody Two-Shoes was the nickname for a poor orphan girl who had but one shoe. She bubbles with happiness when a rich gentleman gives her a pair of shoes. The girl grows up to become a teacher and marry a wealthy man. The officer told Valerie that the story showed how heredity didn't need to limit her destiny. If Valerie chose to be grateful for what she had and worked to make the best of her life, the officer believed she would find peace and contentment. If Valerie let herself envy others for the advantages she thought they had, her future would likely be bleak.

*Lord, thank You for the blessing of peace that
allows me to be healthy and prosper. Amen.*

Pepper with Salt

*"You are the salt of the earth. But if the salt loses its saltiness,
how can it be made salty again? It is no longer good for anything,
except to be thrown out and trampled underfoot."*
Matthew 5:13 niv

Gabby never said no when asked to help a good cause. As an at-home mom, she felt obligated to be available whenever possible. Gabby had two teenage children both active in after-school activities with booster clubs and fund-raisers. She also volunteered at church and for two charities.

Her husband, Mark, believed Gabby did so much volunteer work that she had become overcommitted. He asked to sit down and discuss his concerns. Mark acknowledged that Christians should willingly give of their time and resources in salty service to others. However, he told Gabby that she was so busy trying to do good works that it might be hurting her effectiveness. He referred to Matthew 5:13 when he told Gabby that if she overextended herself she would lose her saltiness and no longer be good for anything.

Gabby defensively explained how she juggled all her volunteer tasks with her family responsibilities. Mark reminded Gabby they had agreed to make their kids her first priority. They made sacrifices to have her at home because it was valuable to their family.

Gabby finally admitted that she had probably taken on more than she could do well. She liked her husband's suggestion that she sparingly pepper her life with service so that she could preserve her salty effectiveness.

*Lord, thank You for showing me how to balance
my responsibilities with my salty service to others. Amen.*

JUST BE PRESENT

Then they sat on the ground with him for seven days and seven nights.
No one said a word to him, because they saw
how great his suffering was.
JOB 2:13 NIV

. . . .

Edna saw a friend rush out of worship on Sunday morning. After the service, she learned that her friend had been called to the hospital by her family. Her husband had been taken by ambulance from his nursing home. Edna asked Pastor Anita if there was anything she could do to help.

Pastor Anita said, "At this point the only thing to do is support the family and pray." Since the pastor had a family dinner to attend, Edna agreed to go and represent the church.

She called ahead and offered to bring food from a drive-through. After picking up their requests, Edna went to the hospital. She asked the family if she could stay and pray for them. They welcomed her presence. Edna sat out of the way and prayed for the Lord's will to be done as He guided the medical professionals and this troubled family.

When Pastor Anita arrived hours later, Edna excused herself and left after sharing hugs.

Like Job's friends, Edna went to sympathize and offer comfort. She accomplished the goal by quietly and patiently sitting with this family. Like Edna, often during emotionally difficult times we give comfort just by our presence. Words aren't required.

. . . .

Lord, thank You for allowing us to show comfort
merely with our presence. Amen.

Actions Speak Louder with Words

*Dear children, let us not love with words
or speech but with actions and in truth.*
1 John 3:18 niv

Everyone knew they could depend on Georgia for help. Her talents were as extensive as the tools she owned. If Georgia didn't know how to do something, she was willing to learn. Georgia described herself as a doer, not a talker.

Even though Georgia worked alongside others, she often felt lonely. Volunteers on a work team would be courteous and appreciative of her contributions, but she didn't feel she connected on a personal level. Georgia assumed that others didn't really like her.

While helping her sister strip wallpaper, Georgia mentioned that she often felt isolated when she was volunteering with a group. Robin gently probed and Georgia gradually shared examples as they worked. When they sat down for a glass of tea, Robin asked if Georgia wanted her thoughts.

After an affirmative nod, Robin took her sister's hands and turned them palm up. "Georgia, you do so much good with these talented hands. But showing Christian love requires you to share your heart with actions *and* words."

Just as we develop a personal relationship with God through talking with Him, Georgia needed to speak from her heart to develop personal relationships. In 1 John 3:18 we're instructed to give love through actions and truth. To show love with truth, Georgia needed to become a doer *and* a talker.

*Lord, thank You for the talents You have blessed me with. Help me share
my Christian love with both actions and words. Amen.*

Leap Day Corrections

*Whoever heeds discipline shows the way to life,
but whoever ignores correction leads others astray.*
Proverbs 10:17 niv

February 29 only happens every fourth year, normally in years evenly divisible by four. Some refer to it as Leap Day. It's the day added to adjust our Gregorian calendar to match the slightly longer solar year. Historic data shows humankind has been adjusting our calendars for over two thousand years.

Why do we care if our calendar is equivalent to the solar calendar? If we didn't add Leap Days, in the span of one century, January 1 would slip back to approximately May 1. Without the addition of Leap Day, the first day of summer and the first day of winter wouldn't occur on the same calendar dates each year. Life cycles would need to shift and evolve.

In Genesis, we're told God created the first day made up of both day (or morning) and night (or evening). After this, God made all His creatures to live within His time structure of days.

Centuries have passed, but we're still the same children God created to live in His world. To thrive, we still must live by the laws and commandments He established for humankind. So to conform to the solar year He gives us, we have disciplined ourselves to adjust our calendar with the addition of Leap Days. This simple correction assures us that our calendar and the regularity of life will not stray from God's plan.

Lord, thank You for giving structure to my world and my days. Help me to exercise self-discipline to make corrections that are prudent. Amen.

Spinning Just for Her

*For by the grace given me I say to every one of you: Do not think
of yourself more highly than you ought, but rather think of yourself
with sober judgment, in accordance with the faith
God has distributed to each of you.*
Romans 12:3 NIV

Miss Ego—let's call her Olivia Braggart—comes into a room looking
great and smelling great. Even the air around her has a rosy-colored hue.
She knows the world is spinning just for her. And so, Olivia naturally
feels she should be the life of the party and even sit at the head table.
Why not? But just when she sashays up to the front and sits herself
down, the hostess—who is slightly mortified at Olivia's audacity—leans
down and whispers that the seat she is now occupying was not meant
for her. It is for her honored guest.

Uh-oh.

Olivia does a whole-body blush. She scurries off, breaking a heel,
hoping no one saw the social blunder. What could have gone wrong in
her thinking? Really, it comes down to one little word, but one big sin.

Pride.

When we place our focus on "me" 24–7, issues are bound to arise.
Let us think on God. Let us think of others. As long as we seek the Lord
and have the mind of Christ, we won't have to worry about being sent
back to the end of the line. With Christ by our side, we will always be
just where we need to be.

Lord, forgive me for my pride and give me a servant's heart. Amen.

CAN'T YOU HEAR HIM WHISPER?

He says, "Be still, and know that I am God."
PSALM 46:10 NIV

Our society is so fast-paced there is little time to take care of our mental and physical health, let alone our spiritual health. We are beings created for eternity, and we are made in the image of a supernatural God, yet paying attention to our spiritual journey gets put off and off and off.

Until something terrible happens. Like a financial crisis. Or infidelity in our marriage. Or bad news at the doctor's office. Or a death in the family. Then we do far more than pause. We go into a full-body panic mode, drenched in fear, racing around, grasping at anything and everything, desperate for answers. For peace.

Had we been in close fellowship with the Lord all along, we wouldn't be so frantic, our spirits so riddled with terror. What we need to do is to be still and know that He is God. Know that He is still in control, even though we think the bad news is in control. It's not. God is.

Life would be more peaceful, more focused, more infused with joy if we were already in the midst of communion with God when troubles come.

Can't you hear Him whisper to you, "Be still, and know that I am God"?

Lord, help me to want to spend time with You every day
of my life—in fair weather as well as stormy. Amen.

Good Ol' Aunt Mable

Be kind and compassionate to one another,
forgiving each other, just as in Christ God forgave you.
Ephesians 4:32 niv

Some days it can be fairly easy to don a smile and carry a basket of sweetness and light to scatter everywhere you go.

That is, until your aunt Mable shows up. Wow, when that woman walks through the door, it's as if a pit bull has had its tail pulled and you're the one with the guilty look. Aunt Mable will twist your words, offer you a few backhanded compliments, point out all your latest transgressions, and judge you within an inch of your life. When she's done with you, there will be nothing left but tears.

Yes, with Auntie Mable around, being a Christian becomes anything but easy.

We all have an Aunt Mable in our lives. The only way to deal with the Auntie Mables is to pray for them. We must have compassion for them, love them, forgive them. Why, you may ask, should we bother? Because that is what Christ has done for all of us. While we were yet sinners, Christ died for us.

He even died for Aunt Mable. He even died for me and you. Because whether we want to admit it or not—there is a little Aunt Mable in all of us.

Lord, help me to remember how Your sacrifice on the cross offered me forgiveness and eternal life. Help me to extend that same loveliness of spirit to all people, even to the folks who are hard to love. Amen.

I Did It My Way

*Those who trust in themselves are fools,
but those who walk in wisdom are kept safe.*
Proverbs 28:26 niv

People tend to think of themselves as intelligent beings—full of insight and understanding, especially if they have acquired academic degrees and accolades. They like to think they can make it on their own. That they are a powerhouse of strength and a font of sound judgment. That they can breeze through life fueled by their own wit and wisdom. People love to say, "I did it my way."

This kind of thinking is folly and anything but wise.

We do need assistance. We need counsel from godly men and women, and most of all we need help from the ultimate guide—whose name is Jesus.

How have you chosen to live your life? Do you tread lightly, knowing you are fallible and fallen and in need of the Lord's daily guidance? Or do you bulldoze forward no matter what, confident that you'll make it in your own understanding? Proverbs 3:6 (nkjv) instructs, "In all your ways acknowledge Him, and He shall direct your paths." What a promise. What relief!

In the end, that is the essence of true wisdom—to say, "I did it God's way."

*Lord Jesus, help me to realize I can't make it on my own in this life.
I need You every hour of every day. Please direct my paths. Amen.*

A SPECTACLE OF JOY

Wearing a linen ephod, David was dancing before the LORD with all his might, while he and all Israel were bringing up the ark of the LORD with shouts and the sound of trumpets. As the ark of the LORD was entering the City of David, Michal daughter of Saul watched from a window. And when she saw King David leaping and dancing before the LORD, she despised him in her heart.
2 SAMUEL 6:14–16 NIV

The world tells us how to live our lives—how to eat, communicate, love, sleep, grieve, and celebrate. The problem is, the world's philosophies, values, and viewpoints don't usually mesh with God's ways. In the book of 2 Samuel, when David danced before the Lord, we sense that even though his wife Michal despised her husband's spectacle of utter joy, the Lord did not. David was celebrating with abandon—although not in the conventional ways perhaps—but he was indeed showing his passionate joy and profound thankfulness to God.

How easy it is to seek the approval of others. How tempting. But how unwise. Let us instead seek to satisfy God, to love Him, to joy in His presence. Life will then be more beautiful. Maybe not as the world describes beauty, but it will possess a loveliness in spirit from the Lord that the world cannot touch. That the world will puzzle over. That the world may even ponder and eventually desire.

Dear Lord, help me to seek Your approval and not the world's. Show me how to praise You for Your goodness and mercy. Amen.

SUNDAY, MARCH 6

DEEP IN OUR HEARTS

For this God is our God for ever and ever;
he will be our guide even to the end.
PSALM 48:14 NIV

You turn a corner on a busy street, and suddenly you don't know where you are. You don't recognize the signs, the buildings, or the landmarks. You go back the way you came. You pause to think, to focus, trying not to panic. But it's no good. You know in your heart that you're off course, and you won't be able to find your way back without help.

And so it goes with our souls. We take many of the wrong paths in life. Then we backtrack. Then we take the wrong roads all over again. And again. We get scared, but we still want to go it alone. Or perhaps we reach out to the wrong people for help.

Still we search.

Deep in our hearts we know the truth, even if we spend a lifetime trying to deny it.

We're horribly lost.

We need someone to rescue us. We need the One who can take us by the heart and hand and give us a way out of our peril. Give us new life. Take us home where we belong.

There is only One who can be called on for that kind of mighty and supernatural rescue.

His name is Jesus.

Take heart. Your rescuer is here.

Lord, please set me free from sin and sadness. Let me walk on higher ground with You by my side, for now and all eternity. Amen.

ITTY BITTY WORDS

*The words of the reckless pierce like swords,
but the tongue of the wise brings healing.*
PROVERBS 12:18 NIV

. . . .

Whoever started the childhood chant—"Sticks and stones may break my bones, but words will never hurt me"—lied. Plain and simple.

Words may seem itty bitty as they escape from our lips, but they have the power to make us cringe and cry and crumble into pieces. Pieces that may never come back together again the way they were meant to be.

Words can destroy a reputation and break a tender (or not-so-tender) heart. Words can create an untold ripple effect of misery. Our words can grieve the Holy Spirit. Surely there is a better way to live.

There is. It's with the power of the Holy Spirit. From the Psalms comes a wonderful daily heart-prayer: "May these words of my mouth and this meditation of my heart be pleasing in your sight, LORD, my Rock and my Redeemer" (Psalm 19:14 NIV).

Our words can heal, comfort, challenge, encourage, and inspire. It's our choice, every minute of every day, which kind of words we will use—those that heal or those that hurt. Let us always speak truth, yes, but let us do it with tenderness. Not with a mind-set that feeds our egos, but with a caring spirit that pleases God.

. . . .

*Holy Spirit, guide me in my thoughts, and may my words
be healing to all I meet. Amen.*

Shout for Joy

*The desert and the parched land will be glad; the wilderness will rejoice
and blossom. Like the crocus, it will burst into bloom;
it will rejoice greatly and shout for joy.*
Isaiah 35:1–2 niv

Is there any season as joyous as spring? Trees unfurl thousands of tiny juicy green flags to wave hello to the world. Flowers make that final push through the dark soil and stretch out their bedecked arms to embrace the sun-warmed air. Farmers plant seeds of promise into the brown, barren land—measuring out hope by the bushel.

You are human. You will go through times of sorrow and despair, times of suffering and boredom. You will work through long days and toss and turn through longer nights. You will worry and fret and stew. You will look around and see only gray.

Spring is our annual reminder that the story isn't over. It's never over. It starts up from page one again every year, ready to be filled with characters and plots and dialogue. No, the story won't always be happy and the characters won't all get along. But isn't it amazing that it happens at all? That our Creator God is willing to keep writing new chapters for us, and that He never runs out of ideas?

A new story starts right before your eyes every spring. Now that's something to shout about.

*Dear Lord, thank You for Your endless creativity that brings us so much
grace and joy. Help me remember in the grayest times that
color is just an inch or so under my feet.*

No More Land of Good-byes

*"My Father's house has many rooms; if that were not so, would I have
told you that I am going there to prepare a place for you?"*
John 14:2 niv

Our birthday, when we take our first screaming gasp of air in this
world, is the same day our bodies prepare to eventually die. Wow, what
a depressing thought, right? And yet it is the truth. This fallen world
involves a daily letting go, even from the beginning.

In fact, one could say that the earth is a land of good-byes. A land
of sorrows, pain, and suffering. Of war, traumas, loneliness, and rivers
of tears that never seem to stop flowing. Sounds bleak, miserable, and
hopeless.

"Where is the hope then?" you may ask. Our hope is in Christ,
who came not only to take away the sins of the world but to bring
us into a new land of promise. A place of welcome, new life, and
unspeakable joy. A place of holy light and pure love. A place for all time.

Each and every person is given an invitation to this heavenly
place, which is being prepared by the Son of God. Will you accept His
invitation? Will you say yes to eternal life?

*Jesus, I accept Your generous and sacrificial gift of salvation,
and I look forward to spending an eternity with You. Amen.*

My Refuge

The LORD is my rock, my fortress and my deliverer; my God is my rock, in whom I take refuge, my shield and the horn of my salvation, my stronghold.
Psalm 18:2 NIV

Here's the scene. You're snorkeling not far from the shoreline in a sparkling turquoise sea. You're enjoying the gentle sway of ocean waves and the pretty fish. But you soon discover that you've drifted beyond the confines of the quiet bay. Suddenly swells are heaving around you, and land looks like a distant memory.

You gulp some water and cough. You fight the waves, but your arms and legs quickly tire. Panic rises inside your belly. Adrenaline pumps. Fear becomes a living thing inside you as you shout, "Help me!" Someone on the shore sees you, but can they reach you in time before you're overcome by the waves?

You pray. Harder than you've ever prayed.

Then you see it. A big hulk of a stone, jutting out of the sea. You swim toward it, and in a few moments you are climbing onto that rock. You're clinging to that bit of sanctuary with every fiber of your being. Refuge never felt so good.

That is like God, our deliverer. He is our rock when we call out to Him, when we're in any kind of need—physically, mentally, or spiritually. Jesus may not rescue us in the way we want or in our timing, but He will never forsake us. It is His steadfast promise to us. Count on it.

Lord, You are my rock, my fortress, and my deliverer. I will take refuge in You. Amen.

As Pure as Rainwater

Hatred stirs up conflict,
but love covers over all wrongs.
PROVERBS 10:12 NIV

. . . .

Have you ever seen a rain barrel filled after a good storm? That water is clean and refreshing. But if you take a big stick and whip up the contents, soon the dregs will rise and whorl. Suddenly what was clean is now a dirty mess. That visual is a good one for Proverbs 10:12, which reminds us that hatred stirs up old quarrels.

When we choose to hold on to grudges, hatred seeps into our hearts. It's like we're carrying around a big stick, and we're more than ready to whip up some dregs by bringing up an argument from the past. This is a common way to live, but not a godly or healthy one.

What's the answer?

Love.

When we love others, we will overlook insults, whether they are intended or not. Does that seem like an impossible task using these feeble shells of ours?

It is impossible in our own humanness.

But with the supernatural power of the Holy Spirit, we can overcome this need to stir up trouble, and we can forgive freely and love abundantly—just as Christ has done for us. So let us come not with a big stick but with a spirit as refreshing and as pure as rainwater.

. . . .

Holy Spirit, please take away any tendency in me to bicker,
but instead make me into a woman who loves with my whole
heart and who is an instrument of Your peace. Amen.

His Loving Eye Is on You

I will instruct you and teach you in the way you should go;
I will counsel you with my loving eye on you.
Psalm 32:8 niv

Imagine you are asked to walk through a long hallway, but then as you travel along, you discover that the hallway is more like a maze with many passageways to choose from. Then you discover that the farther you go into those corridors, the more they are shrouded in darkness. You can't tell for sure which way to go. The shadows become sinister. You hear whispers, but they don't sound encouraging or helpful. Feeling frightened and alone, you frantically run this way and that. You stumble in the darkness and cry out to God.

Suddenly someone switches on all the lights, and you can see clearly. Warm, pure light vanquishes the darkness. Now as you walk along, you can maneuver around the perilous choices and see which path will take you on your way. Your footing becomes stable and your heartbeat steady.

So it goes with prayer. It lights our path. It is a way for God to guide us through life so we will know which course to take—in fact, His will for us.

Have you spent time in prayer today? God's loving eye is on you, and He will counsel you in the way you should go.

Lord, help me to remember to spend time in prayer every day
so I might know Your will. Amen.

REMEMBER THE MIRACLES

*He came to Jesus at night and said, "Rabbi, we know that you are
a teacher who has come from God. For no one could perform
the signs you are doing if God were not with him."*
JOHN 3:2 NIV

People today are cynical about miracles. Even some Christians wonder
if miracles are perhaps a Bible-times phenomenon and no longer part of
modern-day life. Disbelief and cynicism are easy emotions. In fact, some
of the Israelites felt this way even after they had witnessed many signs
and wonders from God. How many miracles does it take for humanity
to finally have faith? The kind of belief that doesn't wobble like a tower
of Jell-O?

If we look, we will see miracles—even daily. Miracles come in all
shapes and sizes. When they do come, thank God for them. Tell others
about them so that they too might be uplifted. Write them down.
Memorize them and keep them close to your heart. That way, when
hardships come—and they will come eventually—you can remember all
that God has done for you.

Then, when the enemy of your soul comes to tempt and discourage
you, you will be able to stand strong. You will keep hold of joy. You will
live with victory.

Acknowledging and celebrating these wonders from God is part of
a contented Christian life. What miracles will you praise God for today?

*God, help me to remember all the miracles in my life,
both big and small. Amen.*

Precious Bundle

But because of his great love for us, God, who is rich in mercy,
made us alive with Christ even when we were dead in
transgressions—it is by grace you have been saved.
Ephesians 2:4–5 niv

It's your first baby, and the nurse has just placed that precious newborn bundle in your arms. You count her wee little toes. You brush your lips against her cheek. You gaze into her eyes. Oh, such pools of delight. You love her—that cherishing kind of love that makes your heart ache. You are filled with such wonder and sighing bliss that you think you might die of an overdose of pure joy.

Yes, you do indeed love your child profoundly, and yet it can't come close to the intensity of affection, care, and devotion your heavenly Father has for you. He delights in you even when you're red-faced and wailing. Even when you're stamping your feet. Even when you stumble and fall into sin.

In fact, His great love for us is beyond human understanding. His love included sending His only Son to die for us so that we could know freedom from sin and death. Imagine. Now that is amazing love.

But just as parents long for their children to grow up and love them in return, so does God. He welcomes your company, not just for the here and now, but for all time.

Thank You, God, for Your great love for me. Amen.

REAL HOPE

If only for this life we have hope in Christ,
we are of all people most to be pitied.
1 Corinthians 15:19 NIV

People hope for all kinds of things. They hope for a good education so they can fulfill their purpose. They hope to fall in love, get married, and have a family. All of those goals seem reasonable, even noble, but what good are they if life were to end when we die? Then an education and a profession would be no more than busyness just to get us through until our death. And why should we bring more children into a world of pain if there is nothing beyond this material world?

This passage in 1 Corinthians offers us a stark and poignant "what if?" scenario. That is, if our hope in Christ is meant only for the here and now, then we are to be pitied. We would be spouting a faith that has no future and thus no real hope. We would be peddlers of a religion as hollow and fake as the building facades on a movie set.

Christianity is a relationship with Christ, and that relationship is not only for today but will take you right into a time that knows no end. As a lover of Christ, you have every right to hope, rejoice, and live and love with a full heart. So get that education. Fall in love and have that family. In Christ, it matters now. It matters forever.

Lord, thank You for the hope we have in You
now and for all time. Amen.

LAUGHING AT THE DAYS TO COME

She is clothed with strength and dignity;
she can laugh at the days to come.
PROVERBS 31:25 NIV

You mean a woman of God can laugh at the days to come? Really? Wow. Most of the world wakes up each morning under a black cloud of regret and a debilitating fear of the future. That sounds more realistic, right? To laugh at the future is hard to imagine. To see hope instead of futility? Promise in the pain? What would that kind of woman look and sound like?

Perhaps a woman of God as described in Proverbs 31 doesn't necessarily have a lot of confidence in herself, but rather in God. Perhaps she trusts so implicitly in His divine plan and goodness that she can sleep deeply. She can wake up refreshed each morning.

And this woman of God knows some truths—that God will indeed work everything for good in her life. She knows that He is watching over her comings and goings, and nothing will befall her that He can't handle. She knows that this earthly life is temporary. She knows that heaven is not only for real but forever. Knowing these truths all the way to her soul gives her peace and joy, and it shows in her countenance. Yes, and even in her laugh.

Jesus, help me trust in You every hour of every day, and let me be so full
of peace that I too can laugh at the days to come. Amen.

EVERYONE'S IRISH

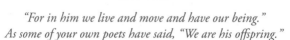

"For in him we live and move and have our being."
As some of your own poets have said, "We are his offspring."
ACTS 17:28 NIV

On this day, many celebrate Patrick, saint of Ireland, and indeed, it seems almost all the world claims to be Irish. Though we certainly are not all sons and daughters of Ireland, we all can be sons and daughters of one King.

In the city of Athens, the apostle Paul found himself in a position not unlike that of Patrick, whose birth was still several hundred years away—a believing man of God in a place full of worshippers of idols. It took courage for Paul to face a city full of such opposition and speak his message clearly and boldly. More than that, it took compassion and love for him to see such people and not despise or belittle them, but instead want them for brothers and sisters.

St. Patrick returned to the land of his former captors with that same compassion and love. Though he suffered and was often in danger of being killed for it, he continued to fight for the opportunity to welcome more people into the family of God.

On this day when we all can be Irish, let us also remember that we all can be children of God. And let us fight boldly and courageously for the chance to welcome more people into our family.

In the words of Patrick: "Christ beside me, Christ before me, Christ behind me, Christ within me, Christ beneath me, Christ above me." Amen.

Rainbows and Unicorns

"Never again will the waters become a flood to destroy all life."
Genesis 9:15 NIV

. . . .

Are there some people you wouldn't mind seeing washed away? Perhaps not utterly destroyed—just swept far, far away.

God experimented with a solution for ridding the world of its evil. He wiped away every living creature, except for the ones he entrusted to Noah's care. Noah was the unicorn in this story—the legendary figure of a blameless man, the only man who "walked faithfully with God" (Genesis 6:9 NIV).

For reasons we can only guess at, God decided the plan to destroy the earth and start again was not one He wanted to repeat. Perhaps He realized that, since "every inclination of the human heart is evil from childhood" (Genesis 8:21 NIV), this whole scenario would likely have to be repeated again and again—and who wants to clean up that mess over and over? Or perhaps He thought of a different solution. Perhaps His experience with Noah was enough to give God hope that He could have a relationship with humans. Perhaps the answer is just that God has grace and mercy in measures we cannot fathom.

Whatever the reason, God set a rainbow in the sky as a sign of His promise. He decided to give Noah, and all of us, another chance.

Perhaps if God can look at all the wickedness of the whole world and decide to give us another chance, we can give others a second chance too.

. . . .

Dear Lord, help me remember my own flaws
and keep me from judging others. Amen.

REFRESHMENT

*A generous person will prosper;
whoever refreshes others will be refreshed.*
PROVERBS 11:25 NIV

Maybe you've hit a low point in your year already. Things aren't going as planned. You feel stuck at your job or stifled in a relationship. Maybe you're having a bad year. Or even just a bad day.

At any moment when you feel disappointed or unlucky or down, try this. Find someone who is in need—maybe someone who is also feeling knocked down—and do something for them. It doesn't have to be a big something. Give them a fountain drink, a small bouquet, a bar of chocolate, or a good book. Maybe just call and say hi or send a card.

The person doesn't even have to be someone you know. Go to a nursing home and read to someone who can't see anymore. Just spend some time listening to a person's story. Go to a bus stop and hand out free bottles of water. Go to the grocery store and offer people help with carrying groceries. Buy someone's coffee in the drive-through line at the coffee shop.

Once you've done some act of kindness or generosity, stop and take note of how you feel. Is life a little bit brighter? If it isn't, try again. If it is, try again. You will soon find that the more you give to others, the better you get at it, and the more you will feel refreshed by God.

*Dear Giver of all good things, thank You for Your blessings.
Help us to see them all around us, especially in
our service to others. Amen.*

THE DOUBTFUL ENTRY

"See, your king comes to you, gentle and riding on a donkey."
MATTHEW 21:5 NIV

. . . .

They were armed with parade signs and had practiced their chants. They'd even arranged a flash mob to lay down cloaks on the entry route. Hyped up by the festival atmosphere, the fans were ready. Whispers of Roman murder plots, government upheaval, and the fulfillment of prophecies only added to their excited anticipation. It was a scene primed for a magic moment—a truly triumphant entry.

Had it been done Hollywood style, there certainly would have been cymbal crashes and trumpet fanfares, with a majestic orchestral swoosh backing the scene—driving the hairs up on the backs of our necks. Perhaps there even would have been a few fireworks, or a lightning bolt, or at the very least a soft, glowing light shining on our champion's face and highlighting the brilliant white mane of His stallion.

Instead, Jesus came clip-clopping into a city full of enemies on a lowly beast of burden, with only the noisy shouts of some common folks and the rustling of palm leaves to announce His arrival.

It's little wonder the Gospel writers record how His authority was questioned soon after this event. The disciples themselves didn't even understand what He was doing.

So what *was* He doing? He tells us. "The one who looks at me is seeing the one who sent me" (John 12:45). He was painting a picture. A picture of a King so powerful, He dared to enter in weakness.

. . . .

God, give me a heart that is humble like Yours. Amen.

EXPECTATIONS

But love your enemies, do good to them,
and lend to them without expecting to get anything back.
LUKE 6:35 NIV

Do you feel entitled to a certain kind of treatment from others? Think about that for a minute. Think about some of the most annoying things that happen to you on a regular basis. You have to wait in line longer than you like at the so-called fast-food restaurant. You order something online, and the store sends you the wrong thing. You do a good deed and no one notices. You give generously (so you think), and no one pays you back.

How much do you expect from others? From strangers? From friends? From enemies? From God?

Whatever your level of expectation, take a step back and evaluate what that says about your relationship with that person. It may be a good thing—for example, you expect faithfulness from your spouse because of the vows you've taken. But it may be that you have placed too much importance on your part in this equation. Should you get something simply because you have given something? Is that the requirement? Or rather, is the requirement to give cheerfully, with or without a reward?

Jesus came to turn the "eye for an eye" kind of justice on its head. He came to say that loving God with all your heart, soul, mind, and strength means giving differently. Giving big. And quite likely getting *nothing* in return.

Dear Lord, help me to give with a heart like Yours. Amen.

MORE THAN SPARROWS

"You are worth more than many sparrows."
MATTHEW 10:31 NIV

- -

Sparrows are not rare birds. The little gray, white, and black bodies can be spotted all over the world. They hang out in hedges and graze on grassland. They are about as common as field mice and rabbits.

As common as they are, God knows these creatures. He knows the seeds they like to eat and when they molt. He knows they like to bathe in the dust and congregate in talkative groups. He knows the feathers on their heads and the bird's-eye views they have seen.

God cares about sparrows. He cares about caterpillars and ants and rabbits and mice as well. If our great God cares about these little creatures that come and go and do as they please, how much more do you think He cares about you? Even when you're struggling to follow Him, and when you sing the wrong notes in all the right praise songs, and when you forget to pray, and when you forget you know Him—in all these times, the God of the sparrows and the grass in the field and the mountaintops and the nations knows you, and claims you as His child.

Never worry about what you are worth to your Father. He loves you more than the wildflowers growing in the field. He loves you more than the flutter of a million sparrows' wings. He sees you and everything you do from his God's-eye view, and He loves you still.

- -

God, thank You for making me feel precious. Amen.

YET

"Though he slay me, yet will I hope in him."
JOB 13:15 NIV

· ·

There are many who know the meaning of these words better than the rest of us.

The family living in Tornado Alley whose house has been torn to shreds no fewer than five times in the last fifteen years.

The mother whose sons and husband were all lost on the battlefield.

The family of the woman who survived a long, wearying struggle with cancer only to be sent back into the hospital by a megavirus.

Have you ever felt under attack? Have you ever felt perhaps God was testing your mettle? How do you hold on to hope when there seems to be no reason to do so? What does that even look like?

Though his case seems extreme, it's unlikely that many of us would react much differently than the course Job took. People going through difficult periods of their lives cycle through anger and bitterness, anguish and sorrow, and resignation and confusion, just as Job did. Though they probably don't sit and cover themselves with ashes, they may hole up in their bedrooms with quilts over their heads.

In the end, what leads Job to hope is God. God is still there. Even through all of Job's complaints and cries and angry accusations, God does not leave. God does not change. God provides no excuses. Bad things will come. But so will God.

· ·

Dear Lord, thank You for holding on to me
when I can't hold on to hope. Amen.

Flowers Fall

*"The grass withers and the flowers fall,
but the word of the Lord endures forever."*
1 Peter 1:24–25 niv

It's funny how people try to make things last that were never meant to do so. For example, people hold on to mementos of special occasions, sometimes keeping the flowers that were worn on the day or that decorated the scene. They will press flowers, dry them, and preserve them in various ways. When that isn't enough, they have silk renditions created. Or they take photographs and hold on to those instead.

We want good things to last. We want people to live long lives and relationships to endure hardships. We root for the longsuffering hero who finally wins in the end. We hold detailed ceremonies to remember those we have lost.

Though these bodies of ours were not meant to continue forever, when we have accepted Jesus as our Savior and Redeemer, we become "born again, not of perishable seed, but of imperishable, through the living and enduring word of God" (1 Peter 1:23 niv).

It's this contradiction—forever souls bound in temporary houses— that makes us long for all good things to never die. But peace and contentment—a cure of sorts for that longing—can be found in the enduring Word of God. The more time we spend there, the more we realize we have all the time in the world.

*Thank You, Lord, for giving us Your Word to guide and sustain
us as we walk in this temporary home. Amen.*

PASSED OVER, NOT FORGOTTEN

"The LORD will fight for you; you need only to be still."
EXODUS 14:14 NIV

The festival of Passover is a time for all followers of God to remember. Among the many great things God has done for His people, we remember how God freed the Israelites from generations of slavery and brought them out of Egypt.

An outsider observing this remembrance might easily ask, "You say God does great things for you every day—why would you need this reminder?"

Passover reminds us of many aspects of God—His power and might, His care for the Israelites, and His tenderness and mercy, among others. But it also invites us to remember a few things about ourselves—that we are weak and in need of a Savior, that we are witnesses, and that we are forgetful. Passover reminds us that despite all of our shortcomings, we have been chosen by God.

It is this last thing we remember as we go forward every day and decide anew each morning to trust Him with our lives—with all of the hundreds of little trials that we stumble through and with all of the huge valleys of doubt and despair that we encounter on our way through our own kind of wilderness. He will not forget us. He is with us. He wants us. Not just for the day of delivery, but for every moment thereafter. For eternity.

Dear God, help us to remember that You are the God
who delivers us, every day. Amen.

Redemption Stories

Let the redeemed of the Lord tell their story.
Psalm 107:2 niv

. . . .

For just about as long as the entertainment industry has been around (or longer), redemption stories have been the basis for popular movies, novels, and plays. Everyone loves to follow the story of the bad guy turned knight in shining armor, the down-on-his-luck everyman who receives big blessings, or the orphan in rags who gains a family and great riches all at once.

If you are a follower of Christ, there's a good chance you've had to exchange something for the path to eternal life. You've had to let something go or give something up. Or perhaps you've been changed in some significant way. No one encounters Jesus Christ and comes away exactly the same.

Let these words encourage you today to tell your story. If you have not told it before, start now. Pick a few small details to share, or give the whole general outline. Tell a loved one. Tell a coworker. Tell your pastor. Tell a friend. Tell a stranger on the subway. Tell anyone who will listen.

You never know how your story might impact someone else. You will never know the strength and love and hope you have to give until you open your mouth and let your truth out.

Everyone loves a redemption story. Why not give them yours?

. . . .

*Dear Redeemer, thank You for dying for us, for saving us,
and for preparing a place for us in heaven. Help me to have
the courage to share my story of You. Amen.*

SUNRISE SERVICE

Just after sunrise, they were on their way to the tomb and they asked each other, "Who will roll the stone away from the entrance of the tomb?"
MARK 16:2–3 NIV

The three women were on a mission. It was all they could do for their Lord now, and they were determined to do it. No doubt they were at risk on their route to the tomb. The body of the Rabbi would have been a target for many with less kind intentions, and the women themselves, as followers of the convicted traitor of Rome, would have been in danger of, at the very least, some rough treatment from the Roman guards.

But these women were not so unlike women today facing a crisis. You do what you can do. You cook, you clean, you offer help of any practical, tangible kind, because facing the actual spiritual and emotional wounds is too heavy to bear all at once. So you do what you can do. Far better to mess one's hands with oils and spices—with the dirt of work—than to wash them with more tears.

These women came to perform a service, but a service had already been performed for them. The stone had been rolled away. The body was gone. The tomb was clean. The only work left to do was to rejoice and tell the news.

*Dear Lord, this Easter Sunday, help me to do the work
You have given me to do. To rejoice in Your resurrection
and to tell the Good News. Amen.*

LIKE A MUSTARD SEED

"The kingdom of heaven is like a mustard seed."
MATTHEW 13:31 NIV

Your church may be a tiny house of worship in the middle of a great big county of nothing notable. It may be a huge palace of praise in a city of cultural patchwork. No matter where we worship, because we are followers of Jesus, we are all part of one family, one body. The Church with a capital C.

We don't always act like it.

Jesus told a parable about what the kingdom of heaven is like. He painted a picture of a tiny, roly-poly mustard seed. Have you ever held a mustard seed? They are so small and so easy to lose. One wrong move and it slips through your fingers and bounces away to who knows where.

Yet if that seed is left to grow, it will become rooted well into the ground. It will sprout a stalk that thickens and strengthens. It will stretch out branches wide and low to the ground that the birds love to perch in.

Each of our churches begins with that small seed of faith. Then we grow and change and stretch and support. But no mustard tree competes with another for birds. And no trees criticize one another and pick apart each other's branches.

If we want to keep growing, we have to keep reaching out our branches and supporting those who want to come and perch upon them. No matter what kind of seed they started from.

*Dear Father, help us to see each other always
as brothers and sisters in You. Amen.*

SINGING TREES

*Let the fields be jubilant, and everything in them; let all the trees of
the forest sing for joy. Let all creation rejoice before the LORD,
for he comes, he comes to judge the earth.*
PSALM 96:12–13 NIV

What are your favorite worship songs? Are they slow and soft, or fast
and bright? Do they bring peace or excitement? What would you do if
your favorite song was performed by a chorus of trees?

It would certainly make for an interesting service. No one would
sleep through that one.

The interesting thing about this idea from Psalm 96 is not just the
singing trees and fields. It's why they are so joyful that seems intriguing.
They are rejoicing before the Lord because He is coming to judge the
earth.

Judging doesn't sound like much fun. Judging sounds like something
that might be followed by the word *sentence*, *punishment*, or *penalty*.
There's nothing joyful about any of that.

The writer of this psalm is rejoicing in this event because of two
things he is sure of: (1) his place before the Creator of the earth and (2)
the truth that God is a just and righteous judge.

Are you sure of these two things? Do you trust God to judge fairly?
Could you sing with joy about your judgment to come? If you answer
no, what can you do today to start trusting God more? What do you
need to do to be sure of your position before God?

*Dear God, I know You are a just and righteous judge.
Help me honor You. Amen.*

Simple yet Powerful Words

Humble yourselves, therefore, under God's mighty hand,
that he may lift you up in due time.
1 Peter 5:6 niv

How can a person talk and talk and talk and yet when it comes time to speak words that have great importance, they are speechless? Two of those weighty words are "I'm sorry."

Without those words—and the sincerity of spirit backing them up—marriages fail, friendships break apart, family members suffer, working relationships become strained, and the church loses its ability to minister to people.

So why do we become tongue-tied on those simple words? Because it is easy to justify our position on any matter. Easy to take our own side in an argument. You name it, and we can find a way to point to someone else as the villain in any given circumstance. We must be the heroes, after all. We know our Bibles. We sit in the same pew every Sunday. We can spot sin in someone else's life faster than you can say, "Judgment Day!" But the truth is, sometimes even as Christians, we choose to play the villain in our life story. We forget kindness. We turn our head on justice. We forget the most important scriptures on love.

We need to take a deep look in the mirror, spiritually speaking, asking the Lord to show us if we are at fault and to give us the courage to make things right with others—to say the simple yet powerful words that can change a heart, a life.

Lord, please give me a humble heart
so that I may always please You. Amen.

BEGIN AGAIN

*I am not writing you a new command but one we have had from
the beginning. I ask that we love one another. And this is love:
that we walk in obedience to his commands.*
2 JOHN 1:5–6 NIV

Most people start off the new year with the best of intentions. "This year
will be different. This year will be better. *I* will be better."

But somewhere along the way, you get distracted. You get tired.
You lose ground. You forget. You fail.

Why not begin again?

You don't have to wait for the next New Year's Day. You don't have
to wait for permission to be reborn. Every day can be your spring.

All you have to do is decide. Decide to be obedient to what God
has told you to do from the beginning. Decide to be honest with
yourself. Decide to stay on the path. Decide to love. Decide to walk.

Examine your failures. Take note of your distractions and
temptations. Plan strategies that will lead to healthy relationships, a
healthy lifestyle, a balanced work life, and a devoted spiritual life.

There is nothing all that special or magical about New Year's Day.
It's just a day. And today is just a day too. It won't be easy, whatever it is.
Every good work requires effort. But you don't have to wait until you're
perfect. In fact, you shouldn't.

Begin again today.

*Dear Lord, show me how to love others I encounter this day.
And help me obey all Your commands. Amen.*

The Worst Joke of All

The fool has said in his heart, "There is no God."
PSALM 14:1 NASB

Faux announcements on social media, practical jokes at breakfast, and pranks pulled on coworkers—these mark the arrival of April 1, April Fool's Day. It's a day to enjoy with good humor. Every once in a while, someone pulls an inappropriate stunt, but as long as no one is really in danger, we can choose to ignore it.

There is one joke that Satan tells every year, and millions believe it. You guessed it. He convinces them that God doesn't exist. Some are called atheists; they totally deny the possibility of His being. Others are called agnostics; they can't decide if He is real or not. Then there are those who say they believe in Him, but deny that He is the God described in the Bible, almighty and powerful and before whom they will stand someday. And so every day of the year, Satan celebrates the foolish who live the way they want and die without eternal hope.

That's why God calls us to spread the truth, to live in such a way that others around us will know His power is at work in us. We have to show up Satan's lies and expose his wretched plot, for only the righteous can smile about eternity.

Heavenly Father, use me today to carry Your truth and show Your light.
Let Your love draw others to You so that Your house may
be full someday. In Jesus' name, amen.

RECONCILED RELATIONSHIPS

*God. . .reconciled us to Himself through Christ
and gave us the ministry of reconciliation.*
2 CORINTHIANS 5:18 NASB

After being inspired by a letter from one her readers regarding a strained family relationship, columnist Ann Landers has encouraged her followers to observe April 2 as Reconciliation Day. Through letters, phone calls, or visits, she advises that efforts be made to mend broken relationships through seeking or granting forgiveness. Many have written to her of the life-changing effects of their efforts. While reconciliation is sometimes a challenge, it is so rewarding. Often women are the ones who reach out for reconciliation in relationships because God designed women to be attuned to the nuances in the family and home. We just instinctively know some things about relationships.

On a different level, as God-followers, you and I have been reconciled ourselves through the sacrificial death of Christ. We have been brought into a restored relationship with our Creator. We can now enjoy the benefits of being part of His family. And we have been given the responsibility of telling others about these benefits. As we interact with friends and coworkers, let's not neglect to tell them that there is good news about the most important relationship they could ever have—one with Christ, who reconciles us to the Father through His Cross.

*Dear God, thank You for letting Jesus go to the cross so that I could have
a relationship with You. Help me to share this good news
with others today. In Christ's name, amen.*

Easter Living

But thanks be to God, who always leads us in triumph in Christ.
2 Corinthians 2:14 nasb

. . . .

Several different magazines describe the joys of various places to live—
Country Living, *Coastal Living*, and *Midwest Living*, to name a few. As a
girl raised in the South, I'm partial to *Southern Living*. These periodicals
tell us what we should buy and how we should decorate and cook in
order to be true to a certain way of life.

Jesus also offered a distinct way of doing life. It could be called
Easter Living. It can be accomplished with no money and is accessible
anywhere on earth. It affects every area of living, from the atmosphere
of one's home to the attitude one has at work. It celebrates death to
self and life in Christ. It unleashes Resurrection power to work. It is
victorious living.

Corrie ten Boom found that this way of living worked even in a Nazi
concentration camp. Deep in Germany, behind wire fences, surrounded
by cruelty and violence, Corrie and her sister Betsie discovered that the
power of Christ leads even prisoners in triumph. As Corrie liked to say,
"Jesus is Victor." He is the Victor over circumstances, tragedies, disease,
sin, and death. No matter what you face today, Jesus has victory for you.
And because He conquered it all with His death and resurrection, He can
make you free indeed.

. . . .

*Jesus, thank You for being the Victor. I accept the way of life
You offer me by Your grace and ask that You will lead
me in triumph over my challenges. Amen.*

THE FLOWER FACTORY

The flowers are springing up, the season of singing birds has come.
SONG OF SOLOMON 2:12 NLT

. . . .

In the area where I live, we have a local decor warehouse appropriately named Flower Factory. Thousands of square feet filled with merchandise greet the shopper; the aisles are packed with everything from wedding items to baskets to Christmas trees. Whatever the actual season outside, there are always flowers. They are silk and plastic, of course, and they aren't actually made at that location; they are simply sold there.

God, on the other hand, manages an authentic flower factory. He is the designer and sustainer of it all. He puts the blooms to bed in the fall and wakes up the seeds in the spring. He watches over the ground through the frosts and smiles as the sun warms the earth again. And, of course, He sends those "April showers" to speed up the growing process.

Without Him, nothing grows. Satan is skillful only at destruction and decay. He comes to "steal and kill and destroy." But Jesus came to give us "a rich and satisfying life" (John 10:10 NLT). He also grows people. Just as the flowers spring up with new life, He offers us opportunities to sink our roots down into His grace and bloom even more beautifully.

. . . .

Lord, I'm delighted with the beauty of the flowers this spring. I want to reflect Your glory like they do. Please work in my life and let the beauty of Jesus shine through me. In His name, amen.

THE TANTRUMS OF SPRING

He has made everything beautiful in its time.
ECCLESIASTES 3:11 NKJV

. . . .

While I enjoy the blossoming of nature and the reminder that God makes all things new, spring weather is not my favorite. Its fits of temper remind me of a toddler needing a nap; its fluctuating temperatures put me in mind of a woman suffering with hot flashes. Spring just can't make up its mind what it wants to do.

I know the back-and-forth of the weather in spring is all part of the cycle as the globe rotates around the sun and gets situated for the heat of summer. In spite of the temperamental outbursts, spring gradually arrives in full force and we can rejoice in wearing white again and throwing open the windows to let in the refreshing, bloom-scented breezes. When there's a break in the rain showers, some even pin freshly laundered sheets on a clothesline in the backyard. Others may clean out closets or wash windows and curtains and walls. Whatever ritual one uses, the arrival of spring and the promise of summer often provide the motivation to get started.

I believe God intends for the seasons He created to provide us with natural restart points. They are great opportunities to assess what needs changing and go forward with renewed energy. Now then, it's time to put away the tantrums and do something constructive. After all, a new season awaits.

. . . .

Father God, thank You for seasons and restarts and renewed energy. Help me to accomplish something wonderful today. In Your name, amen.

PLAN YOUR EPITAPH DAY

*I have fought the good fight, I have finished
the course, I have kept the faith.*
2 TIMOTHY 4:7 NASB

. . . .

It seems a bit macabre for a bright spring day, but the calendar of quirky holidays says this is "Plan Your Epitaph Day."

We don't do grief well in this country, and so most of us recoil from talk about epitaphs. We are uncomfortable with discussions of death, preferring to focus on closure and celebration of life and moving on, and we often shortchange our psyches in the process.

One way to help us cope with death is to accept the reality of our own and make preparations for what comes afterward. This is not morbidity but rather wisdom. For those of us who know Christ and realize that death is the doorway to eternal existence with Him, planning a funeral or writing a will need not make us depressed. Rather, it is a testimony to the way we have lived our lives.

The apostle Paul wrote a kind of epitaph while he sat on death row in a Roman prison. He wanted young Timothy to know that he was satisfied with what God had allowed him to do. Oh, that you and I might feel the same. That is the real point after all. Maybe writing an epitaph is as simple as writing a mission statement for life and planning each day to fulfill it. What would yours say?

. . . .

*Lord, I know that my life is a gift from You, a trust for which I am
responsible. Help me to fulfill Your purpose for me. Amen.*

Wellness from Within

*Do not be wise in your own eyes; fear the Lord and turn away from evil.
It will be healing to your body and refreshment to your bones.*
Proverbs 3:7–8 nasb

Today, April 7, is World Health Day. Sponsored by the World Health Organization (WHO), this is a date set aside each year for global health awareness. Each year there is a different theme, and there are international, regional, and local events. The themes have ranged from infectious diseases to road safety to healthy hearts and aging. By spotlighting various aspects of health on this day, health organizations hope to draw attention to practices and habits that contribute to better living for everyone.

Unfortunately, a person may be full of physical vitality and yet sickly in his or her spiritual being. While the market for whole food supplements and organic vegetables and potent vitamins and tinctures has exploded in the last couple of decades, the awareness of what brings spiritual health has never reached international proportions. Nonetheless, God, our Creator, tells us that honoring Him and living by His Word brings health and refreshment, and often this extends even to the physical body. Caring for the body as the temple of the Lord should keep us from destructive habits and should foster a sense of dignity and well-being that guides us in our personal choices. When the physical life succumbs to the decay in our broken world, the spirit will live on, nourished and eternally fit as it returns to the God who gave it.

Father God, thank You for the body You have given me. Help me to care for it well and to nourish my spirit on Your Word. Amen.

STONES OF WORTH

*For no one can lay any foundation other than the one we already
have—Jesus Christ. Anyone who builds on that foundation may use
a variety of materials—gold, silver, jewels, wood, hay, or straw. But on the
judgment day, fire will reveal what kind of work each builder has done.
The fire will show if a person's work has any value. If the work
survives, that builder will receive a reward.*
1 CORINTHIANS 3:11–14 NLT

April is a sparkling month when it comes to birthstones. Diamonds and
crystal are valuable pieces of rock.

Look at precious stones from another viewpoint. Under the
inspiration of the Holy Spirit, Paul wrote to the Corinthian church
about the materials they were using to build their lives. Of course,
Christ is the undisputed foundation of all who claim to follow Him.
He is secure, faithful, and everlasting. No life built on Him need fear
that the foundation will collapse. It is solid in any and every season.
But what is built on top of the foundation has to do with our everyday
choices. If we are honoring God and building for eternity, we are
using high-priced materials that will last. But if we are focusing on
this temporal world, we are throwing together a shack of plywood and
thatch, a house that will crumble and dissolve. The fire of judgment will
reveal who really does belong to Him. So today, no matter the month of
your birthday, choose the costly materials that will shine for eternity.

Lord, let my house be built on You and made to last. In Jesus' name, amen.

SIMPLE JOYS

So I decided there is nothing better than to enjoy food and drink and to find satisfaction in work. Then I realized that these pleasures are from the hand of God.
ECCLESIASTES 2:24 NLT

I live near the large Amish community of Holmes and Wayne counties in Ohio. These hearty people are an ongoing source of intrigue for most of us. Their commitment to simpler ways causes us to examine our own busy lifestyles and wish for a return to less complicated times. Their unpretentious ways of dress invite us to rethink our fashion motivation. Their delicious baked goods remind us that family and table are wonderful rituals that we should not neglect.

Why is it that we get so bogged down in our modern way of life? Our advances in technology give us more gadgets to manage, our commitment to wellness and fitness and good teeth brings more and more health appointments to our schedules, our desire to raise fully prepared children adds lessons and sports to the family calendar, and on it goes. When you add social events and church attendance and all the usual household tasks to that list, there isn't a lot of time or mental energy left for delighting in simple joys. Yet that is what we all crave at the end of the day, isn't it?

There is no quick solution, but let's commit to work toward the goal of relishing the simple things. After all, they are pleasures from the hand of God.

Lord, thank You for the delights of family and home. Show me how to use my time wisely so I may fully enjoy them. Amen.

WOMEN TRANSFORMED BY GRACE

Soon afterwards, He began going around from one city and village to another, proclaiming and preaching the kingdom of God. The twelve were with Him, and also some women who had been healed of evil spirits and sicknesses: Mary who was called Magdalene, from whom seven demons had gone out, and Joanna the wife of Chuza, Herod's steward, and Susanna, and many others who were contributing to their support out of their private means.
LUKE 8:1–3 NASB

The scriptural account records that Jesus changed the lives of all who came into contact with Him. Some of these He changed simply by entering their world, and others were changed in more dramatic ways. Of course, Mary, His mother, was the first woman whose life was radically altered by His incarnation. The sisters Mary and Martha knew Him as a frequent guest and friend. Other women contributed to His ministry and daily life through financial support; they followed Him, weeping, as He carried His cross and came with spices to prepare His body that misty third morning.

Then there were the women whose lives He drastically changed— the woman at the well in Samaria, the woman caught in adultery and thrown at His feet, the widow whose son He raised from the dead, and the woman with the bleeding disorder who was made well from touching His robe. As Creator, Jesus understood the inner longings of a woman's heart and offered redemption for hurts and the promise of hope and healing. He still does today.

Jesus, thank You for understanding me and for giving Your life to redeem me. Please transform me with Your grace. Amen.

Fading Glory

*Be merciful to me, Lord, for I am in distress; my eyes grow weak
with sorrow, my soul and body with grief.*
Psalm 31:9 niv

. . . .

My paternal grandmother was diagnosed with Parkinson's disease a few
years before her death. As the days went by, she experienced the hallmark
symptoms of this debilitating condition—shaking hands, staring eyes, and
deteriorating cognition. Since she was an integral part of my childhood
and adolescence, it was painful to see her well-being and dignity erode. I
did not want to see this fading of her personal glory. But it happened.

Death is at work in our world; the principle of decay is constant. It
is a result of sin that has broken the perfection of our world. All around
us every day, we are reminded that things are not as they should be.
Today is the birthday of Dr. James Parkinson, who first described the
disease in an essay in 1817. On this day every year, efforts are made to
raise awareness of this disease and to encourage research to find a cure.
One of the prominent symbols of Parkinson's disease is the red tulip.

As you go about your responsibilities today, remember to pray for
those whose lives are irrevocably touched by degenerative diseases. If you
are able, offer to relieve a friend who is serving as caregiver for an aging
parent. When you see a red tulip amid the profusion of spring blooms,
take a moment to remember that this world is not the end and that all
who know Jesus will one day trade their fading earthly bodies for one like
His—resurrected and whole.

. . . .

*Oh God, thank You for the victory over death that was won by Jesus Christ.
I celebrate the sure hope of eternal life in You. Amen.*

LIFE-CHANGING POETRY

The law of the LORD is perfect, restoring the soul;
The testimony of the LORD is sure, making wise the simple.
The precepts of the LORD are right, rejoicing the heart;
The commandment of the LORD is pure, enlightening the eyes.
The fear of the LORD is clean, enduring forever;
The judgments of the LORD are true; they are righteous altogether.
They are more desirable than gold, yes, than much fine gold;
Sweeter also than honey and the drippings of the honeycomb.
Moreover, by them Your servant is warned;
In keeping them there is great reward.
PSALM 19:7–11 NASB

April is National Poetry Month. Don't worry; you don't have to read Longfellow or Dickinson or Keats or Shelley. You can celebrate great poetic literature in your regular devotional time when you read Psalms, Proverbs, Ecclesiastes, and Song of Solomon.

God created all things, and that includes language in its various forms. He is the One who has given us the desire and ability to communicate. Every word of His Book is God-breathed, and in it we see various types of literature—historical accounts, personal narratives, persuasive writing, and, of course, ancient Middle Eastern poetry.

Why not celebrate National Poetry Month by reading a psalm or proverb every day this month? When you do, aside from ingesting great literature, you will be absorbing divine words that will change your life.

Lord, thank You for Your Word, which communicates truth in so many different ways. Speak to me through it and let me know the reward of obeying it. Amen.

GRITTIN' IT OUT

It is God who arms me with strength,
and makes my way perfect.
PSALM 18:32 NKJV

Do you know what grit is? Have you thought much about it?

Grit is that tough and tenacious quality that gets us through the difficult times. Though the circumstances and challenges differ, women in every generation have used it aplenty.

Think of the grit of the women on the *Mayflower* who endured seasickness and squalor and privation to help birth a nation. How about the women who traveled west on wagon trains and put up with dust and hardship and often left their china on the mountainsides and their children buried under the wagon ruts? Then there are the women who came through the Great Depression and tried to steady their men who had no income and no hope, and the women who sent their sons off to fight the Great War and watched them return debilitated by mustard gas and shell shock. We could also talk about the women in the 1940s who waved good-bye to sweethearts and husbands and then marched off to war plants to fight for freedom on the home front. These great generations knew a lot about grit and the God from whom such stern strength comes.

These women stepped up to the task to which they were called. May we commit to doing the same when the day to show our grit comes. May we rest in the Strength that never fails.

Father, thank You for being my Strength in both good days
and bad. I depend on You. Amen.

A MOMENT TO CONSIDER

*"And why are you worried about clothing? Observe how the lilies
of the field grow; they do not toil nor do they spin, yet I say to you that
not even Solomon in all his glory clothed himself like one of these."*
MATTHEW 6:28–29 NASB

In this sermon, Jesus wasn't specifically talking to women; rather, He
was addressing people who didn't have many resources but had many
needs. His message was to trust God for food and clothing and shelter.
How can we apply what He said to our concerns today?

Some would feel the message is that we shouldn't really care about
what we wear; that as long as it's decent and serviceable, we should be
content. There is a measure of truth to that when one considers the
millions around the world who live in poverty. Yet God created women
to care about beauty and to be His beauty-bearers to the world. It is a
natural thing for women to desire to be beautiful. The trouble comes
when our caring turns to comparing.

Jesus used the lilies of the field to demonstrate how the Father
provides. He doesn't compare one to another; He created them all and
delights in the beauty of each. How foolish it would be for the flowers
to measure themselves against each other! After all, the field isn't theirs
and the glory isn't their own. It all belongs to Him. Today, let's trust the
Gardener and His individualized care. The lilies do.

*Father, I am Yours; let me honor You with what I wear and resist
the temptation to compare myself with others. In Jesus' name, amen.*

The Tax Man Cometh

Render to all what is due them: tax to whom tax is due;
custom to whom custom; fear to whom fear;
honor to whom honor.
Romans 13:7 NASB

. . . .

Today is the annual day of reckoning for American taxpayers. Accounting offices and tax preparers will get hardly any rest and the post office will see record lines. The American people are "rendering" to the government what is due.

The people of Jesus' day understood the system of taxation very well. Under the thumb of Rome, they were subject to taxes for the emperor as well as to the local Jewish tax collector. Fraud and extortion were the norm, and there was no justice system to which one could appeal. They had to pay, and if they could not, the officials might take their children to work off the debt. At least we are spared that tragedy today, though when we see the amount owed on the Form 1040, it seems as though it might cost the proverbial arm and leg.

You've heard the saying that nothing is for sure but death and taxes. It seems that as long as the earth remains, there will be tribute to pay. So let us follow the example of our Lord, who gave the government its due and yet understood that true wealth is accumulating in heaven where there is no tax.

. . . .

Dear Lord, thank You for providing me with income in 2015.
As I pay my taxes this year, remind me that my
true riches are eternal. Amen.

THIS IS THE DAY THAT THE LORD HAS MADE. . .AND I JUST MESSED UP!

This is the day which the LORD has made;
let us rejoice and be glad in it.
PSALM 118:24 NASB

Have you ever wondered how a perfectly good day can get so messed up?

The answer can usually be laid down to human behavior. All it takes is a sharp word to a family member or an unhelpful attitude or unkind action and the situation quickly degenerates. Personal failure has odd tentacles. The guilty feeling from knowing the problem was self-instigated fosters a desire to shift the blame and then in the end leads to self-incriminating despair at again being the cause of strife.

Human relationships, while having the strength to withstand much trauma, are remarkably fragile when it comes to insult. Friends and spouses and children can be hurt greatly when we are careless with our words and attitudes. So how do we fix the day?

We can turn to our God who is the essence of redemption. Since He sent Jesus to redeem our souls, He is able also to redeem even the smallest earthly concern. Coming to Him for mercy is the first step in righting the wrong. Exchanging our failure for His grace reminds us that all is not lost. The day is His, after all, and He offers the hope we need to live it through to the end.

Father God, thank You for Your abundant mercy and constant grace.
Redeem my failures today and help me not to repeat them.
In Jesus' name, amen.

HEAVEN—THE ALWAYS PRESENT

But you must not forget this one thing, dear friends:
A day is like a thousand years to the Lord,
and a thousand years is like a day.
2 PETER 3:8 NLT

Humans have always been intrigued by what is commonly called the "afterlife." How about the ancient Egyptians who prepared the bodies of their dead pharaohs to live in the great beyond and entombed them with rooms of treasures and foodstuffs to take along? We are still digging up what they buried for the ages. Generations after them also thought about what comes after death. Philosophers offered their best ideas and religions promised peace and reward to their faithful. But only Jesus could offer any concrete evidence that His followers would live forever. He spoke about a place in heaven for those who loved God, and then He rose from the dead to prove He had the power to take them there.

Heaven is the hope of all believers in Christ. Many songs have been written about it, and they bring us comfort when we say good-bye to friends and family members. One written by Billy Sprague has the captivating title "Heaven Is a Long Hello." This lyric encapsulates the thought that there will be no past tense there as we know it here. We will not have to say good-bye or be separated or "leave the party," so to speak. In that land, there is always a glorious "now." We will be beyond the realm of time because we will have stepped into eternity where God dwells.

Jesus, thank You for preparing a home in heaven for me.
I can't wait to see You. Amen.

THE SPECTRUM

Defend the weak and the fatherless;
uphold the cause of the poor and the oppressed.
PSALM 82:3 NIV

According to numbers released from the Centers for Disease Control in 2014, about 3.5 million people in America live with an autism spectrum disorder, and prevalence in the US is estimated at 1 in 68 births. The numbers have increased dramatically every year since 2000.

April has been designated as National Autism Awareness Month, and while you may not be on the spectrum yourself, you likely know someone who is affected in some way by this complex developmental disability.

While Christ walked the earth, He healed many people, among them those who were suffering from mental illness or disabilities. We don't know if He touched any who had autism, but it is very possible that He did. We do know that parents often brought their children to Jesus for His healing, and He responded with compassion in every instance.

Today, why not be His hands and reach out to someone on the autism spectrum with His love? There may be opportunities through your church or through the local support group. Giving a break to an exhausted caregiver or donating time to help provide resources for affected families will bring joy both to others and to yourself. Helping those who are neglected and giving aid to the suffering are acts of service that show God's heart to a hurting world. Let Him use you to serve.

Lord, I want to be Your hands of compassion. Direct me to an area
of service that You know I can fill. In Jesus' name, amen.

HOUSEKEEPER OR ZOOKEEPER?

And we know that God causes all things to work together for good
to those who love God, to those who are called
according to His purpose.
ROMANS 8:28 NASB

You may feel like your home is a zoo, but imagine what it was like for
Noah's wife. She really did live in a zoo! There have been many women
to whom God has given difficult assignments, but think about the
details of life on the ark with the animals. We can only hope that Mrs.
Noah was an animal lover; if not, and even if so, surely God gave her
extra help to carry out her task.

For about a year, Noah and his family cared for the animals and
waited for the waters to recede. As the oldest woman on board, Mrs.
Noah would have been the "mother" to whom they turned for nurture
and counsel. She would have been a mentor to her three sons' wives.
She would have been Noah's confidante and helper. It was a tall order.
Yet the Bible does not record her emotions or her actions or even her
name. It does indicate that she was faithful to fill her place, even if that
meant sleeping in a zoo.

Where has God placed you today? What assignment has He given
you to fulfill His plan? Whatever and wherever, you must rely on His
strength and carry out His purpose; the end of your story has not yet
been written. Who knows, you might end up loving your zoo!

God, I accept Your call on my life.
Use me today for Your glory. Amen.

DONATE LIFE

*"The Spirit of God has made me, and the breath of
the Almighty gives me life."*
JOB 33:4 NASB

. . . .

God is the giver of life. Despite the theories and philosophies and
postulations to the contrary, life must come from other life and cannot
start on its own. God the Creator breathed His own life into man, who
then became an eternal being.

Since the fall of man and the entrance of sin into our world, the
globe has been plagued with death. Through the millennia, humans
have found ever crueler and more sophisticated ways to destroy life. In
the past century, death was given euphemistic names to mask what was
really taking place. Hitler's henchmen called their killing operations
"Special Actions." Planned Parenthood calls its services "termination of
pregnancy." Doctors who offer death assistance to terminal patients call
the suicide a "release." In spite of the name, it is still death.

Among other notable titles, April has been chosen as Donate Life
Month. Americans are encouraged to save lives by being donors of
organs, eyes, and tissue. More than 124,000 men, women, and children
are waiting for these life-saving donations. In a culture where the idea
of life from conception to natural death is becoming less accepted, it is
good to remember that there are many ways we can honor and preserve
life. Maybe being an organ donor is for you; maybe not. Whatever
your decision, you can pray for those today who are waiting for those
wondrous words, "We have a donor!"

. . . .

*Creator God, You have given me life.
May I use it to bless others. Amen.*

Unfading Beauty

*You should clothe yourselves instead with the beauty that comes
from within, the unfading beauty of a gentle and quiet
spirit, which is so precious to God.*
1 Peter 3:4 NLT

. . . .

Perhaps Sarah was the only elderly woman who was so beautiful that an
Egyptian pharaoh wanted her for his harem! Most of us don't have to
worry about that. We know that whatever physical beauty we possess
is fleeting. Despite the commercials and the boutique counters in
the department stores and the advances of Botox and collagen, aging
happens to every woman.

God understands that our bodies pay a heavy price for the brokenness
caused by sin. He knows that we grieve as we see our youth slipping
away. Yet He does not want us to make this temporal body the focus of
our living. After all, the body only houses the spirit, and one day we will
exchange this primitive model for a glorified one.

I love vintage photos and am intrigued by the youthful beauty seen
in the picture albums of the elderly. Looking at them in younger days, full
of life and vitality, and then glancing at them today brings one to the stark
reality that beauty fades and only a shadow of the former glory exists.

That's why God's Word tells women to spend most of their effort
on beautifying the spirit, which can grow lovelier with every passing
year. For only eternity will reveal the glories yet to come.

. . . .

*Father, let me not mourn the passing of time as a foolish woman.
Rather, let me beautify my spirit for Your glory. In Jesus' name, amen.*

EARTH DAY REFLECTIONS

He established the earth upon its foundations,
so that it will not totter forever and ever.
PSALM 104:5 NASB

At its heart, Earth Day is an insult to the Creator.

Now, I'm all for stewardship as it applies to our planet. The Bible tells us that God placed humankind in management over the vegetation and the animal kingdom; in other words, God assigned man and woman to care for their environment. So good waste management and wise timbering practices and compassionate care of animals are all in keeping with humankind's original job description.

But I have a problem with the elevation of conservation and "green" living to the point where it gives humans the responsibility to uphold the earth and values the flora and fauna of our globe more than the human life found on it. God is the Creator and Sustainer of our planet. He will keep it on its course and in existence for as long as He wills it. He expects us to do our part and He will do His. At the very core of Earth Day there seems to be an attitude that dismisses God and grabs the authority for "saving" the planet. As the apostle Paul wrote in Romans, those who embrace this attitude do not want to glorify Him as God and so they worship the creature rather than the Creator (Romans 1:20–25).

Those who know the truth recognize that the heavenly Father is the One we worship, not Mother Earth. Every day of the year, we should celebrate His glory.

Heavenly Father, the world is Yours and all that is in it.
May I be a faithful steward of it. Amen.

PASSOVER BEGINS

*"The blood shall be a sign for you on the houses where you live;
and when I see the blood I will pass over you, and no plague will
befall you to destroy you when I strike the land of Egypt. Now this day
will be a memorial to you, and you shall celebrate it as a feast to the
LORD; throughout your generations you are to celebrate
it as a permanent ordinance."*
EXODUS 12:13–14 NASB

To Gentiles, the story of Passover is an amazing account of God's miraculous deliverance of the Jews from Egypt. For Jews, Passover is a vibrant observance that reminds them who and whose they are.

Passover is an eight-day festival celebrated in spring. The first and last two days are full-fledged holidays, and the middle four days are intermediate days. There are holiday candles and special meals and specific rules and rituals to be observed. It is a holy and happy time.

In recent years there has been renewed interest among believers in commemorating the season of Passover with a family or church *seder*. Participating in the ceremonies for cleansing leaven and eating bitter herbs brings the symbolism alive and helps one envision that night long ago when the death angel struck the firstborn of Egypt and God's people walked freely out of bondage.

Even if you have no Jewish blood, you can embrace that feeling of joy that the ancient Hebrews felt. If you are a believer, the God who delivered them is the One who walks with you.

*Lord God, thank You for delivering Your people from bondage
long ago and for delivering me from Satan's dominion.
I worship You as God Almighty. Amen.*

THE CHALLENGE TO LOVE

[Love] bears all things, believes all things,
hopes all things, endures all things.
1 CORINTHIANS 13:7 NASB

In the animated movie *The Prince of Egypt*, Zipporah, wife of Moses, is portrayed as a feisty, dark-skinned girl who sings and dances and charms the ex-prince turned shepherd. Whether this is true or not, we do not know. Exodus 2:21 simply says that Reuel, the priest of Midian, gave Zipporah, one of his seven daughters, to Moses as a wife. We know that she gave birth to two sons, Gershom and Eliezer, and that she went with her father and sons to Moses' wilderness encampment after the Exodus.

The only other time she is referenced in scripture is in Numbers 12:1, where Aaron and Miriam object to the fact that Moses had married a Cushite woman. Many scholars believe that Cush was the land of her origin and that it could be somewhere in present North Africa.

Whatever her ancestry and ethnicity, Zipporah was the wife of a remarkable man. She had the opportunity to support and affirm the deliverer himself. It must have been a challenge to love the man who talked with God at the burning bush and challenged Pharaoh in his courts! Considering that leaders are often unemotional and determined, it surely was no easy task.

Whom have you been given to support and affirm today? A husband, a parent, a sibling, a grandparent? God will use the person you are to complement someone else. Will you accept the challenge?

God, I want to love the people You've put in my life.
Let me do that today. Amen.

ARE YOU AWARE OF STRESS?

You will keep in perfect peace all who trust in you,
all whose thoughts are fixed on you!
ISAIAH 26:3 NLT

. . . .

I suppose there aren't enough months in the year to focus on all our
ailments and national concerns, so the calendar-makers piggyback them
to give everyone a fair hearing. Are you ready for this? April is also Stress
Awareness Month. And as you might guess, during this month, health
care professionals try to increase awareness of the causes and cures for
what is called our "modern stress epidemic."

We're all aware that stress is widespread and affects us in many ways.
Stress management is difficult to implement. Taking a vacation only helps
a few weeks out of the year. Relaxing on the weekend only increases the
anxiety of Monday morning. Displaying beachfronts on our computer
desktops only reminds us that we are office bound. And talking with a
therapist is only a release valve for continuing pressure. Yes, stress is a
problem, and it is here to stay.

For Christians, stress seems to fly in the face of Jesus' promise of
peace and abundant joy. Yet the peace He gives keeps the stress from
destroying us. He keeps the threads of our sanity from unraveling, but
He expects us to do what we can to help ourselves. This month, take a
good look at your schedule and your routines and ask God for wisdom
so you can appropriately manage your stress.

. . . .

God, grant me the serenity to accept the things I cannot change,
courage to change the things I can, and wisdom to know the difference.

DETERMINED AND SURRENDERED

*"And then, though it is against the law, I will go in to
see the king. If I must die, I must die."*
ESTHER 4:16 NLT

Esther might have won the beauty contest in ancient Persia, but she also
had guts to go with her glitz. Raised by her uncle Mordecai, a devout
follower of Yahweh, she had principles that held her firm in the time of
testing.

You know the story of her marriage to King Xerxes after the
banishment of Queen Vashti, and of her sudden introduction to royal
life. You know also of the subplot of the wicked Haman who had a rabid
hatred for the Jews and who despised one Jew in particular and secretly
plotted his demise. And then there was Mordecai, who worked as an
official in the palace and got the intelligence report to his niece that she
was the only one who could save her people from extinction. She was the
only one who had access to Xerxes. Well, actually, she only had access
when he summoned her. But desperate times required desperate measures,
and after days of fasting, Esther dressed to the nines and walked in to
catch the king's eye and plead her case.

Of course, we know the end of the story, but she didn't know it
at the time. She was completely surrendered to whatever her fate may
be. This was the moment for which she had been summoned to the
kingdom.

Like her, you are called to surrender yourself to God's purpose.
Have the guts to surrender and do your part in His kingdom.

Lord, I give myself completely into Your hands. Amen.

HATS OFF TO SECRETARIES!

Masters, treat your servants considerately. Be fair with them.
Don't forget for a minute that you, too, serve a Master—God in heaven.
COLOSSIANS 4:1 MSG

Today is Administrative Professionals Day, the day to tell a secretary you know how much she or he is appreciated. Maybe you don't have a personal secretary, but there is one in your office or one at your children's school or one who works at your church who would love to get a little note or encouraging word. If you have the resources to splurge, flowers or chocolate would likely be appreciated!

When the New Testament was written, the concept of secretary as we know it today didn't exist. Many of those who assisted with management duties were slaves or servants. God's message to those masters then and to employers today is one of fair treatment. After all, each Christian, employer or employee, serves Christ. And we expect Him to treat us with love and kindness. We are then to pass on this same love and kindness to others in the workplace.

The office or factory is often a place of murmuring and discontentment. The Christian plays by a different set of rules, and the workplace should be a place where she glorifies God by how she works and how she interacts with others.

Lord, please help me to be Christlike in my workplace today,
and help me remember to appreciate the contributions
of others. In Jesus' name, amen.

A RETURN TO HYMNODY

Let the word of Christ richly dwell within you, with all wisdom teaching and admonishing one another with psalms and hymns and spiritual songs, singing with thankfulness in your hearts to God.
COLOSSIANS 3:16 NASB

Christian music today is a broad genre. There seems to be a style to fit every taste and background. It would serve all of us well to stay familiar with some of those hymns written more than a hundred years ago. Their solid lyrics contain bedrock doctrine and their unvarnished melodies have ministered to the faithful for generations.

When one mentions hymns today, many think of any song found in a hymnal of yesteryear. But, properly defined, a hymn is a song sung to or about God. A hymn differs from the testimonial feel of old gospel songs and choruses. A few you might have heard of are "A Mighty Fortress Is Our God," "Holy, Holy, Holy," and "How Firm a Foundation."

There is a trend today among contemporary Christian artists to update gospel songs with newer tunes, and there's nothing wrong with that. After all, worship has gone through many trends and fads down through time. But if you want to get a fresh look at the Christian life through the eyes of great people of the past, pick up a hymnal at a thrift shop and read the words in your devotional time. The poetry will delight you and the words will captivate you. At least, they have that effect on me.

Thank You, Lord, for the gift of music.
Speak to me in some song today. Amen.

THE GOD OF THE TREES

*Out of the ground the LORD God caused to grow every tree
that is pleasing to the sight and good for food.*
GENESIS 2:9 NASB

Today, the last Friday in April, is Arbor Day. The Arbor Day Foundation says that they "inspire people to plant, nurture and celebrate trees." The first celebration of Arbor Day was in 1874 and marked the efforts of J. Sterling Morton, a pioneer in Nebraska. Today, the organization is a thriving one and promotes conservation efforts and healthy foresting techniques.

A tree is a remarkable symbol of life and beauty. The many species remind us of the variety in people. The tree's resilience in many types of weather makes us remember that the inner life is what keeps it going and the source of that life is nutrition that it draws up from its roots. The shade of a tree shows us that we can contribute to the comfort of others. The many uses of the wood and bark of trees hint that even in death, there is purpose and beauty.

The genius behind the tree is, of course, our Creator God. Genesis tells us that He caused every kind of tree to grow. And it is He who can make us as beautiful and resilient as one of them. Psalm 1:3 (NASB) says that the righteous person will "be like a tree firmly planted by streams of water." Now that is something to celebrate!

*Dear God, thank You for the gift of trees. Nurture me so that I can be
a stalwart testimony of Your grace. In Jesus' name, amen.*

LOOKING FORWARD TO THE WEDDING

"Look, the bridegroom is coming!
Come out and meet him!"
MATTHEW 25:6 NLT

Since my childhood, I have listened to teaching on the return of Christ. In the 1970s a lot of emphasis was put on the theme of prophecy—gospel songs on the topic abounded and the first Christian apocalyptic movies were made. In recent years, there has been a renewed interest in eschatology, no doubt in some part owing to the phenomenal success of books and movies on the topic.

There is no question in my mind that Jesus will return. He promised He would, and He does what He says. The apostle Peter warned us that unbelievers would scoff at the idea but that they would be taken unaware, for to them, Christ would come as a "thief in the night."

For those of us who are part of His Church, the Bride, the day of His return is a welcome event. Just as a bride anticipates the day of her wedding and feels the pounding of her heart when she imagines the arrival of her groom, so the followers of Christ are looking forward to the day when He comes to take us to be ever with Him.

No one knows the exact day or hour, but we know that it is getting closer with every passing minute. We must look for Him. We must be prepared to welcome Him and enjoy His presence forever!

Jesus, I am looking forward to Your return! Thank You for loving me
and choosing me. It won't be long now. Amen.

A FRESH START

See, I am doing a new thing! Now it springs up; do you not perceive it?
I am making a way in the wilderness and streams in the wasteland.
ISAIAH 43:19 NIV

There is something about a fresh beginning. At the start of the new year, people decide to make positive changes in their lives. The new school year seems to usher in another round of hope for achievement and organization. For a while at least.

God specializes in giving us a new start. Lamentations 3:22–23 tells us that His compassion is new every morning. We can never make a mistake so big that God can't give us a fresh start. Nothing is too big for the blood of Jesus to cover. He wants to give us a new life, right where we are.

As we trust in Him, He will make us into new creatures. That's not something we can do ourselves. Our pasts can't hold us back. While Satan loves to remind us of our past and the mistakes we've made, God is turning the wilderness of our lives into beautiful growth with His living water. Remember to trust God for the changes He is making in you and to thank Him for His unfailing love.

Heavenly Father, we thank You that Your love never runs out on us.
Thank You for covering our sins with the blood of Your Son
and giving us new life every day. Amen.

The Gift That Keeps on Giving

Just as people are destined to die once, and after that to face judgment, so Christ was sacrificed once to take away the sins of many; and he will appear a second time, not to bear sin, but to bring salvation to those who are waiting for him.
Hebrews 9:27–28 niv

After we've been Christians awhile and traveled down the road of our spiritual journey, it's easy to lose sight of what started us on our way. Christ's blood paid the price for our sins and is the cost of our spiritual journey. From His death, we receive several benefits.

We get forgiveness of sins. Not only did Jesus pay the price for everything we ever have done or ever will do wrong, but God annuls our sins. He treats them as if they never happened. This means we are rescued from the judgment we deserve for our sinful rebellion. In addition, we are brought into God's family.

After Jesus rose from the dead, He made a promise to return and give us a permanent place in heaven. He sent the Holy Spirit to live inside us and to act as the deposit on the contract that He will return one day to fulfill.

The journey of faith is not free, but Jesus has paid the price. We receive freedom now and hope for the future.

Precious Jesus, thank You so much for paying the penalty for our sins. May we never become complacent and forget the price You paid. Help us to be continually grateful. Amen.

Great Is His Faithfulness

Because of the LORD's great love we are not consumed,
for his compassions never fail. They are new every
morning; great is your faithfulness.
LAMENTATIONS 3:22–23 NIV

Have you ever felt you were being consumed by rage, hurt, jealousy, pain, loneliness, or grief? Have you ever said, "One more thing, and I'll fall to pieces. I can't handle this"?

The good news is we don't have to handle it. God's compassion never fails. He is greater than anything that threatens to consume us. His mercy never runs out. It is new every morning.

When the Israelites were wandering in the desert because of their disbelief in God's ability to deliver the Promised Land into their hands, God was still faithful. He fed them manna daily, but they had to go out of their tents and gather it. And it was only good for a day.

In the same way God is faithful to us, regardless of what we have done. And like the manna that came every morning, new mercies are available to us every day. We just have to ask for them. We can't let our pain, shame, and anger keep us from running to God daily for new mercies to sustain us. He will not let us be consumed. He is faithful.

Oh Lord our God, we are such faulty, frail humans. You know that we are
but dust. We thank You that we don't have to do anything but run to
You and receive Your mercies that never run out. Help us not to
let anything keep us from running to You. Amen.

THE WARRIOR SINGS

*"The LORD your God is with you, the Mighty Warrior who saves.
He will take great delight in you; in his love he will no longer
rebuke you, but will rejoice over you with singing."*
ZEPHANIAH 3:17 NIV

What kind of picture does this verse create in your mind? The Lord is a mighty warrior who leads the armies of angels. Yet He is with us. One of Jesus' names is Immanuel, literally the "with us God." He takes delight in us. He doesn't rebuke us. He rejoices over us with singing.

This verse from Zephaniah is like a sampler of God's attributes. Look them over again. How does each of these characteristics show up in your relationship with Him? What attribute do you need to know more about? Which do you struggle with?

We sing worships songs to God, but have you thought about His joy over you being so great He bursts out into song? Or maybe He sings you a sweet lullaby like a parent does to a small child. Next time you sing a worship song, think about what kind of song God would sing about you. Let that fuel your worship of Him and deepen your relationship with the One who loves you so greatly.

*Heavenly Father, it is almost too much for us to comprehend that You,
the Creator of the universe, could sing about us. We want to understand
that, even in just the small way our minds can handle. Show us Your
love and help us to love You more deeply. Amen.*

NATIONAL DAY OF PRAYER

*I call on you, my God, for you will answer me;
turn your ear to me and hear my prayer.*
PSALM 17:6 NIV

Have you ever tried calling someone's name in a crowded room? You yell and wave until everyone is looking at you except the person whose attention you're trying to get. Or you call, leave a voice mail, text, and send an e-mail, all without getting an answer. Is anything more frustrating?

With God we can be confident that He hears us. He stands ready to listen to us all the time. In fact, He welcomes our prayers. He encourages us to pray to Him and pour out our hearts, our concerns, our praises, and our dreams. Prayer connects us deeply to God. Just as you would have a weak relationship with a friend who only called when she needed something, our relationship with God grows and deepens through regular prayer.

One simple way to organize your prayer time is with the simple acrostic ACTS. A—Adoration. Tell God how much you love Him and why. C—Confession. Confess areas in which you've fallen short and messed up. T—Thanksgiving. Thank God for the many ways He has shown you His love. S—Supplication. An old-fashioned word that simply means to ask for something. Whether or not you use this format, take time to regularly connect with God throughout your day.

*Lord, thank You for listening to us when we pray. You are never
too busy to hear evern the smallest request. Help us to
remember to come to You with everything. Amen.*

THE GOOD SHEPHERD

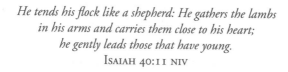

He tends his flock like a shepherd: He gathers the lambs
in his arms and carries them close to his heart;
he gently leads those that have young.
ISAIAH 40:11 NIV

How we view our own earthly fathers often influences how we view our heavenly Father. If our dad was attentive and present, we have an easier time seeing God as loving and interested in our lives. But if he was angry, distant, or absent, we tend to see God as upset with us and waiting to punish us the moment we mess up, or as too distant to care about us as individuals.

God has many attributes: holy, righteous, just, loving, and merciful to name a few. One way we can get to know God better is to spend time studying each of these characteristics. Today's verse shows us a loving Shepherd, gently tending His vulnerable lambs, carrying those who can't walk. The Bible often uses the image of the good shepherd to describe our relationship with God. A good shepherd provides everything the sheep need: food, water, rest, protection, and care.

If you struggle with seeing God as loving you deeply and caring for every detail of your life, meditate on scriptures that show God as the good shepherd and ask Him to reveal this part of Himself to you.

Heavenly Father, we thank You for being the Good Shepherd. Your love for
us is far more than we can ever imagine. Let us feel Your presence in
our daily lives and catch a glimpse of how much You love us.

Joy and Thankfulness

*Then Hannah prayed and said: "My heart rejoices in the Lord;
in the Lord my horn is lifted high. My mouth boasts over my enemies,
for I delight in your deliverance. There is no one holy like the Lord;
there is no one besides you; there is no Rock like our God.*

1 Samuel 2:1–2 niv

Hannah had prayed for years for a child. In those days, not bearing a child was a sign of disgrace, a sign that you had somehow displeased God. Hannah felt this stigma keenly.

God answered her prayers, and she followed through on her vow to deliver the child, Samuel, to live at the temple in service to the Lord. The name Samuel means "heard by God." While it is difficult to imagine how a mother could give up her only child in this way, Hannah is rejoicing.

Hannah's focus is not on herself. She is praising God. She is telling others what He has done for her. She has surrendered all that is precious to her to the Lord and is trusting in Him.

How hard it is for us to do this! We worry and we fret and we wonder where God has gone when we don't see Him answering our prayers in the way we think it should happen. Let's follow Hannah's example and praise the Lord. Let's tell others of how He is working in our lives.

Lord, we so often forget to praise You and thank You for all that You have done for us. Help us to remember to keep our trust in You. Amen.

THE BEST PARENT

*"Can a mother forget the baby at her breast and have no compassion on
the child she has borne? Though she may forget, I will not forget you!"*
ISAIAH 49:15 NIV

. . . .

Everyone has a mother. She might not have raised you or even been a
good mother, but everyone was given birth to by a mother. Mother's
Day is a day when we acknowledge and appreciate how hardworking
and sacrificial moms are. But sometimes it can be a painful reminder of
the deficiencies of our parents. Or of ourselves as parents. Or of the loss
of a parent. Maybe your mom left your family when you were young, or
was so consumed by her own pain that she didn't know how to be a good
parent to you. Maybe you're a mother with a child who has made painful
and disappointing choices and you blame yourself, at least in part. What
is supposed to be a day of celebration comes mixed with pain.

When we turn our lives over to Jesus, we get adopted into a new
family with a perfect Father. No matter what our childhood years were
like, God loves us better than any earthly parent can. He will never
leave us. He walks beside us through every situation. Let Him heal your
hurts.

. . . .

*Heavenly Father, we thank You for welcoming us into Your family
and for being the perfect Father to us. Help us remember to
thank You and to come to You with all of our needs. Amen.*

AMAZING LOVE

*"See, I have engraved you on the palms of my hands;
your walls are ever before me."*
ISAIAH 49:16 NIV

We do all sorts of things to keep reminders of our loved ones around us.
Children's handprints are memorialized in plaster of paris or in paint.
We keep letters and mementos tucked in drawers. Flowers are dried and
pressed. But most often we put up pictures: on walls, on the refrigerator,
on our computers, in our wallets, even on our phones.

Now think about how many times a day you look at your hands.
We wear wedding rings, class rings, and mother's rings to remind us of
our connection to our loved ones in a most obvious way. When God
says He has tattooed our faces on His hands, He is telling us we are
never out of His thoughts. He thinks of us constantly.

The phrase "your walls are ever before me" refers to the walls of
a city. In ancient times, a city without walls was vulnerable to attack.
God's keeping an eye on our walls means that He is keeping us under
His protection. He never takes His eyes off us.

As humans, there is a limit to our love, our attention, our protective
eyes, but God's love is limitless. He loves us in a deep, amazing way, with
an attention that never strays.

*Dear God, we can't begin to fathom Your love for us. Help us to see
glimpses of it throughout our day and to smile and
thank You for Your amazing love. Amen.*

EVERYTHING YOU NEED

You can be sure that God will take care of everything you need,
his generosity exceeding even yours in the
glory that pours from Jesus.
PHILIPPIANS 4:19 MSG

Have you ever gone through a period in your life when you were completely dependent on God to supply everything for you? Perhaps you lost your job or had an extended illness. It can be humbling to be unable to provide for yourself and your family.

The Israelites faced similar circumstances when God freed them from slavery in Egypt. As He led them through the desert toward the Promised Land, He provided water and food in miraculous ways. Every morning, one day's supply of manna would appear. Any attempt to save it until the next day was futile; the manna would rot. God wanted them to rely on Him daily for their provision. Yet the Israelites' response wasn't to be grateful but to complain they didn't have enough variety!

God often takes us through the desert before we get to the Promised Land. It's in the desert that we learn the lessons we will need to use in the Promised Land, most of which involve trusting Him. It's in the desert that we learn God is who He says He is. It's in the desert that we learn to obey Him, not because He says to, but because it's what will ultimately give us the life we were designed to live.

Lord, we don't always live our lives as if all of our provision comes
from You. Remove our fear and help us to trust in You
and take You at Your word. Amen.

WHERE GOD'S WILL BEGINS

Do not conform to the pattern of this world, but be transformed by the
renewing of your mind. Then you will be able to test and approve
what God's will is—his good, pleasing and perfect will.
ROMANS 12:2 NIV

We speak often of behavior—do this, don't do that—but we don't often talk about the root of our behavior: our thoughts.

With today's technology, it is easy to be inundated by the world's views and values. They're everywhere: TV, movies, our computers and phones. To live the transformed life, we have to be intentional about what we let into our minds and what we keep out. Is what we're watching on TV drawing us closer to God or moving us farther away? Is the latest book we're reading helping us to understand God's will or showing us the world's values?

Many people like to characterize God as a killjoy, the One who has the list of Do's and Don'ts. But at the end of Romans 12:2, you see that God's will for us is good, pleasing, and perfect. Is that something you can say about the last movie you saw? When we follow God's will for our lives, it is the path that is the best one for us. God's instructions are intended to help us and keep us from harm. It starts with our thoughts.

Dear God, please help us to check what we are putting into our minds.
So much can seem harmless. Help us to thirst after those
things that draw us closer to You. Amen.

Encouragement from the Scriptures

*For everything that was written in the past was written to teach us,
so that through the endurance taught in the Scriptures and
the encouragement they provide we might have hope.*
Romans 15:4 niv

You know those days when nothing goes right? Sometimes those days stretch into weeks and months. You don't get the promotion. Your car breaks down. Someone you love gets sick. Disappointment settles in and brings its brother, Discouragement. Things are not going according to your plan, and you may wonder if God even hears your prayers.

Looking at the heroes of the Old Testament, you'll see that God's plan for those people wasn't smooth sailing either. Joseph was sold into slavery, falsely accused by Potiphar's wife, and unjustly imprisoned. Moses tended flocks in the wilderness for forty years after murdering a man and before leading God's people out of slavery. David was anointed king but had to run for his life and wait fifteen years before actually sitting on the throne.

Those stories give us hope and encouragement. Our plans are quite different from God's plans, and His ways of doing things are quite different from what we would often choose. We see how things worked out for the people of the Old Testament. We can take encouragement from the fact that the same God is at work in our lives.

*Heavenly Father, it can be difficult to have hope during trying times.
Remind us to trust in You and cling to Your Word
for encouragement. Amen.*

Sustainer and Provider

*My flesh and my heart may fail, but God is the strength
of my heart and my portion forever.*
Psalm 73:26 niv

As we grow older, we realize there are limits to our physical bodies. Our minds aren't as sharp as they used to be. An injury weakens a body part. Loss breaks our hearts. This life is hard.

Fortunately, we have more than this life to sustain us. God provides more than just what we need physically. He strengthens our hearts and walks with us, even during the difficult times.

Psalm 73 was written by a Levite, who was supported by the offerings worshippers brought to the temple. He is saying that the Lord is more than any portion someone could bring in. He is the sustainer and preserver of all who trust in Him. He is far more than any earthly provision, and there is no limit to His ability to provide for us physically and emotionally. He never gets tired. He never runs out of resources.

When we go through difficult times, we may have trouble trusting God for a solution we can't see. But His Word promises He will sustain us. We can tie the anchors of our hearts to this hope during the blowing storms of life.

*Lord God, we thank You that You are not limited by earthly resources
or physical barriers. You love us with a limitless love, even when we
cannot see it. Help us to see Your love today to encourage
our hearts and give us hope. Amen.*

HOPE FOR THE SOUL

We have this hope as an anchor for the soul, firm and secure.
It enters the inner sanctuary behind the curtain.
HEBREWS 6:19 NIV

In just a few words, this verse paints a rich word picture to comfort us. "This hope" refers to the verses before where God secures His promise by swearing by Himself, giving us two trustworthy things to place our hope in, His Word and Himself.

Anchors are also a symbol of hope. During a storm, a strong anchor locked into a solid foundation keeps the boat from being blown off course or onto the rocks. Sailors' hope during a storm is the anchor.

"The inner sanctuary behind the curtain" would be familiar to these Jewish Christians—the audience of the book of Hebrews—as the Holy of Holies where the high priest went once a year, after the sin sacrifices were offered, to enter the presence of God. When Christ died on the cross, the curtain separating the two areas tore from top to bottom, symbolizing direct access to God for all believers. So instead of anchoring into solid rock, like a ship would, we anchor our hope directly to God.

Our hope is founded in the unshakable character of God, who loves us so much He sent His Son to die for us. His Word is true. He will do what He says He will do.

Heavenly Father, we are grateful for the sacrifice of Your Son,
making it possible for us to have a relationship with You. Remind us we
can trust You completely, and help us to rest in that truth. Amen.

Joy in Trials

*Consider it pure joy, my brothers and sisters, whenever you face trials
of many kinds, because you know that the testing of your faith produces
perseverance. Let perseverance finish its work so that you
may be mature and complete, not lacking anything.*
James 1:2–4 NIV

· ·

James begins his letter by encouraging his brothers and sisters in Christ to
find joy in their trials. The word *consider* tells us to move this discussion
about trials out of our emotions and into our heads.

Stop and think about this for a minute. Trials are going to come.
That is a fact of this life. We can't waste our time trying to avoid them. So
instead, let's remember we have the ultimate victory in Christ. Nothing
that happens on earth will take away our heavenly reward and the joy we
will have in heaven.

With Christ, the fruit of our trials can be growth, maturity, peace,
and the fruit of the Spirit instead of despondency, discouragement,
depression, and hopelessness. Ask God for wisdom for the next step.
Draw close to Him. Let perseverance finish its work to increase your
maturity. Take real steps of obedience and faith, because the key to joy
is obedience.

· ·

*Lord, as hard as it is, help us to find joy in the difficult things that come
our way, because we know You have given us the ultimate victory.
In the process, we can become more like You. Amen.*

JOY IN SERVING

Now John also was baptizing at Aenon near Salim, because there was plenty of water, and people were coming and being baptized.
JOHN 3:23 NIV

. . . .

John the Baptist was single-mindedly focused on what God had told him to do. He went to a place that had the two things he needed to fulfill his mission: water and people wanting to be baptized.

Sometimes we make serving God more complicated than it needs to be. We don't need to wait for conditions to be right or to have more knowledge or experience or resources. We can serve right now where God has us. He will grow us into what He needs us to be.

John had joy because he was doing what he was supposed to be doing. He knew his mission had a season. He was preparing to let someone else, Jesus, take over. It was not about John. It was about God. Mothers with small children can relate to this. The ministry of raising children is just for a season, as we prepare them to be responsible adults. The goal is to work ourselves out of a job.

What talents and interests do you have? What resources has God given you? How can you use what you have right now to serve Him? Be open to see what God brings your way. Serve God and find your joy.

. . . .

Dear God, make us aware of talents and resources we can use to serve You. Open our eyes to the opportunities You have placed around us, and show us the joy in serving You. Amen.

No More Tears

*" 'He will wipe every tear from their eyes. There will be no more
death' or mourning or crying or pain, for the old
order of things has passed away."*
Revelation 21:4–5 niv

This world is sadly full of sorrow and disappointment. But God doesn't allow our pain to be purposeless. It helps us need Jesus more. It drives us to a closer, more dependent relationship with Him, even when we can't possibly understand the reason for the pain we are experiencing.

Pain, especially when it's seen in our rearview mirror rather than in front of our faces, helps us have greater compassion for others' suffering. It also gives us common ground to give comfort and empathize with others who are in painful circumstances.

It won't always be like this. Someday we will live with Jesus in a perfect life with no sorrow, pain, or disappointment. We get a "no more tears" promise that is greater than any baby shampoo could deliver. Someday we will have joy greater than anything this earth can offer because it won't be tinged by sin and death. That is a promise we can hold on to.

Heavenly Father, thank You so much for defeating death and sin so we can have a glorious future with You in heaven, where we will truly have no more tears. Help us cling to Your promises and comfort others who are going through painful situations. Amen.

RUN YOUR RACE IN COMMUNITY

*Let us draw near to God with a sincere heart. . . . Let us hold unswervingly
to the hope we profess. . . . And let us consider how we may spur one
another on toward love and good deeds, not giving up meeting together,
as some are in the habit of doing, but encouraging one another.*
HEBREWS 10:22–25 NIV

God has marked out a journey of faith for each of us. He has also
given us a community to help us along this journey. If you look at the
verse above, it may seem that the section about "not giving up meeting
together" only goes with the "encouraging one another" part. However,
grammatically in the Greek, the first three phrases are all the benefit of
"not giving up meeting together."

When we remain in community with other believers, we draw near
to God. We hold on faithfully to our hope. We spur each other on.

This section of Hebrews is closely related to Psalm 40:9–10, which
talks about sharing with our community how God has saved us, how
He has helped us, and how He loves us and is faithful. When we share
with each other how God is working in our lives, we are encouraged on
our journey. This kind of sharing deepens our faith in God and gives us
hope. Take advantage of the community God has placed you in on your
journey of faith.

*Dear God, sometimes it's hard to make time for church and small groups
in our busy schedules. Help us realize how vital other believers are in
our journey of faith. Remind us to share with each other
what You have been doing in our lives. Amen.*

The Blessing of Peace

"The LORD bless you and keep you; the LORD make his face shine on you and be gracious to you; the LORD turn his face toward you and give you peace."
Numbers 6:24–26 niv

These verses are the priestly blessing God told Moses to instruct the priests to give to the people. This beautiful gift from God is a taste of heaven to carry us through until we get there. The word "peace" here is the Hebrew *shalom*. Here *shalom* carries its full meaning of more than peace, but also rightness, well-being, and wholeness.

The repetition of the Lord's name leaves no doubt as to who is doing the blessing. And no doubt as to the One to whom we belong.

When God blesses us, He beams proudly at us like a father with his child. He wants us to have a close, personal relationship with Him. And when our relationship with Him is right, we have that all-encompassing peace, the peace Paul tells us in Philippians 4:7 passes all understanding.

When God blesses us, other people notice. How are we telling others of His goodness to us? How are we using His deeds to encourage other believers and point nonbelievers to Christ?

Heavenly Father, Your blessing us with Your peace is beyond our ability to understand. You walk with us through all of life's difficult circumstances. We thank You for Your goodness toward us. Help us remember to share with others what You have done. Amen.

PEACE WITH GOD

Therefore, since we have been justified through faith,
we have peace with God through our Lord Jesus Christ.
ROMANS 5:1 NIV

The type of peace this verse is talking about isn't a feeling. It's the kind of peace that's like a treaty. When we ask Jesus to be Lord of our lives, our status and relationship with God change. We go from being His enemies to being His friends. Additionally, we have a sense of relief that His wrath and the punishment for our sins are no longer hanging over our heads.

We also can celebrate that peace with God is not just a onetime event. Rather, it is an ongoing source of blessing. Peace *with* God leads to peace *from* God. This peace is not just the absence of turmoil and trouble, but a real sense that God is in control. It's a small representation of heaven here on earth. His peace brings the confidence that He is working things out in our lives, even if we can't understand it all.

Satan would love to steal our peace. He can't change our relationship with God, but we can give Satan a foothold when we worry and ruminate and fuss over our circumstances instead of turning them over to God. Give your troubles to God and rest in His peace.

Dear God, as Your Son told us, we will have trouble in this world.
But You have overcome the world. Remind us to rest in Your presence
and in the knowledge that You are working everything out
according to a plan far beyond our comprehension.
Thank You for Your watchful love. Amen.

PEACE BEYOND COMPREHENSION

*Do not be anxious about anything, but in every situation,
by prayer and petition, with thanksgiving, present your
requests to God. And the peace of God, which transcends all
understanding, will guard your hearts and your minds in Christ Jesus.*
PHILIPPIANS 4:6–7 NIV

Within the first hours of the day, many of us can find opportunities to worry. As we learn to take every situation to God, He exchanges our worries for His peace.

We come before God and bring Him our needs, knowing He is the only One who can grant our request. We are to do this with thanksgiving. When we remember all God has done for us and provided for us, the worries that cause us to focus on what we don't have slip away in the presence of our mighty God.

God has compassion on us and knows we have many things to worry about. He tells us many times to come to Him. In 1 Peter 5:7 He tells us to give Him our cares. In Matthew 6:25 He tells us He will provide for us and meet our needs.

God promises that peace will permeate both our hearts, where our feelings can churn painfully, and our minds, where we can turn situations over endlessly. Along with giving us His peace, God takes our minds into protective custody, cutting off worries before they can enter.

*Lord Jesus, thank You for giving us Your supernatural peace.
Remind us to bring all of our cares to You and to
thank You for everything You've done for us. Amen.*

PRAISE AND THANKSGIVING

Enter his gates with thanksgiving and his courts with praise;
give thanks to him and praise his name.
PSALM 100:4 NIV

In Old Testament times, people went to the temple to meet with God. God's presence resided there just once a year after the sacrifice had been made on the Day of Atonement, but people came many times a year for festivals and to offer sacrifices for sin. The gates were the entrance to the temple grounds, and through the gates were the courts. They were the outside area where the people gathered. Part of this area was dedicated to altars for sacrifices.

Now that God lives within us through His Holy Spirit, we don't have to go to the temple or church to find Him. He is always with us. How, then, should this verse impact our relationship with God now? When we go to Him in prayer, let's consider starting with thanksgiving and moving into praise. Thanksgiving is thanking God for what He has done for us and how He has provided for us. Praise is identifying and acknowledging the characteristics of God, such as Creator, Healer, righteous, merciful, and loving.

We are commanded to give thanks and praise God's name. As we do so, our worries, fears, confessions, and requests fall into their proper place.

Heavenly Father, thank You that we can worship You without going to a building. You are always with us. We praise You for Your mercy in making a way for us to have a relationship with You. Remind us of who You are and help us to cling to You. Amen.

SHARPENING YOUR IRON

As iron sharpens iron, so one person sharpens another.
PROVERBS 27:17 NIV

. . . .

God never designed us to travel this journey of life alone. We need community. The book of Hebrews says we need to spur each other on to good works. We also need each other for accountability.

God uses other people to grow our character. Other people stretch us and challenge us. They point out our blind spots. They may make us uncomfortable at times.

Sometimes our churches are too big for us to develop true community, which is best done in smaller groups. Serving at church through various ministries or getting involved in a small group or Sunday school class is a good way to find community. Not every group will be a good fit, but don't give up. Pray and ask God to show you where you belong.

In a community group you can deepen your knowledge of worship and the Bible. You can reach out to your broader community and serve as a group. You can support each other with prayer and share each other's burdens. God will use these people to bring you closer to Him.

. . . .

Dear Jesus, You prayed that we would be one as You and the Father are one. Help us to find the community You want us to be united with. Open our hearts to let others in, and make us willing to grow and let others speak into our lives. Show us how we can impact Your kingdom when we work with others. Amen.

THE SACRIFICE GOD DESIRES

*Therefore, since we are surrounded by such a great cloud of witnesses,
let us throw off everything that hinders and the sin that so easily entangles.
And let us run with perseverance the race marked out for us, fixing our eyes
on Jesus, the pioneer and perfecter of faith. For the joy set before him
he endured the cross, scorning its shame, and sat down
at the right hand of the throne of God.*
HEBREWS 12:1–2 NIV

Keeping the rules perfectly isn't what pleases God. Jesus went beyond keeping traditional Jewish law to total surrender and sacrifice. His obedience to God's will is why He is considered the pioneer of our faith journey.

The sacrifice God desires from us is a full surrender to Him. He wants us to follow, by faith, the journey He's laid out for us. When we follow this path by faith, we please God. He wants our attitude to be one of acceptance, not reluctance or annoyance that we don't have someone else's journey. When we fix our eyes on Jesus, we can journey with faith, grace, and trust.

Those who have gone before us on their journeys are cheering us on. The telling of their stories is meant to encourage us. Share your journey with others and encourage them.

Lord Jesus, thank You for Your ultimate sacrifice and for never leaving us alone on our journey. Give us strength to take one more step even when it's hard. Help us to remember that You know best. Remind us to share with others what You have done for us so we can encourage one another. Amen.

REFINED BY GOOD

*Let us not become weary in doing good, for at the proper time
we will reap a harvest if we do not give up.*
GALATIANS 6:9 NIV

One cartoon shows a man digging in a mine. We can see from a cutaway
that he is inches from striking it rich. But he drops his pick and walks
away, thinking he'll never get anywhere.

It's easy to get discouraged. Sometimes it feels like we are the only
ones doing the right thing. Sometimes it seems doing the right thing
works against us. We want to give up and just go along. We aren't getting
anywhere. But many times people give up just before the fruit begins to
show. God wants to encourage us to keep on going. He promises that we
will see a harvest of our actions.

Galatians 6:9 reminds us that there are seasons. Just like a farmer
plants her seed in one season and harvests the crop in the next, so it is
with our actions. We don't necessarily see the benefits of doing the right
thing right away. Some benefits we might not see until we get to heaven.

In the meantime, doing good benefits us. It refines us, getting our
hearts aligned with God's. We act on His interests instead of our own, and
we start seeing the world through His eyes. Keep looking for opportunities
to do good and don't give up. Trust in God's promises.

*Heavenly Father, help us see the world through Your eyes.
Give us the wisdom to know the right thing to do. Amen.*

TAKING JESUS AT HIS WORD

*The royal official said, "Sir, come down before my child dies."
"Go," Jesus replied, "your son will live." The man took
Jesus at his word and departed.*
JOHN 4:49–50 NIV

The royal official must have been desperate. He had probably made offerings to the many Roman gods but his son was still sick. He'd heard about a prophet the local Galileans called Jesus. Everyone was looking to see what miracles He would perform.

The official found Jesus and begged Him to come heal his son. But Jesus didn't do the expected. He didn't go to heal the man's son. Instead, He simply said that the son would live. The man may have had a moment of confusion at the unexpected turn of events, but he took Jesus at His word. He believed that Jesus' word could heal his son, even though he'd expected that Jesus would have to touch his son to heal him. When he arrived home and found his son well, he and his whole household believed.

Sometimes we are like this official. We look to Jesus as a last resort, and then we expect Him to act in a certain way. But as we look through the Gospels, we see that Jesus healed in a variety of ways. Still today He works any way He chooses, not just the way we expect.

Are you looking for Jesus to act in a certain way to answer a prayer? Ask God to open your eyes to the unexpected ways He is working.

*Lord Jesus, thank You for being intimately involved in our lives.
Remind us to trust You for everything. Amen.*

I Shall Return

And the Lord replied, "A faithful, sensible servant is one to whom the master can give the responsibility of managing his other household servants and feeding them. If the master returns and finds that the servant has done a good job, there will be a reward. I tell you the truth, the master will put that servant in charge of all he owns."

Luke 12:42–44 nlt

General Douglas MacArthur was a military adviser to the Philippine government just before World War II broke out. After the Japanese bombed Pearl Harbor and their invasion of the Philippines seemed imminent, MacArthur escaped at the last possible moment and narrowly missed being spotted by the Japanese. He sent word back to the Philippine people: "I shall return."

Two years later he waded into the water on the shores of the Philippines and said, "People of the Philippines, I have returned." MacArthur made this promise so the people of the Philippines wouldn't think he was abandoning them to the Japanese troops. He wanted them to have hope. And he kept his promise.

In a much greater way, Jesus told His disciples that He would return. He wants us to keep our hope in Him and to be prepared. He expects us to be good stewards or caretakers of the time, talents, and resources He's entrusted to us. When He returns, we will give Him an account of what we did with what He gave us.

Heavenly Father, help us to remember that all we have comes from You and we are merely caretakers. Show us in what areas we need to recognize Your ownership, and help us to be faithful stewards. Amen.

MOVE THE STONE

"Roll the stone aside," Jesus told them. But Martha, the dead man's sister, protested, "Lord, he has been dead for four days. The smell will be terrible."
JOHN 11:39 NLT

Jesus had been a frequent visitor to Martha's home. Now He has come again to raise her brother from the dead. If you asked Martha, if Jesus had come when they first asked Him to, her brother wouldn't be dead. Now He wants to open up the tomb. Martha doesn't understand any of it.

When Jesus asks for the tomb to be opened, Martha doesn't express amazement that Jesus intends to raise her brother from the dead. Instead, she's worried about the smell.

Aren't we often like that? God tells us to do something, to take a step of faith, to do our part so He can work. Instead of focusing on what God's going to do, we worry about how it's going to affect us.

It's also interesting that Jesus asked for the stone to be moved. If He was about to resurrect a dead body, moving a stone from in front of the tomb was a small thing. But He wanted their participation. He wanted them to put their faith in action. If they believed He was really going to raise a body that had been dead four days, then moving the stone from the tomb was the first step to show their faith.

Dear Lord, show us where we need to step out in faith and give us the courage to do it. Help us to trust You with everything. Amen.

THE BATTLE BELONGS TO THE LORD

*The commander of the LORD's army replied, "Take off your sandals,
for the place where you are standing is holy." And Joshua did so.*
JOSHUA 5:15 NIV

Joshua has some big sandals to fill. Moses is gone and now Joshua is in charge of the nation of Israel. Surrounded by enemies, the tiny nation has its first battle for the Promised Land coming up. Even though he's seen God work in miraculous ways, Joshua must be at least a little afraid.

And then he hears the same message his predecessor, Moses, did. "Take off your sandals. You're on holy ground."

Moses heard it coming from a burning bush. Joshua hears it from the commander of the Lord's army. If he wasn't scared before, he certainly is now. But ultimately this messenger and his message give comfort to Joshua. He has been anointed to be Israel's leader in the same way Moses had been. The battle isn't Joshua's to win or lose. He just needs to be faithful. The battle is God's, and He's already won it. Joshua just needs to follow orders.

We can have the same comfort that Joshua had. Whatever battle or challenge we may be facing, we don't face it alone. God is with us every step of the way. He will never leave us or forsake us.

Heavenly Father, thank You for always being beside us. Remind us of Your presence and help us to bring all of our cares and concerns to You. Amen.

FAITHFUL IN SERVICE

Then the LORD said to Joshua, "See, I have delivered Jericho into your hands, along with its king and its fighting men."
JOSHUA 6:2 NIV

Joshua trusted God. Which was a good thing, because his marching orders must have seemed like some of the craziest ever. March around a city in a certain order a certain number of times, make a lot of noise, and the walls will collapse. It probably didn't sound like any battle plan he'd ever heard of. But Joshua was faithful and obedient. God told Joshua in advance of the battle that it would be won. Joshua just needed to be faithful to do what God had said.

Today we honor the men and women who have given their lives in service to our country. They made the ultimate sacrifice to preserve our freedom. They were faithful in their service, just as Joshua was faithful to obey God. We may not all be called to such a sacrifice, but we all face battles of various sizes. We can know, like Joshua, that God is always with us. He goes before us and the battle is His. Our job is to be faithful and obedient.

Dear Lord, we are so thankful to the men and women who were faithful in their service and gave their lives to protect our freedom. Help me to be faithful in my obedience to You and remember that no matter the size of the battle I'm facing, You are with me. Amen.

DON'T WASTE YOUR TALENTS

*"His master replied, 'Well done, good and faithful servant!
You have been faithful with a few things; I will put you in charge
of many things. Come and share your master's happiness!'"*
MATTHEW 25:23 NIV

Imagine inheriting a fortune and then burying the money in the backyard. You don't want to make a mistake in spending it, so you hide it. Most of us would agree this kind of thinking is ridiculous. We would spend the money, either putting it to good use or just for our pleasure.

The verse above is near the end of the parable of the talents. This servant used the talents the master had given him to create more talents. In biblical times a talent was a measure of weight used for precious metals. It was often used as money.

The spiritual gifts, or "talents," God has given us are precious. Yet like a bar of gold sitting in a bank vault, they do no good unless they are used. Every believer receives spiritual gifts, or "talents," after receiving Christ. The purpose of these gifts is to build up the Body of Christ.

When it comes to our spiritual gifts, many of us still have them buried in the backyard. We don't think we're good enough yet or we're afraid of making a mistake. But notice the servant didn't get judged on how well he did. Just on whether or not he used his talents.

*Heavenly Father, give us the strength to step out and use our talents
without comparing ourselves to others. Help us to glorify You
in everything we do. Amen.*

THE CHOICE TO BE CHEERFUL

A cheerful look brings joy to the heart; good news makes for good health.
PROVERBS 15:30 NLT

· ·

"So how are you feeling now?" Jolene asked her grown son on the phone. He seemed to be gasping for breath.

He sniffled as he answered, "I just got back from a three-mile run. I feel just okay, not good."

"Have you been taking the vitamin shakes I sent you?"

"Sometimes."

"A positive attitude helps," his mother chirped. "Live longer, better, and have more fun. Look at the good! I do!"

"Mom, I know how to take care of myself! You think that Pollyanna stuff cures everything. Well, it doesn't."

Jolene smiled, realizing her son was well enough to run and sass his mother. He would recover—even without a great attitude.

King Solomon, inspired by God, penned this divine wisdom over three thousand years ago. Researchers today know that a positive attitude affects both the length and the quality of one's life. Attitude plays a big role in winning over disease. Attitude is also a choice.

When faced with challenges, choose to stand up straight and smile. Feel the blessings in a positive attitude.

· ·

Lord, I pray that in every situation in my life,
You point me to praise and the positive. Amen.

THE BLESSING BLUES

Bless those who persecute you; bless and do not curse.
ROMANS 12:14 NIV

"Roger's not even part of the family. He's adopted! He shouldn't get part of Mother's property!" Rena complained. "I want my share and everything else I deserve!"

Normally calm, Roger was rattled. Chosen by their mother for his financial expertise, he was astonished when his stepsister stopped probate. Now that their mother's house was in escrow, Rena stopped the sale. Her actions hurt the family, including her children.

The next morning, Roger prayed, "Lord, get her good!" Then he realized his mistake in Jesus' words, "Love your enemies, do good to those who hate you, bless those who curse you, pray for those who mistreat you" (Luke 6:27–28 NIV).

"You're kidding, Lord. I've got the blessings blues and You want me to pray good things for her!" He began with clenched teeth, "Lord, bless Rena and her attorney. Let this come out Your way." As he asked God for a blessing on Rena day after day, Roger felt his own resentment melt away. He could smile. His sense of humor returned. He became willing to let God handle the situation entirely. He let go of worry and let God manage the issue.

Blessing those who mistreat you is impossible—except with God. In His strength, we can overcome.

Lord, I ask You to strengthen me as I pray with a sincere heart for You to bless those in my life who may be dishonoring or mistreating me. Amen.

Paid in Advance

*In fact, the law requires that nearly everything be cleansed with blood,
and without the shedding of blood there is no forgiveness.*
Hebrews 9:22 niv

"For your birthday," Carol told Sylvia, "I'm treating us to a girls' day
out, including pedicures, lunch, and shopping!" The women looked
forward to the chance to visit as well as a shared luxury experience.

When the friends appeared at the nail spa, two new employees
greeted them and ushered them to fiberglass chairs. Their work was
excellent. Though the Asian staff of the salon in the past had proved to
have a reasonable command of English, the two new nail technicians'
English was limited to pointing to the nail colors and saying "Hello"
and "Pay now."

When Carol had paid for the services at the desk and the friends
were walking down the sidewalk, one technician ran after them, grabbed
Carol by the elbow, and cried, "Pay now! Pay now!"

"I already did!" she told the woman and guided her back to the
salon desk. There the technician understood when another staff member
explained in her native language about the gift certificate.

Just as Carol had already prepaid for the pedicures, God's only
Son's sacrifice paid it forward for all time with forgiveness of sins—for
everyone who accepts Him. Nothing else is needed to be forgiven and
bridge the relationship gap between us and God.

*Jesus, thanks for Your gift of life, love, and forgiveness for us.
May we be empowered to tell others more about You. Amen.*

LOVE IN WORDS AND ACTIONS

" 'Love the Lord your God with all your heart and with all your soul and with all your mind and with all your strength.' The second is this: 'Love your neighbor as yourself.' There is no commandment greater than these."
MARK 12:30–31 NIV

"I'll let you paint this room in exchange for the guest bed," Marilyn said, "but if you track mud in or get even one drip on the rugs, I'm not giving you the bed. You'll be paying me for the damage!"

"No problem," Jill responded confidently. "The bed looks new. How often did guests sleep in it?"

"Never. Family didn't stay here when they came through town. They didn't stop to visit, either. Some family!"

While Jill worked, she overheard Marilyn with a plumber. "I paid good money for you to fix the clogged drain. A month later, it's clogged again. I expect you to fix this right this time and not charge me more!"

Though it appeared that Jill won in this trade because she got a new bed without a cash outlay and Marilyn won because she could make the guest room into a den by adding furniture, Marilyn is the real loser—in relationships.

As Jesus taught about relationships with others, he took down walls. Jesus gave love, forgiveness, and physical and spiritual healing without expecting anything in return from people—men, women, children, the diseased, the poor, or foreigners.

He left us with orders to love all our neighbors—and to show that love in words and actions.

*Father, help me to see value in others
and respond to them as You do.*

Don't Be a Hoarder

Better what the eye sees than the roving of the appetite.
This too is meaningless, a chasing after the wind.
Ecclesiastes 6:9 NIV

. . . .

Nellie scarcely wrinkled the flannel sheet that covered her, but her possessions at home—saved for decades—bulged from every cranny. With Nellie in the hospital and destined to go to an assisted living facility, her daughter Ellen attacked one bathroom cupboard with heavy-duty contractor bags. She threw out outdated medicines and creams, broken combs, and frayed toothbrushes.

King Solomon, whose wisdom and net worth wowed the world, penned these words of caution about the futility of wanting more. Heeding this caution isn't easy when the world promotes the grandest vacation, newest car, and best kitchen ever.

Jesus urged us to focus on building treasures on earth that won't rust, rot, or be stolen. What could be of such great value? Jesus Himself modeled these treasures: when He fed the crowds that followed Him, meeting the needs of those who were hungry, sick, disabled, discouraged. He showed love and kindness, as well as forgiveness and acceptance. These are all things we can do when we see a need in others.

Hoarding earthly goods leads to trash—not treasure. But taking action to follow Jesus' lifestyle of genuine care for others leads to a priceless investment. And God smiles.

. . . .

Lord, give me the vision to recognize my gifts
and to see others' needs as You do.

MOTHER: A CHILD'S FIRST TEACHER

She speaks with wisdom, and faithful instruction is on her tongue.
PROVERBS 31:26 NIV

Once inside the century-old candlelit church, two women tiptoed down the wide aisle between wooden pews. One visitor whispered, "You can really feel the presence of God in this church."

"I think so, too," her friend agreed. "And look at this—Mary, mother of Jesus, teaching her young son about God!"

It was like no other statue either had seen in any church. The marble statue of Mary glowed in the candlelight as she pointed to scriptures from which she was teaching the boy Jesus—perhaps ten years old.

Whether or not the artist's rendition is accurate for the culture of the time, the message is clear: teaching godly values and a righteous lifestyle begins at home. A mother is a child's first teacher. What a responsibility!

Today's mother has to handle many things at once. Most work, keep up the house and family, pay bills, plan and prepare meals, and spend time with their husbands.

Sometimes it may seem that the least of all her jobs to squeeze in is to spend time nurturing her children. But God doesn't think of it as a small job at all.

Godly women who guide and mentor their children—or grandchildren—leave a godly legacy, influencing generations to come.

Through our love and teaching, God's words become real ones to live by.

Lord, remind us of the importance of being a woman who leads by example and love as we teach children Your commands.

God Sees Your Beauty Always

For you created my inmost being; you knit me together in my mother's womb. I praise you because I am fearfully and wonderfully made.
Psalm 139:13–14 niv

. . . .

As Brenda prepared for work, she noticed cars and people crowding her neighbors' lawn. They were having a large yard sale.

"How much for the oak dresser?" she asked Marlene, indicating the neglected piece pushed up against the house.

Her neighbor glanced at the tall antique dresser with a beveled mirror that had been in storage for years. She cringed at the broken drawer pulls and lumpy black finish. Besides noticeable kid scratches, one gleeful grandchild had left a permanent marker scribble on the top.

"Sorry. It's in terrible condition. Five bucks."

Brenda saw instead the graceful lines. She visualized new glass drawer pulls set in a glowing chestnut finish. Beauty was locked inside the vintage piece.

Weeks later, after much stripping, sanding, patching, and staining, Brenda finished the antique dresser. Marlene stopped by. Her neighbor was astonished. "I should have asked you for more." Brenda just smiled.

Just as Brenda invested time, skill, and patience to bring out the dresser's best, God, too, sees our potential and brings out the best. His sanding and finish work take away any ugliness and create a glow that all can see and that no cosmetic makeover can give.

. . . .

Lord, my heart is joyful that You, my Creator, see the beauty and value in me each day. You never stop working on making me the best I can be.

THERE'S NO PLACE LIKE GRANDMA'S

"The eternal God is your refuge, and underneath are the everlasting arms."
DEUTERONOMY 33:27 NIV

"There's no place like Grandma's," ten-year-old Ben piped up. "I can hardly wait to see what fun she has cooked up for us today!" he told his mother as she was driving him there.

Though Ben's room overflowed with souvenirs from theme park vacations, Grandma offered no such extras. What she did share was her time, home, encouragement—and fun!

"After I have a bad day," Ben continued, "Grandma hugs me and says, 'Ben, you're still going to grow up to be a wonderful man.' I feel better then."

When Ben arrived at Grandma's at the same time as two cousins, Grandma hugged the boys and ushered them into the kitchen, where she was making flour paste. She smiled and said, "We're making piñatas today! When they're dry and done, we'll fill them with candy and toys!"

The unanimous response: "Hooray!"

Like Grandma's investment in her grandsons and her provision of a refuge through good days and bad, God believes in us and gives us safe places to rest.

God's refuge of strength and protection has stood unchanged for millennia. He's worth our trust. Though the world pulls us to trust in money, careers, and causes, all become shaky investments of time and effort. Trusting in God never fails. He provides the solid foundation that stands for all time—and is a safe place always. Just like Grandma, God supports and encourages us inside hugs from His strong arms.

Lord, each day, help me seek and find Your plans for me.
Send me into the world in Your strength.

I WAS SORT OF BLIND, BUT NOW I SEE!

"But blessed are your eyes because they see, and your ears because they hear."
MATTHEW 13:16 NIV

Jean, not yet old enough to drive, coached her Grandma around on the streets of the city. Most often, they weren't going far. But even short treks could become white-knuckle experiences, such as when Grandma asked, "Jean, is that a tree or a person ahead?"

After they safely passed by the obstacle—a light pole—Jean suggested, "Grandma, I'll go with you to the eye doctor."

The doctor explained, "Mrs. Brown, you have cataracts. The lens of the eye makes things look cloudy as if you were looking through sheer curtains. Yours are like trying to see through three layers of sheer curtains. You won't be able to renew your driver's license without getting both cataracts fixed."

When the doctor removed the patch after her first cataract surgery, Grandma cried, "I can see!" Like her eyesight, her driving vastly improved after that.

When Jesus walked on earth, he healed many from physical blindness. He also recognized those whose spiritual blindness kept them from seeing and hearing the truth of His words. Some decided, in spite of His teachings, that Jesus was a threat to their investments, business, or positions. Jesus applauds those whose spiritual eyesight is 20/20. He spotlighted the disciples, whose hearts and lives were changed because of Jesus. They saw. They heard. They believed.

We have the treasure of God's Word, which gives us clear vision here all the way to heaven.

Lord, thank You for Your truth and direction each day.

KEEPING GOOD SECRETS

*"Be careful not to practice your righteousness in front of others to be seen by
them. If you do, you will have no reward from your Father in heaven."*
MATTHEW 6:1 NIV

"I insist on knowing who is responsible for this!" the general store's
owner, Clara, demanded. When she talked, even the ancient rafters of
her establishment trembled. You would have thought her outburst was
caused by a broken window, a noticeable amount of goods shoplifted, or
a burglary at the store.

Instead, she held a decorated paper bag filled with homemade
cookies, child-made window decorations sparkly with glue and glitter, a
comb, a small bag of pistachios, and a card.

Her employee, Robbie, offered timidly, "There were some little kids
tiptoeing around town not long ago. They had a bunch of bags."

In a town so small, secrets were hard to keep. "So it must be that
kids' church group. Well," she said, her tone softening, "that was a nice
thing to do for me."

Though Clara was not in need of cookies, she needed to know that
God loves even her.

Jesus added to the concept of giving in secret by explaining that if
we are giving to the needy, we are not to make it a public show. Giving
to the poor and making payments of tithe were often accompanied
by trumpets. Such actions were for show only. The donors felt no
compassion or kindness toward the poor.

Jesus cares what we think when we give. Why are we doing it? For
God or for us?

Heavenly Father, show me how to give You glory when I help others.

GOD'S YARDSTICK

*"Do not judge, or you too will be judged. For in the same way
you judge others, you will be judged, and with the measure
you use, it will be measured to you."*
MATTHEW 7:1–2 NIV

Showing up in the late afternoon just before closing, the couple had
traveled far to the home improvement store in town with their emergency.

"It's hot and we need to put an air conditioner in the window," the
man began.

"What kind of window? Does it slide to the side or does it need to
slide up?" Doris asked.

"The up kind," his wife responded.

"A casement," Doris remembered from her recent on-the-job training.
"What size?"

The man pulled from his pocket a bootlace that was frayed on one end.

"Like this," he said as he stretched it across the counter. It could
only be as accurate as elastic.

Doris thought, *Stupid! To come all this way without the window size!*

She looked up. They saw her attitude. "Sorry. You have to have the
right measurement to fit the window. You don't want to have to rebuild
the whole wall. Take this free yardstick and come back. We'll be glad to
help you."

God's command not to judge is assessed by our own actions. When
others know less than we think we do, give us a hard time, or don't agree
with us, we must not judge them. Using our standard of measure, God
will measure us—and reward us according to what we do.

*Lord, help me not to judge others but to give them
a second opinion as You do with me.*

Praise to the Women!

After this, Jesus traveled about from one town and village to another,
proclaiming the good news of the kingdom of God. . . . These women
were helping to support them out of their own means.
Luke 8:1, 3 niv

When a coworker at her building trades job commented, "You're just a woman," Kristin got mad. Though she sold power tools, she was terrified of them because of careless customers who came to the store with digits missing.

But Kristin couldn't be afraid of the noisy power tools that could cut 4x6x8 posts easier than slicing butter with a warm knife.

A few months later, when the teacher took attendance at Kristin's college shop class, he remarked, "Out of twenty-one students, only five are men! What impressive projects you ladies are building!"

Kristin created shelving for her home office with edges rounded on a router table. She fell in love with tools. She celebrated by buying a compound miter saw.

In Jesus' time, women had few rights and little importance. Yet Jesus included them in His ministry: the women learned from Master Rabbi Jesus; they helped support the ministry. They fed the followers with meals from scratch. When Jesus disappeared from the tomb, the disciples doubted, but the women were the first to see the risen Jesus, and they believed Him to be the Messiah.

Though some may say, "You're only a woman," think of Jesus' take instead: "You're important enough to share in My kingdom!"

Jesus, thank You for giving women importance
and respect on earth and in heaven.

GET INTO THE MOVIE FREE? DREAM ON

My son, do not despise the LORD's discipline, and do not resent
his rebuke, because the LORD disciplines those he loves,
as a father the son he delights in.
PROVERBS 3:11–12 NIV

"Dad, will you please let us go to the show on Saturday? It's only three bottle caps apiece. We can get into the movie free! You have pop machines in your gas station. You throw away lots of bottle caps each day. Dad, please!" Maggie's face was hopeful.

Her father met her look squarely and replied, "No, honey. If you and your brother and sister want to go to the show bad enough, you can work for it. We have chores here, and our neighbors need help, too."

"But Dad. . . ," Maggie began.

"Maggie, it's important for each of you to do your part—by working to earn your way. No free pass."

Maggie's dad was successful in teaching his children by firmly saying "no" when needed. Dad's discipline guided them to responsible adulthood, just as God's "no" stands firm as He guides us along a responsible Christian walk.

When God provided manna daily for the Israelites who fled to the desert, the food was raw. They picked it, pounded it, and then baked it into cakes.

Their food in Egypt had included garlic, leeks, fish, and grains of the fertile Nile Valley, but even there, people worked to eat. The severe desert conditions honed God's people into sojourners of strength as they trusted Him daily for His provision.

Lord, thank You for loving me enough to
sometimes answer "No" as You teach me.

Honor the Bible and the Flag

Your word is a lamp for my feet, a light on my path.
PSALM 119:105 NIV

. . . .

Bobby's timid voice could hardly be heard when teachers called on him. But Sunday, after much coaching, the seven-year-old spoke in a loud, clear voice as the crowd quieted to hear him. Bobby proudly held the Bible high. "I pledge allegiance to the Bible, God's Holy Word! I will make it a lamp unto my feet and a light unto my path and will hide its words in my heart that I might not sin against God. Amen."

This pledge to the Bible is based on Psalm 119:11 and 105. In the same way children learn respect for the Bible from church and home, respect for our country and its flag should begin at home, too.

Today, June 14, is Flag Day in the United States. It is a day to honor the flag and those who have helped keep it flying. In 1855, a Wisconsin schoolteacher named B. J. Cigrand started the "Flag Birthday"; it was the 108th anniversary of the official adoption of the Stars and Stripes. Teaching patriotism caught on, beginning with teachers and children. In 1916, President Woodrow Wilson designated June 14 as Flag Day.

Just as we accept responsibility for teaching kids to honor our country's flag, we must take initiative in teaching them respect for the Bible. Who can show the way better than us, by modeling its teachings and hiding its words in our hearts? The Bible is a timeless guide for making wise decisions in every situation and generation.

. . . .

Lord, thank You for our flag and the freedom it represents.
Thank You also for Your Word and the wisdom it imparts.
Please light my path with Your words for all to see.

DRUNKARD'S PATH QUILT PATTERN

*Bear with each other and forgive one another if any of you has
a grievance against someone. . . . And over all these virtues put
on love, which binds them all together in perfect unity.*
COLOSSIANS 3:13–14 NIV

The church-sponsored quilting class was using creativity and scraps to
provide gift quilts for new mothers at the local hospital.

"Any mom would be thrilled to have such a special gift from a
stranger!" said Linda.

"I don't think so," Danielle commented. "That pattern is called
'The Drunkard's Path.' It means there is a drunkard in the house. It's
like a curse!"

Linda was so upset, she left the class early. Later, she went online and
learned that the pattern she'd made into a quilt was not "The Drunkard's
Path."

By the next class, Linda had finished the quilt. She also had studied
Colossians 3, which advises us to clothe ourselves with compassion,
kindness, humility, gentleness, patience. . .and especially love. What a
stretch with Danielle!

When Linda arrived, Danielle was complimenting another quilter,
"Your machine quilted this! Congratulations on learning how to do it!"
The lady knew how to encourage—not just criticize. It was a start.

As Linda adjusted her vision, she saw many things to love about
Danielle.

*Lord, help me to adjust my vision to love and have
patience with all those around me.*

LISTEN TO GOD?

WHO HAS TIME?

After the earthquake came a fire, but the LORD was not in the fire.
And after the fire came a gentle whisper.
1 KINGS 19:12 NIV

Susan greeted the couple as they entered the home improvement store: "What can I help you find?"

"We need patio furniture," the wife began. "We have a big yard."

"Great! We have comfortable weatherproof furniture. Have you considered one of these colorful hammocks? Just kick back and enjoy!"

"We don't have time to lounge around," the husband responded. "We're just too busy. What we need is a patio table and six chairs for when the kids and grandkids come up."

Susan reflected on the patio trend in home magazines. Even with garden makeovers focused on creating a pleasant retreat, spaces were furnished with many chairs—never just a hammock or space for one.

With today's pace, we are pressured to do more and more multi-tasking. What's missing is time to think, reflect, appreciate, and listen to God—alone.

Being able to hear God's voice—even in a whisper—is one key to keeping close to Him. We just need to take the time to relax and enjoy His company and our own.

Lord, thank You for coming to me in a whisper at times.
I will take time to listen.

DON'T GIVE UP! GOD SEES YOUR POTENTIAL

"The LORD does not look at the things people look at. People look at the outward appearance, but the LORD looks at the heart."
1 SAMUEL 16:7 NIV

. . . .

"I'm sorry, miss," the newspaper editor began as he addressed one of his journalism students. He couldn't remember her name. "You're just not cut out for the writing life. I can't pass you. Find another field of study."

The college student's eyes misted. "But I was tops in journalism at my junior college."

"You've got straight F's because you're a poor proofreader. That's where good writing starts. Change fields of study."

Miss J.'s heart was on the ground. She graduated in another field. Years later, she enrolled in a non-credit class: magazine writing. Her first story was purchased by a popular magazine. Over the decades, hundreds of articles followed, as well as anthologies and an award-winning book.

Miss J. smiled the day she was asked to be a writing workshop leader—in the city where she washed out in journalism. God had seen all along what she could be.

Our Creator sees more of our hearts and potential than anyone on earth. Just as He saw a king in David—while his siblings might have thought of him as only a pesky little brother—God sees the best of what we can be. He believes in us.

When it comes to believing what others believe we can and can't accomplish—trust in God instead and soar without limits!

. . . .

*Heavenly Father, thanks for my skills and the way
You lead me in using them.*

PATIENCE AND PERSISTENCE

*Never be lacking in zeal, but keep your spiritual fervor, serving the Lord.
Be joyful in hope, patient in affliction, faithful in prayer.*
ROMANS 12:11–12 NIV

Marnie's eyelids were drooping toward the end of class, even though it was just 5 p.m. She had worked from 6:00 a.m. to 2:00 p.m., rushed home to eat, then traveled to her college classes.

Her professor dismissed class and touched Marnie's arm. "The dean of students wants to see you right away."

Marnie saw the dean studying her college schedule.

"I see that you are taking twenty-one class hours this semester. You're working full time as well, is that right?"

"Yes."

"We don't advise our students to take more than eighteen credit hours. So we're asking you to drop a couple of classes—for your own good."

"I have straight A's in all my classes. I'm working and paying for college as I go. Just which classes do you think I should drop?"

His mouth snapped shut. "Never mind. Good job!"

Marnie became the only sibling of five to attend college. With the same zeal that she applied to school, she sought God's way for her life while helping those in need.

Paul urges us to persist in our quest for God, following His commands for handling situations and relationships. The path may seem as difficult as Marnie's struggle with full-time work and school. But at graduation, God is waiting there with the words, "Well done, good and faithful servant!" (Matthew 25:23 NIV).

Lord, always help me to keep my eyes looking up—at You!

A FATHER IN DEEDS

For you know that we dealt with each of you as a father deals with his own children, encouraging, comforting and urging you to live lives worthy of God, who calls you into his kingdom and glory.
1 THESSALONIANS 2:11–12 NIV

Dressed in black bike shorts and a colorful jersey, the middle-aged deacon, Dan, stopped to invite a neighbor's son for a bicycle ride in the country.

"Thank You, God!" the teenager responded as he looked to heaven. "Saved from more Saturday chores!"

Len's mother glared at him.

"Sorry, Mom. I was just making a funny." Len wheeled his bike outside.

"It will just be about eight miles today," Dan commented. "It's a good ride up and down rolling hills."

When they returned, Dan told Len's Mom, "Len is quite a rider! He can race on one of my bikes anytime."

The teen who hated organized sports zeroed in on bicycling after that. He raced. He went to school to learn to fix and build two-wheelers. Bikes became Len's career.

A simple ride coupled with the deacon's positive influence guided the teen to learn that becoming a man who follows God can be fun.

With nearly one-third of American families headed by single parents, the influence of a father may come from someone other than a biological parent. Focus your thoughts today on the men who have taken on the role of a father through their deeds—shaping you and your children.

Heavenly Father, give me the opportunity to thank men and fathers who make a difference.

NEED CASH, NOT GAS!

Let us not become weary in doing good, for at the proper time
we will reap a harvest if we do not give up.
GALATIANS 6:9 NIV

. . . .

Paula was refueling her car several hundred miles from home when she heard two men at the next pump lament, "How are we going to get back to Pine Springs?" They talked so loudly that other customers at the pumps heard them. Their vehicle—a shiny late-model pickup truck—was parked under the cabana next to the pump.

Pine Springs? she thought to herself. She lived in Pine Springs! Though the town had just a little over five thousand people, she didn't recognize the men.

"I put two gallons in, but that's not enough to get home," the second complained. They publicly aired their dilemma and asked travelers to give them gas money.

Paula was skeptical. "How is it they can't make the three-hour trip home?"

Sometimes we can get disgruntled about those who always seem to need help. Jesus commanded us to help those in need. Kindness and compassion during a crisis can change a life. Yet discernment is necessary.

One church determines who to help on this basis: *Are they telling the truth? Is their situation temporary or are they frequently in crisis after help? If able, are they willing to work for what has been given them?*

. . . .

Lord, help me see when someone truly has a need—
and show me what to do.

Y'ALL COME IN!

Do not forget to show hospitality to strangers, for by so doing some people have shown hospitality to angels without knowing it.
HEBREWS 13:2 NIV

Ruby clanged the triangle dinner bell, calling her family inside. Her husband, Rex, the ranch foreman, had been showing his boss, Richard, around the cattle ranch.

"I'll be going now," Richard told Rex as he checked his watch. "Where is a good place to eat around here?"

"Nearest town is about an hour away. Everything closes at noon. If you don't mind simple fare, join us for lunch."

When Rex ushered the wealthy man inside for a meal, Ruby blushed. "It's only chili and corn bread." Their ten children had settled in chairs of all types and styles—even metal folding chairs—around the well-scrubbed table covered in plastic.

Richard tasted the buttered corn bread moist with garden sweet corn and the chili beans seasoned with fresh green chili peppers, onions, garlic, and cumin. He groaned with pleasure and smiled. "Thanks for sharing this meal with me. It's so much like my home when I was growing up!"

Hospitality is for everyone—poor and rich alike. In the Bible, not to offer hospitality to all when it was needed was unthinkable.

Today, we can still share what we have. No fancy home or table is needed. Gourmet food is unnecessary. Showing hospitality is a giving of self. The Lord provides the when and the how.

Father, give me more opportunities to give of myself and show hospitality.

NO CELLOS ALLOWED

Yet to all who did receive him, to those who believed in his name,
he gave the right to become children of God.
JOHN 1:12 NIV

As Rick and Ron hefted their orchestra instruments to the bus stop for their first week at a new school, they felt anxious. Would the students at their new school accept newcomers?

Ron hefted his cello up the steps to the aisle while his brother followed with a violin case.

The bus driver riveted an unfriendly glare at Ron. "No cellos allowed on this bus! That fiddle is too big, too."

"How are we supposed to get to school?"

"Walk due north on the dirt road there."

When their mother asked them how their first day was, the boys—who had never been in trouble in school—reported, "We got kicked off the bus!"

Though the driver stopped anyone with too much cargo, Jesus takes down the restrictions: *All* who welcome Him into their lives become children of God. All have ahead a new life and a fresh start.

Reflect on the gift of a new beginning. Let go of regrets or mistakes. God forgives you. He still loves you and holds you close as His child. It doesn't matter if you're a newbie. You're accepted and cherished—always.

Lord, thanks for infusing me with Your love
and providing me with a family.

It's Not Official until It's on Facebook

Hold on to what is good, reject every kind of evil.
1 Thessalonians 5:21–22 niv

Social media—it's how to get the buzz out. Businesses are begging, "See our social side! Like us on Facebook!"

One source reports that Facebook could be a country, with over 200 million users a year. In less than an hour, the whole world knows the news on the Internet. And between Facebook friends, reminders pop up that it's someone's birthday, they've posted pictures, or they have a new gripe or family addition.

But whatever the news, good or bad, the challenge for all Christians is to monitor one's words—whether spoken or written—and include God in all parts of our lives. After one woman posted a picture of herself up to her neck in bubbles in a Jacuzzi tub with the caption, "TGIF. Do something fun this Friday," one response was, "So now you're posting naked pictures on Facebook?" It is a startling reminder that the world watches.

King Solomon's writings in Proverbs 10 through 24 include at least fifty references to the necessity of guarding one's words and actions. Examples include, "The wise store up knowledge, but the mouth of a fool invites ruin" (Proverbs 10:14 niv), and "The lips of the righteous nourish many, but fools die for lack of sense" (Proverbs 10:21 niv).

When it comes to social media, that advice still stands. That's the official word from Facebook Friend God.

*Lord, guide me to choose wisely the words
and actions of my daily life.*

LOVE IS A MANY-SPLENDORED THING

Flee from sexual immorality.
1 CORINTHIANS 6:18 NIV

When Sheila finished yet another sexually graphic romance novel from a popular writer, her husband, Dennis, was dismayed. She whined, "Why can't you be more like that?" Dennis could never measure up.

What was the fictional guy like? He was taller than she was, with thick hair she loved to entwine in her fingers; his touch and kisses scalded her with passion, and without a shirt, he had a six-pack that didn't come from cans in the refrigerator.

But fictional romance is no more real than catalogs for "average women" using size 2 models who had surgery to enhance their measurements.

Paul primarily addressed men when he approached this topic of honoring God with the body—and mind. But women face temptation, too. Sexual sin can be crowded out when we allow the Holy Spirit to rule our bodies and thoughts.

Pastor Jimmy Evans, author of *Marriage on the Rock*, discourages women's romance reading because it opens the door for sexual sin.

What is a woman to do? Choose wisely. Honor God and the commitment to one's helpmate. Turn away from temptation from unsuitable media overload.

Appreciate the love of the man scuffing around in a worn bathrobe who cleans up after the baby or the dog, washes dishes, helps around the house, and cares for his wife when she's sick.

Now isn't that better than the fictional version of Mr. Right?

Lord, indwell me with Your Holy Spirit. Remind me to choose wisely and honor You and my mate with my actions and choices.

TAKING TIME TO LISTEN

Love is patient, love is kind.
1 CORINTHIANS 13:4 NIV

. . . .

At home before and after work, Janice was bombarded with questions from her children. Sometimes she had to research to find intelligent answers.

"Why is God invisible?"

"What time is God's bedtime?"

"Are God and Santa Claus in the same family?"

When she switched to professional mode and headed to school, where she taught older children, she was all business.

Teaching has long been associated with time and dedication. "It's really a *mission*, not a job," her supervisor once said. "The kids really know if you care about them."

But years of demands on her time, meetings after school, and training weekends and summers caused her patience and care to wear thin. So when Leroy asked as she was unlocking the classroom, "Can I come into your classroom and play your word games?" Janice snapped, "No, you're not even in my class. I've got a lot of work to do before the bell rings."

"Boy, Mrs. R., why are you always in such a hurry? Nobody else is."

His words hit her. Though she practiced patience and kindness with her own children, she wasn't bringing those to the schoolchildren. That would change, beginning now.

Patience, caring, and love go together. Turning to look at someone when they are speaking and giving them your attention is a way of showing love. And it's not just for kids.

. . . .

Lord, show me how to share love and patience with those around me—just as You have done for me.

"Shape Your Booty Camp"

Do you not know that your bodies are the temple of the Holy Spirit,
who is in you, whom you have received from God? You are not your own;
you were bought at a price. Therefore honor God with your bodies.
1 Corinthians 6:19–20 niv

"Cellulite season," Jackie, a mother of three, lamented. "The body-shapers under my clothes aren't working!" With her husband to help with the family and home, she signed up for "Shape Your Booty Camp."

Jackie felt as if she'd been thrown into Olympic training against her will. Her humble five ab curls and two-minute cardio workouts left her breathless. She watched others effortlessly pump through push-ups and aerobics. Gradually, Jackie got stronger and better. She acquired more energy and bounce. She was better able to keep up with her demands as a working wife and mother.

God gives women the important roles of mother, model, teacher, caregiver, and missionary to others. Being able to keep up with those roles takes care and maintenance. Just as the family car needs shop time for oil changes, new tires, and transmission service, the family caregiver also needs time for physical and spiritual upkeep.

Women tend to set aside their own needs and care for the care of others. Busy women need time for themselves, too—so they can do what God has chosen them to do. Love and serve and touch the world.

Isn't it worth a trip to the gym?

Lord, help me to schedule time to care for my body
as well as to serve others.

COINCIDENCE OR GOD?

The old has gone, the new is here!
2 CORINTHIANS 5:17 NIV

. . . .

"Uh-oh!" the young woman breathed. Jana was stranded with a blown engine forty miles from the nearest town. Now she saw a heavyset man stalking her at the rest stop. He was twice her size. Today, one might call on a cell phone and lock the doors. But the new 750cc motorcycle was as wide open as the countryside.

With Jana's communication systems down, how could she call for help? Though raised as a Christian, she'd thumbed her nose at God for ten years. Would He even hear her? "Please, God," she prayed as she saw the man was just twelve feet away, "help me!"

Noise and chaos filled the air as a diesel tow truck pulled up, full of rescuers who cried, "It's true! A lady all the way from Arizona on a motorcycle!" In all the commotion, the stalker turned, got in his truck, and drove away.

Fed and housed at the business owner's house, Jana asked herself, "Coincidence or God?" But deep down she knew God had rescued her—physically and spiritually.

God can make you a new person and set you on an astonishing path. His vision for your life and potential is limitless. No matter where you have been or what you have done, God makes you new and clean when you accept Jesus. He also can guide you to break through the barriers of fear to accomplish new achievements and goals.

. . . .

Lord, light the path ahead that You have planned for me.

On Solid Rock

"Therefore everyone who hears these words of mine and puts them into practice is like a wise man who built his house on the rock. The rain came down, the streams rose, and the winds blew and beat against that house; yet it did not fall, because it had its foundation on the rock."
Matthew 7:24–25 niv

In the Sonoran Desert thrives the ironwood tree. Though it is of little use commercially, the tree is an essential hub of plant and animal life. Just as God does, the ironwood tree nourishes and protects every living thing in its heavy shade.

Because of the ironwood's deep roots, the tree stands firm through floods and winds—just like God. He is the same today and always. Ironwoods also enrich the soil by infusing it with nitrogen like God's rich nourishment in our lives. The tree changes the harsh land around it so that living things can thrive. God changes lives for the better. The ironwood lives long and remains hardy. God has been with us since the beginning (John 1:1–2) and will carry us through to the end (Philippians 1:6).

As you build a foundation in your life, look to God's words. They provide a foundation of solid rock: words that survive all storms, words that grow us, guide us, protect us, and provide for our flourishing.

God's Word even outlasts the ironwood tree.

Lord, I thank You for Jesus' words and teaching that guide me to Your kingdom.

EXUDE ENCOURAGEMENT

Let us consider how we may spur one another on toward love and good deeds, not giving up meeting together. . .but encouraging one another.
HEBREWS 10:24–25 NIV

Soon after reading specialist Janey hired Sheila Thomas as a classroom aide to help children with learning problems, Janey realized Mrs. T.'s heart was wounded.

"I left home in my senior year," she confided to Janey. "My stepfather wouldn't leave me alone and Mom didn't believe me."

Shelia's success as an aide, mother, wife, and scout leader was legendary. Yet her journaling—no matter what the topic—bled with pain. With Janey's daily encouragement, Shelia became more confident. She began to visualize a different future ahead.

At the end of Shelia's first school year with the reading teacher, Janey encouraged Sheila to write her life story and enter it in a statewide contest. She didn't just place. "cfWow, Mrs. T.! Grand prize! You won over everyone in the state!"

At Janey's urging, Shelia enrolled in college and graduated with honors. Shelia became the teacher she had always wanted to be.

Encouragement promotes growth and confidence. Everyone benefits from words that lift and nourish. Everyone needs encouragement to hurdle the negatives that hit them in words, situations, and relationships. Look for the gifts in others. Compliment others on the things they do well, their progress, and their achievements. Give others the vision God sees in them. Sincere words can change a life. God will show you how.

Lord, give me the words of encouragement others need.

Taking Character to Heart

*But the seed on good soil stands for those with a noble and good heart,
who hear the word, retain it, and by persevering produce a crop.*
Luke 8:15 niv

. . . .

Character education is popular today. Schoolchildren are taught positive values such as responsibility, honesty, fairness, caring, teamwork, and helpfulness. Character programs were first designed to reduce classroom discipline problems, drop-out rates, and juvenile delinquency. Our society wants caring, contributing citizens. The bottom-line motivation is monetary: it's cheaper than maintaining jails and inmates.

But God cares about individuals—each person—their future and their community contribution as well as their character path. His training program and hands-on challenges produce people who make a difference.

Consider Queen Esther, who confronted her husband, the king of Persia, to save her people. Or Mary and Martha, who shared meals with Jesus and His disciples numerous times (Luke 10:38). Or the woman at the well, who persuaded the entire village to meet Jesus (John 4). Or Mary Magdalene, who believed what she saw at the tomb and boldly announced Jesus' resurrection (John 20:10–18).

God's training helps individuals grow through helping others. It is the real deal. The legacy of God's character education stands for all time.

. . . .

*Lord, make me a bold woman of character who invests time
and effort in those things that are precious to You.*

Looking Beyond Earthly Reassurances

Some nations boast of their chariots and horses,
but we boast in the name of the Lord our God.
Psalm 20:7 nlt

David, the writer of this psalm, did not find his hope in things that came from this earth—things he could see with his own eyes or create with his own hands. He did not find it through a solution his mind could conjure. He had faith in the Lord, and that was enough. We can only imagine how comforting it would be to look upon our defending army during a time of war, but he chose to look beyond the army and instead fixed his eyes on the Lord.

Through any trial or pain, the Lord sees all, and He loves his people in a deep, unfailing way. Although a thousand may fall, our fate and lives rest in Him and Him alone. We cannot look to earthly things to predict our future, finances, employment, etc. God's plans far exceed anything we could plan, and if we trust and follow Him, we will end up in a place we never would have come to on our own.

Breathe in. Breathe out. Rest and believe. It is through fixing our eyes on God and looking to Him for direction that we are reassured and can experience peace.

Lord, please set my eyes on You. Help me not to seek reassurance through earthly things but to understand on a deeper level that You control all. You hold my heart and care about each step I take. My hope is in You alone.

SEEKING ADVICE

*The LORD says, "I will guide you along the best pathway for your life.
I will advise you and watch over you. Do not be like a senseless horse
or mule that needs a bit and bridle to keep it under control."*
PSALM 32:8–9 NLT

. . . .

There is a key word in this passage: "advise." The Lord says He will
advise us and watch over us. But what if we don't take the time to ask
for His guidance? How many times have we been sidetracked, lost, and
confused simply because we never asked for the Lord's advice?

In the hurried lives we live, it's easy to fall into a routine and switch
over to autopilot. Our calendars are teeming with activities and deadlines,
and all too often we simply enter survival mode. You could say that we
become similar to the mule in this scripture—putting hardly any thought
into our days and simply being guided by chaos and distraction.

God has more for us. If we take the time to seek out His counsel,
He will advise us. He will guide us along the best pathway for our lives
and watch over us. He will give us purpose, and our lives will be filled
with adventure and divine encounters.

. . . .

*Lord, thank You for opening my eyes to the reality that You desire to guide
my life. Forgive me for being so busy, and help me to slow down and seek
Your counsel. I want to walk this journey of life with You.*

A PERSISTENT LOVE

"O Israel," says the LORD, "if you wanted to return to me, you could.
You could throw away your detestable idols and stray away no more."
JEREMIAH 4:1 NLT

. . . .

Reading the Bible can be scary at times, as we see God threaten to destroy entire nations. All throughout Jeremiah, the Lord speaks of the punishment that is about to befall His people. He goes on and on about the destruction that will come to their cities and families. Yet He continually says things like, "If you return to me, I will restore you so you can continue to serve me" (Jeremiah 15:19 NLT).

God's love for us is vast and deep, and He offers more than second chances! Even though some may never decide to choose Him—and He must deal with them as He sees fit—He continually offers us the chance to return to Him. What wonderful news this is for us!

If you are feeling like you are past redemption, take heart! Read through the book of Jeremiah and be reassured that He desires you. Use a highlighter to mark every time He offers redemption. As you do this, you will begin to see that He ultimately desires for you to be with Him.

. . . .

Lord, I am amazed by Your love for me! Every day You are ready
and waiting for me to trust only in You. Father, I choose to do so today.
Thank You for not giving up on me and for giving me second chances.
May I walk in confidence of Your great love today.

Independence from Sin

God's free gift leads to our being made right with God,
even though we are guilty of many sins.
Romans 5:16 NLT

Speaking to his church, a pastor once asked his congregation what the worldly view of man was. He got answers like "good-natured," "successful," "deserving of wealth," "powerful." Then he asked them what the biblical picture of man was and received a starkly differing picture: "sinful," "evil," "weak," "fickle," "deserving of death." As the pastor wrote down these answers in two columns on a whiteboard, the congregation grew quiet.

You see, although our society convinces us that we are, in fact, good people and deserving of all things good, we are, in truth, evil and deserving of death. From the moment of Adam's first sin, we all have been flawed.

However, because of Christ's sacrifice on the cross, we can once again be in relationship with God! We are now independent from sin. We are able to enter into God's presence not because of anything we have done, but only because of what Jesus has done. By recognizing that it is only by Christ's sacrifice we are made clean, we can have a relationship with God.

He chooses you. He loves you. Choose today to dwell on this love.

Jesus, thank You for enduring the pain You did on earth so that I could
be reconciled to You. May I walk in humble faith forever with You,
and rest daily in the love You have for me. May I know on
a deeper level what Your sacrifice has done for me.

Let God Reign!

*Oh, how great are God's riches and wisdom and knowledge!
How impossible it is for us to understand his decisions and his ways!
For who can know the Lord's thoughts? Who knows enough to give him
advice? And who has given him so much that he needs to pay it back?
For everything comes from him and exists by his power and is
intended for his glory. All glory to him forever! Amen.*
Romans 11:33–36 NLT

It's easy for us to believe that we carry the world on our shoulders. We tend to believe, though we may not admit it, that we alone make the world turn. We convince ourselves that worry, finances, or power will put us in control. But in truth, God is the One who controls all.

What a blessed peace awaits us! As you go about your day, rest in the assurance that God is in control—not you. God understands every feeling you experience, and He can comfort you. God knows the best steps for you to take in life, and He is willing to guide you. He is above all and knows all, yet He is never out of reach.

Set your eyes firmly on the Lord, and He will care for you.

*Lord, please let this truth sink deep into my heart today so that I may
live in joy and peace. Please guide me by Your wisdom and provide for
me according to Your riches. I praise You because You are good!*

A LIVING SACRIFICE

And so, dear brothers and sisters, I plead with you to give your bodies to God because of all he has done for you. Let them be a living and holy sacrifice—the kind he will find acceptable. This is truly the way to worship him. Don't copy the behavior and customs of this world, but let God transform you into a new person by changing the way you think. Then you will learn to know God's will for you, which is good and pleasing and perfect.

ROMANS 12:1–2 NLT

We often stop after this verse when referencing how to be a living sacrifice for God. But if we read on, we get a better idea how this plays out in our daily life: by using the gifts God has given us, loving others, holding tightly to what is good, working hard to serve the Lord, rejoicing in our confident hope, being patient in trouble, blessing our enemies, and not thinking we know it all. Finally, by not letting evil conquer us, but conquering evil by doing good.

Doesn't that feel refreshing? These are all wonderfully tangible ways that we can please God. Our community could be a better place if we hid these words in our hearts and daily lived them out—and how encouraged we would be! Romans 12 encourages us both to love others and to hold tightly to what the Lord has promised.

You spell out clearly what You desire from us, and it is all for our good. Through following You we experience a full, abundant, and vibrant life. Thank You!

REJOICE!

Always be full of joy in the Lord. I say it again—rejoice!
PHILIPPIANS 4:4 NLT

Do you ever feel like life is a fifty-pound backpack? Life can get heavy if we aren't careful, with everyday worries wearing us down and making us exhausted. Even small decisions tend to grow in our minds to be more important than they really are. Big decisions can completely take us over so that even the most wonderful news becomes tainted.

Look away from the cares of this world! Rejoice in what the Lord has done! Instead of lending every thought to the troubles at hand, praise God for the ways He has provided in the past and doubtless will again in the future!

Begin to count your blessings, and feel the weight lifting off your shoulders. Feel the freedom you have to enjoy your life. Enjoy your home and the comfort it brings. Enjoy your family, pets, and things you have. Allow yourself to fully feel the joy that comes with the first snow, the first warm breeze of spring, or the first rays of sun in the morning. There are so many wonderful things to enjoy even as you read this!

Life is complicated, yes. But it should never be allowed to rob you of the joy the Lord provides. "I say it again—rejoice!"

Lord, You are so good! Teach me Your ways and show me Your faithfulness, that I may be full of joy because of You. You created this earth to be enjoyed, and enjoy it I shall!

BE WISE WITH YOUR WORDS

Obscene stories, foolish talk, and coarse jokes—these are not for you.
Instead, let there be thankfulness to God.
EPHESIANS 5:4 NLT

When we come across passages like this, we tend to get defensive and think things like, *This isn't speaking about me. Such things don't bother me.* But let's take a moment to think of the reason this verse could have been written.

Have you ever been in a crowd of friends, having a wonderful time, when suddenly the crude jokes started flowing? Or someone began telling you some inappropriate story that made you squirm? The once good, joyful atmosphere suddenly takes on a heavy, almost sickening feel. Such stories don't encourage. In fact, they do the opposite. They discourage, depress, or, worse, push others toward sin.

What do you want to be known for? Are you the one bringing life to the party by smiling, uplifting others, and speaking about wholesome things? Or are you the one bringing it down, swiftly and surely? Are you the one pushing others toward sin?

Whether we choose to believe it or not, our lips hold incredible power. Use them for good! Honor the Lord and your friends with the words you say. You will gain honor, not only in the eyes of the Lord, but also in the eyes of your peers.

Lord, I realize that my lips bear great power. Forgive me for any foolish words I have spoken, and please redeem them. Bless my lips to speak only what is true, uplifting, and good, that I may bring life.

AN HONORABLE LIFE

There was a man named Jabez who was more honorable than any of his brothers. His mother named him Jabez because his birth had been so painful. He was the one who prayed to the God of Israel, "Oh, that you would bless me and expand my territory! Please be with me in all that I do, and keep me from all trouble and pain!" And God granted him his request.

1 CHRONICLES 4:9–10 NLT

This passage is all that 1 Chronicles has to say about Jabez. He was an honorable man, and God granted him his request. God blessed him, expanded his territory, was with him in all he did, and kept him from trouble and pain. Isn't that amazing?

We can always appreciate the reminder that God hears the honorable. As the psalms show, He doesn't do the same for the wicked. "To the pure you show yourself pure, but to the crooked you show yourself shrewd. You rescue the humble, but you humiliate the proud" (Psalm 18:26–27 NLT). It's important for us to notice that it was because of his good character and respect for the Lord that God noticed and heard Jabez.

We are not asked to be perfect. We are simply asked to live a pure life and to honor the Lord in all we do.

Oh, that You would bless me and expand my territory! Please be with me in all that I do, and keep me from all trouble and pain.

Waiting

Wait patiently for the LORD. Be brave and courageous.
Yes, wait patiently for the LORD.
PSALM 27:14 NLT

* *

Waiting is rarely easy. Waiting means that something we desire is being delayed—postponed—and we don't know when it will arrive. It can be even harder when we are waiting for news that could be terrible—news that could change our lives for the worse.

Isn't it interesting that David linked being brave and courageous to the act of waiting? He is telling us that even though we don't know the timing or outcome of whatever it is we're waiting on, we should be brave in the face of it. We should not cower in a corner but move forward with courage. He also says to wait *patiently*. Here are some other words for *patient*: *calm, composed, enduring, uncomplaining,* and *understanding.* Waiting is not a passive thing! There is a call to action during this time.

There is good in waiting. Take this opportunity to lean into God. At first you may find that spending time with Him is hard, because you feel like He is keeping things from you. But soon you will find that waiting on God is one of the most rewarding things you could ever do.

* *

Lord, through faith in You I can be brave in facing the unknown and I can move forward with courage. Help me to be patient as I trust Your timing and Your ways, and help me to lean on You more and more.

UNFAILING LOVE SURROUNDS US

Many sorrows come to the wicked, but unfailing love
surrounds those who trust the LORD.
PSALM 32:10 NLT

When you read this verse, what is the first thing that comes to mind? Maybe that evil people will face many sorrows, but you will be surrounded by the Lord's unfailing love. You will be surrounded with love because you are a good person, and far from evil! Right?

What if this verse is saying something else? As we read through the Bible, we see that we are all wicked. "No one is righteous—not even one" (Romans 3:10 NLT). No one is *good*. That is, except through the grace of God. Maybe, then, this verse is saying that many sorrows will come to the wicked—to humankind—but those who choose to put their trust in the Lord, in Christ Jesus, will be surrounded by His unfailing love. Those people may face trouble because they are still in a world full of fallen people, but they will not face it alone.

No matter what you may be facing, let this be your anthem. Let this be the promise you hold close to your heart. Let it be a verse you recite to yourself as you fall asleep at night. "Many sorrows come to the wicked, but unfailing love surrounds those who trust the LORD."

I have this promise to hold on to. Lord, remember me. Remember how
I put my trust in You and seek You day and night. Surround me with
Your unfailing love, that I may walk through this life
knowing that I am secure in Your hands.

WRESTLING WITH PRAYER

I am praying to you because I know you will answer,
O God. Bend down and listen as I pray.
PSALM 17:6 NLT

Do you ever find it hard to pray? It can be difficult to believe that God would take the time to listen to our honest plea, and so we rarely try. Oftentimes, when we do muster up the courage, we feel as if no one is listening to us. It is only the still air and our pained hearts.

Our society of computer screens and Internet searches makes it even harder for us to pray. Praying takes time and effort and then forces us to wait on God for an answer. This is rarely a sought-after option when we have answers available to us just a few clicks away. Although it is good to seek wisdom from others, God ultimately desires that we come directly to Him. This passage states it beautifully: "My heart has heard you say, 'Come and talk with me.' And my heart responds, 'LORD, I am coming' " (Psalm 27:8 NLT). This is an invitation.

Both of these passages from Psalms are wonderful ways to open up in prayer, as they reaffirm our faith and remind us of the truth that God does listen and care. If you are in dire need of answers, or simply a connection to the Father, go directly to Him.

I am praying to You, Lord, because I know You will answer.
Bend down and listen as I pray and present You with my requests.
I have felt Your invitation, and so I come.

OUR DAILY BREAD

"Give us this day our daily bread."
MATTHEW 6:11 NKJV

A young woman gazed out her window as the morning sun just began to touch the snow-covered peaks of the Colorado Rockies. Her thoughts could hardly be collected and organized, and so she just stared and prayed, "Lord, give us today our daily bread." Her husband was in a job where he was criticized daily and treated like dirt. Each day felt like Russian roulette, as they never knew if their cars would get them to work or not. Money was tight. Their grocery budget was minimal. Being new to the area, they had no one to turn to.

"Give us this day our daily bread."

Each day, the Lord answered this prayer. He gave them what they needed, whether it be patience, mental or physical strength, food, or faith. A bill never went unpaid. A stomach never went hungry. A body never went unclothed. The Lord provided all their needs.

Eventually, slowly, their situation began to improve. They were able to buy a new car, she picked up more hours at work, and he found a new job. A community began to form around them. Looking back, she remembers it as one of the best years of her life. It was a year she walked closely, intimately, with her Savior.

Father, I ask today that You would give me today's bread. Fill me with what I need to make it through the day, that I may praise Your name forever.

CHOOSING FAITH

Be still in the presence of the LORD, and wait patiently for him to act.
Don't worry about evil people who prosper or fret about their wicked
schemes. Stop being angry! Turn from your rage! Do not lose your
temper—it only leads to harm. For the wicked will be destroyed,
but those who trust in the LORD will possess the land.
PSALM 37:7–9 NLT

Our faith is tested when life doesn't go the way we expect it to, when people who aren't following God prosper, and we seem to be an afterthought. At times we even go so far as to blame God for the things that are going wrong.

Even though it seems like the wicked are prospering and we are sitting on the sidelines, our daily grind is not in vain. Each day we are faithful is another seed planted. It may take time for it to grow, but grow it will. There will be a harvest.

Faith sees the facts but trusts God anyway. Faith is forcing yourself to worry no longer but to pray in earnest and leave the situation in His hands. Faith is choosing to trust and rest in His plan, rather than fret about what could happen. We must choose faith even when we don't feel it. It is through choosing faith that we please God. Choose faith, and see what He will do.

Lord, despite what logic or the world tells me, I choose now to let
my worries go and have faith in You. I trust that You will take care
of every need, and I lay down all my burdens at Your feet.

A HEART OF FAITH AND HONOR

"He lifts the poor from the dust and the needy from the garbage dump.
He sets them among princes, placing them in seats of honor.
For all the earth is the LORD's, and he has set the world in order."
1 SAMUEL 2:8 NLT

This is just a part of the prayer that Hannah, mother of Samuel, prayed as she left her son to live with Eli the priest and serve the Lord all his life. Samuel was her firstborn, a child she desperately prayed to God for, and she fulfilled her promise and left Samuel in the care of Eli.

Have you ever considered how hard it was for her to pray this prayer of praise to God? She finally had a child, but she was committed to her promise to offer him in service to the Lord. She would not be the one to raise him and experience all of his "firsts" in life. And yet she prayed this prayer that does nothing but honor the Lord. Even if there were moments when she wished she hadn't made such a promise, she praised Him. "My heart rejoices in the LORD! The LORD has made me strong" (1 Samuel 2:1 NLT).

We can learn so much from Hannah in the short space she is written about in 1 Samuel. She honored the Lord above all else and trusted His ways. May God give you a heart of courage that honors Him and strengthens you.

Dear Lord, thank You for hearing my prayers and remembering me
in Your faithfulness. May I be like Hannah, who fervently
pursued and honored You.

FOCUSING ON TODAY

Don't brag about tomorrow,
since you don't know what the day will bring.
PROVERBS 27:1 NLT

. . . .

What do you have on your plate today? What about tomorrow? Do you remember the plans you have next week? And that trip you have later this month? What about the work thing you have next year?

If we take an honest look at this verse, we see there is no point in worrying about tomorrow, just as there is no point in worrying about next year! *Nothing* is set in stone. Even today is a fluid river of moments, susceptible to change.

We will find that we can be happier in life by simply taking each day as it comes. If we are not focused on our calendar of events, and instead decidedly focused on each moment of *this* day, we will have the ability to enjoy moments that otherwise would have passed us by. The hilarious thing your child just said that bubbles into laughter. The sweet message from your husband that warms your heart. A lunch date with a friend that encourages your soul. These are all moments we can revel in and enjoy, rather than thinking about the next thing on the list or schedule.

Today, let's keep our focus on only the events of *today*. We will find fulfillment, laughter, and a reduction in stress if we refuse to borrow the worries of tomorrow.

. . . .

Lord, thank You for encouraging me to live life moment by moment.
Help me to recognize the blessings that abound in each day.

PREPARING FOR THE BATTLE

A final word: Be strong in the Lord and in his mighty power. Put on all of God's armor so that you will be able to stand firm against all strategies of the devil. For we are not fighting against flesh-and-blood enemies, but against evil rulers and authorities of the unseen world, against mighty powers in this dark world, and against evil spirits in the heavenly places.
EPHESIANS 6:10–12 NLT

Putting on the armor of God does not mean that all of a sudden we are safe and the enemy will not threaten us. On the contrary, Paul did not tell us to hide in a cave, but to fit our bodies with the armor of God. In this way we will be able to stand firm against everything the enemy tries against us.

Let's take a look at our shield. The devil shoots fiery arrows at us, but we have the ability to lift our shield—our *faith*—to keep them from taking us out. It is through engaging our faith that we are able to remain standing. The devil will still throw lies, threats, and condemnation at us, but we believe by faith in the truth that the Lord has told us.

Life is a very real battle, but the Lord has given us everything we need to stand firm and conquer. We need to put on His armor and walk and fight with confidence in our Savior.

Lord, please teach me more about Your armor. Equip me to move forward in confident faith and unshakable courage.

An Ever-Flowing Spring

> *"The LORD will guide you continually, giving you water when you are dry and restoring your strength. You will be like a well-watered garden, like an ever-flowing spring."*
> Isaiah 58:11 NLT

It's easy to fall into the trap of looking to earthly things to restore us. Instead of immediately looking to the One who made us and knows every detail of what we need, we often look other places. The Lord is our water when we are dry. He restores our strength. As we look to Him, we will become like a lush, well-watered garden. Fruitful. Energetic. Growing.

This is one of those verses to keep close to your heart during a busy season. When it feels like your next day of rest is far off, this is a promise to cling to and draw strength from. Every day, as often as you can, make space for quiet moments with the Lord. A few moments can give you everything you need. Even as you fall asleep at night, this passage can be one you recite to bring you into a peaceful rest.

The Lord will restore you as you choose to take time to meditate on His Word and sit in His presence. When you are seeking out the right Source, you will find you can make it through even the most rigorous of weeks.

My eyes are set on You, and You restore me. As a gentle rain brings life to the driest soil, so Your very presence and love bring life to my soul.

The Ultimate Security

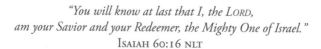

"You will know at last that I, the Lord,
am your Savior and your Redeemer, the Mighty One of Israel."
Isaiah 60:16 nlt

Do you ever wonder what life would be like if we *knew* that the Lord was our Savior and Redeemer, the Mighty One of Israel? What would our lives look like if we believed this with every fiber of our being? Take a moment to think about that. How would your attitude about today change? This passage goes on to say, "I will make peace your leader and righteousness your ruler" (Isaiah 60:17 nlt).

It is a worthy goal to seek the Lord in everything we do, to get to know Him better with each passing day. What would our lives look like if we knew, really *knew*, that He alone is our Savior and Redeemer? Fear would be far from us, for we would understand that even mountains tremble before our God. Worry would drain away as we understood that He is the One who provides for every one of our needs. Even in the face of death, if that was what the Lord willed, we would be at peace, for then we would be even closer to meeting Him face-to-face. We would move forward in every opportunity with confidence. We would battle with courage, knowing our ultimate security is in God.

Lord, may I know at last that You are the Lord, my Savior and Redeemer.
You are the Mighty One of Israel and forever my deepest desire.

HE KNOWS YOU

How precious are your thoughts about me, O God. They cannot be
numbered! I can't even count them; they outnumber the grains
of sand! And when I wake up, you are still with me!
PSALM 139:17–18 NLT

Did you know that you have a history with God? Your relationship is
ever growing, ever changing, and He knows you. He knit you together
in your mother's womb. He's watched as you've grown up. He's seen
every good day. Every bad day. Not a moment passes that He's unaware
of what you're up to.

And He still loves you. When you live in relationship with Him,
covered by the sacrifice of Christ, He doesn't see the things you've done
wrong. Don't walk into this day feeling the weight of your failures and
imagining there is no way He could continue to love you. He does love
you, even through the worst of times. Sending His Son while we were
still sinners is proof of that love.

So instead of coming before Him full of shame and with a heavy
heart, come before Him in humble thankfulness and confidence that He
loves you so much. When you come before Him, He is pleased to see
His daughter—spotless and whole. He is willing—and desires—to have
a deep and thriving relationship with you.

Lord, I can never fully understand the grace with which You love me.
I am forever amazed and filled with joy. Let our relationship grow
deeper through this day and the days ahead.

THE BATTLE IS REAL, BUT SO IS OUR REFUGE

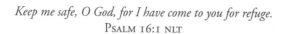

Keep me safe, O God, for I have come to you for refuge.
PSALM 16:1 NLT

Have you ever had days, weeks, or months when this was all you could pray? Or maybe in the heat of the battle, the intensity of the chase, the thought of running to Him for safety never even crossed your mind. Perhaps you believed this was a battle you could win on your own. Yet with each swing of your sword, you felt your strength fail.

Life is hard, and it's okay to admit that. The enemy we face on a daily basis is cunning and unrelenting. How wonderful it is that David looked to the Lord for his protection. And it wasn't protection in a spiritual sense—David's very life was at stake! He prayed to the Lord to keep him safe.

Maybe it feels like the Lord is far away—too intangible to be sought out for emotional strength, much less physical needs. My sister, He is never too far. He is a physical God who is able to keep you secure. He is ready and waiting to be your refuge. Whether your need is tangible or emotional, go to Him.

Lord, I come to You for refuge. Open Your doors to me and take me in. Keep me safe from the enemy who pursues me day and night. Let me hide myself within Your fortress, where You will keep watch over me.

We Won't Be Shaken

"I know the Lord is always with me. I will not be shaken,
for he is right beside me."
Psalm: 16:8 nlt

. . . .

When crisis strikes, people often drift away from the Lord. Heartbreak doesn't heal overnight. As each day passes, another part of them either dies or regains life. Though they may believe nothing ever could have prepared them for such pain, the everyday choices they've made throughout life determine what they will be like on the other side.

Every day we have a choice to trust God and the opportunity to put things in His hands and look eagerly for the way He will work them out. Every day we are developing a relationship with Him. We are choosing whether we will invest or neglect. Build up or break down. Draw closer or walk farther. It is how we handle ourselves in our daily lives that determines the amount of faith we'll have when a crisis comes.

Maybe our hearts will still break, but we will know who to turn to. We will trust and believe when everything is dark, because we have walked many roads with Him. We know His character. We know He is good. We know that though we don't understand, *He does*. And because He does, we can rest in His love. We don't need to know the reason, only that He is with us.

. . . .

Though darkness surrounds me, I know the Light. I know that You are
always with me. I will not be shaken, for You are right beside me.

REMEMBERING HIS PROMISES

Tell everyone about God's power. His majesty shines down on Israel;
his strength is mighty in the heavens. God is awesome in his sanctuary.
The God of Israel gives power and strength to his people. Praise be to God!
PSALM 68:34–35 NLT

Do you ever find yourself dreaming of a place of safety? A place where you can close your eyes, rest your head, and let go of the stress and angst that follow you around like a shadow? It rarely matters what kind of season you are in—busy or calm—you always seem to feel an inner longing to find a place where there is nothing but peace.

Before you move on to the next thing on the list, take a moment to close your eyes. Don't reach for a book. Refuse to look at your phone. Keep your thoughts from wandering away. Simply fix your heart on the One who loves you. Think about His compassion. Dwell on His promises. Consider His majesty, and the army of angels He commands. Have faith in the One He sent so you can forever be with Him.

Whether you need comfort, encouragement, or protection, He is the answer. Look first in His direction for clarity and understanding. He is close at hand and forever unchanging.

Lord, thank You for showing me that You are my everything.
Through every day, through every year, I need only to fix my eyes
on You—the author and perfecter of my faith.

FINDING JOY

*And now, dear brothers and sisters, one final thing. Fix your thoughts
on what is true, and honorable, and right, and pure, and lovely,
and admirable. Think about things that are excellent and worthy of
praise. Keep putting into practice all you learned and received from
me—everything you heard from me and saw me doing.
Then the God of peace will be with you.*
PHILIPPIANS 4:8–9 NLT

Your mind is powerful. The thoughts you choose to dwell on have the
power to determine the outcome of your day. They can pave the way for
a calm and grateful heart, or set a course for cynicism and disbelief.

There is such a benefit to fixing your thoughts on things that are
good, pleasing, and perfect. God was not being legalistic when he said to
think on these things. He was giving us sound advice. He was showing us
the path to peace. What makes your heart beat a little faster? What brings
joy to your heart and a smile to your lips? What makes your eyes crinkle
with laughter and your feet step a little lighter? Think about these things.

Life is meant to be enjoyed. Relish the simple things! God made
the playful puppies, galloping horses, and singing birds. He enjoys
them, and He invites you to enjoy them, too.

*Oh Lord, You delight in every detail of my life! Surely that includes
every wonderful moment and every bubble of laughter.
May I fully indulge in the joy of life today.*

He Is Good

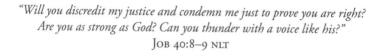

"Will you discredit my justice and condemn me just to prove you are right? Are you as strong as God? Can you thunder with a voice like his?"
Job 40:8–9 NLT

While God loves us unconditionally and wants to bless and love us, we must remember that He is first and foremost the one and only God. He is the last word—the final judge. Have you spent time reading through the Old Testament? There we see God display His power. We see Him destroy entire people groups. We see Him do some scary stuff that is hard to accept.

Seeing this side of God can strike fear in us—and it should. We should learn to fear God, because as the scripture says, His ways are higher than our ways, His thoughts higher than our thoughts. He will do things we don't understand.

But while He is huge and terrifying and sometimes confusing, we know we can trust Him. As you continue to read through the Bible, you'll also see that He protects, provides for, and unconditionally loves the people who trust Him. Not the people who are perfect, *the people who trust Him.*

Thank You that Your ways are higher than my own. Please give me a heart of understanding, that I may be open to all You do.

Sweetly Broken

In him our hearts rejoice, for we trust in his holy name.
Let your unfailing love surround us, LORD,
for our hope is in you alone.
Psalm 33:21–22 NLT

We all struggle with sin, but we are clean in the eyes of the Father when we acknowledge what Christ did for us. It's a loving action to share that hope with our husbands, friends, and family. In the eyes of the Lord, no sin is less or greater. Every sin is equal. That means we are on the same playing field as the rest of the human race before God.

As we begin to see ourselves in the light that we are no more worthy of God's love than the next guy, a compassionate, grace-filled heart begins to grow inside of us. The woman whose husband struggles to be free from addiction can look at him not with judgment or hurt, but with compassion and love. His struggle is no different than her own. As he seeks to be free, she determines to be his support, his cheerleader, the one who points him toward heaven. She knows he can be set free, for the Lord has set her free from her own sin. The Lord has shown her hope.

If you know this hope, spread it. Encourage those around you.

I know hope because of Your love. I am sweetly broken,
because through my brokenness I have found the depth of Your love.

REMEMBER

*"In the future your children will ask you, 'What do these stones mean?'
Then you can tell them, 'They remind us that the Jordan River stopped
flowing when the Ark of the LORD's Covenant went across.' These stones
will stand as a memorial among the people of Israel forever."*
JOSHUA 4:6–7 NLT

After God did this miraculous thing for the Israelites, He instructed them to build a memorial so that what He did for them would be remembered for generations. Future generations would remember that God took care of His people. The memorial would serve as a symbol of His power and faithfulness and would give hope to those in the future.

What has God done for you? It is just as important for us to build memorials in our lives—memorials that declare the goodness of God. These things remind us that during hard times God is still the same yesterday, today, and forever. They remind us in times of plenty that it is because of His goodness we can shout and dance with joy.

There is no right way to remember what God has done. It can be through journaling or a photograph. It could be a vase sitting in your living room filled with little slips of paper full of the ways God has provided on a daily basis. Each of these ways is a means to an end, and that end is remembering the faithfulness of God.

*You have been so good to me, Lord! As I go through today, remind me.
Remind me of the big and the little things, that my faith
in You may grow and my joy increase.*

Boldly We Come

*God's free gift leads to our being made right with God,
even though we are guilty of many sins.*
Romans 5:16 nlt

. . . .

Why do you think it is that as a general population of people, we often assume that God is out to get us? We tend to jump immediately to the notion that God is angry with us and ready to bring down the hammer. We become afraid to go to church or read the Bible—thinking that as soon as we enter the building or crack the cover, we will drown in waves of guilt and condemnation.

We even become too afraid to pray.

This must be one of the devil's most effective schemes—to convince us to fear talking with God—when talking with God is what will ultimately transform us from the inside out. Indeed, prayer is what we were created for. We were created for a relationship with Him—the entire Bible is the story of our being restored to that relationship.

The next time you are afraid to pray, refuse the fear. Know in confidence that, unlike the devil, you are covered by the blood of the Lamb and can enter freely into His presence. You can enter freely because He chose to open the way to you.

. . . .

*I will enter into Your presence and sit and talk with You. I can feel
You restore my soul, because this is what I was made for.
This is what I've been missing.*

WHERE WE FIND OUR WORTH

Don't be selfish; don't try to impress others. Be humble, thinking of others as better than yourselves. Don't look out only for your own interests, but take an interest in others, too.
PHILIPPIANS 2:3–4 NLT

It's not abnormal to want to be recognized, adored, or even famous. People do crazy things to get their five minutes of fame. To be treasured and loved is one of our deepest desires as human beings, so it's not surprising to see people who will do anything they can to fulfill this longing.

What is abnormal is finding a woman who—instead of qualifying herself—edifies, encourages, and celebrates others. A woman who, throughout a conversation, may never once bring up her own accomplishments, but who goes home in full confidence of who she is and has lost nothing from never being the topic of conversation. If anything, she is more full of life and purpose because she was able to give another what we all so desperately need: love and acceptance.

Put others first. That is a very real way we can give honor to the Lord. Make it your goal to put yourself aside and listen to a friend. Encourage them in every area you can, and simply love on them.

God, please help me find my value, confidence, and purpose in You alone. My value is not made less when I build others up. To the contrary! Through putting others first, I am taking after Your own example.

THIS CORNERSTONE, THIS SOLID GROUND

"We can rejoice, too, when we run into problems and trials, for we know that they help us develop endurance. And endurance develops strength of character, and character strengthens our confident hope of salvation. And this hope will not lead to disappointment. For we know how dearly God loves us, because he has given us the Holy Spirit to fill our hearts with his love."
ROMANS 5:3–5 NLT

Hope shows us that life is worth living. It promises that better things are yet to come. It whispers, "I'm not done yet." Hope is the assurance that even though sometimes it may not feel like it, every moment matters. No trial we experience is in vain.

Through it all, hope sustains us. It breathes new life into our weary souls. It keeps us moving, keeps us searching, and keeps us loving. Hope prompts us to reach out to someone who doesn't have any, that they may see the light.

> *In Christ alone my hope is found,*
> *He is my light, my strength, my song;*
> *This cornerstone, this solid Ground,*
> *Firm through the fiercest drought and storm. . .* (Stuart Townend)

Hope. Without it, the best of us lose heart. With it, even the most dire situations can be overcome.

Lord, You are my hope. My future rests secure in You. There is nothing the enemy can do to steal this confidence I have in You. You have already won, and so I will celebrate Your victory.

Beautifully Imperfect

*Yet I am confident I will see the LORD's goodness
while I am here in the land of the living.*
PSALM 27:13 NLT

Being in process is not pretty. In fact, sometimes it's downright ugly.
When life gets too busy and overwhelming, oftentimes we snap. There is
only so much our minds can sort through, and only so much our tired
bodies can handle.

Remember—we must give ourselves grace. We must allow ourselves
to be imperfect. Yes, we want to handle every situation with finesse and
poise, but sometimes trying to achieve that goal only makes the situation
worse. We are exhausted in every way and we cannot handle it the way we
want. If we are completely honest, we only show our worst to one, maybe
two people we trust. Everyone else gets the dressed-up version and the
still-smiling face.

We are imperfect, so let's find some comfort in that. We can accept
that we are broken and work from there. A lot of the time we stress
ourselves out by trying to be flawless. When we put that type of obsessive
striving aside, we can sort through the pieces with a clear head because
we're not hindered by trying to do it "just right." There is freedom in
giving ourselves permission to be imperfect.

*Oh God, I need You more than ever. I am broken into a thousand pieces.
I will find comfort in Your peace that passes understanding,
and in Your love that knows no limits.*

THERE'S YOUR SIGN

*"For I know the plans I have for you," says the LORD. "They are plans
for good and not for disaster, to give you a future and a hope."*
JEREMIAH 29:11 NLT

My cell phone was blowing up with text messages from my youngest
daughter, Allyson. I could almost hear the fear woven into each text. Ally,
in her final semester of college, was experiencing the panic that many
seniors go through. Remember that season?

You've worked ridiculously hard to get into your college of choice,
you've studied many hours to make good grades, and suddenly it's your
final semester and you have to keep your grades up while preparing
your résumé and portfolio so you can begin your job search. It's
overwhelming

I was typing responses as quickly as I could when my phone rang.
It was Ally; she was sobbing.

I tried to reassure her that God had a plan.

"I know," she said. "I just wish He'd give me a sign or something."

"We don't need a sign, Ally. We have His Word," I said. "That's all
you need."

Later that night, Ally sent me a picture text of that day's devotion
that said: *"Approach this day with awareness of Who is Boss. . . . Don't try
to figure out what is happening. Simply trust Me."*

And the scripture for that day? Jeremiah 29:11—Ally's life verse.

I texted back, "There's your sign. :)"

Don't you love it when God speaks so directly to us?

If you need guidance from our heavenly Father today, just ask Him.

Lord, I know You have the plan, and I'm so thankful. Amen.

BE A FAITH PRODDER

So encourage each other and build each other up,
just as you are already doing.
1 THESSALONIANS 5:11 NLT

I was once again reminded this week how much I adore a feisty woman of faith named Wilma Cheek. As I sat across from her at Bible study, I couldn't help but smile, taking notes every time she shared another pearl of wisdom. For example, as we all talked about the good and bad aspects of Facebook, Wilma picked up her Bible and said, "I don't need Facebook; I've got Faithbook."

That's classic Wilma.

She has always encouraged me in my Christian walk, sharing her testimony, praying for me, and offering those "words in due season."

I once heard Pastor Keith Moore say that we all need "faith prodders" in life, comparing those folks to a rancher with his cattle prodder. In my life, Wilma has been a very important faith prodder, and she continues to prod this blonde bovine every chance she gets.

For that, I am ever so grateful.

I'm sure you have faith prodders in your life, too, and I hope you honor them. But let me ask you this—are you a faith prodder in anyone else's life?

If not, maybe it's time.

No matter how unqualified you think you are or how nervous you feel talking to others about your faith, God can use you. In fact, there are certain people who won't receive words of life from anyone else but you. So why not be like Wilma today? Be a faith prodder.

Father, help me to be a Faith Prodder in someone else's life. Amen.

ON CALL

*The earnest prayer of a righteous person has great
power and produces wonderful results.*
JAMES 5:16 NLT

. . . .

Has God ever prompted you to pray for someone, though at that exact moment, you had no idea why?

That's what happened this past summer. I was on my way to Bible study when I had an intense urge to pray for my oldest daughter, Abby. I prayed in my car for several minutes until I felt a peace come over me. A few minutes later, my cell phone rang.

It was Abby, and she was hysterical.

Through sobs, she shared how she had almost been in a very serious car accident just moments before. The key word in that sentence is "almost." I truly believe that angels picked up her little VW Bug and moved it out of the way of that oncoming car. I was so thankful that I had listened, obeyed, and prayed.

The world calls that "a woman's intuition."

We Christian ladies call it God.

What about you? Are you an on-call prayer warrior for God? When He wakes you up to pray for your family or someone you hardly know, do you just roll back over and say, "I'll pray in the morning," or do you get up and pray right then?

As you can see, sometimes your prayer could be the difference between life and death. So let's make a commitment today to be on-call prayer warriors, ready to pray anytime, anywhere, for anyone.

. . . .

*Lord, help me to be sensitive to Your voice and quick
to obey the call to prayer. Amen.*

DARE TO DREAM

I can do all things through Christ who strengthens me.
PHILIPPIANS 4:13 NKJV

Whenever I speak about being a writer at Young Authors Day programs, I always take time for a question-and-answer segment at the end of my presentation. After I answer their questions, it's my turn. That's when I ask the kiddos about their hopes and dreams.

It's amazing the answers I receive! You know what I've discovered?

Little bitty kids can have great big dreams. Some children answer "firefighter," "nurse," "teacher," "author," "police officer," or "movie star." Still others say "model," "race car driver," "professional baseball player," "scientist," "president," and so many more awesome occupations.

Bottom line—children know how to dream big.

Do you know why? Because no one has told them yet that they can't dream big. They don't have that inner dialogue that says, "You can't be a movie star. You're not pretty enough. You'll never be able to accomplish your dream." They truly believe they can do anything. And you know what? They're right!

God's Word says that we can do all things through Christ who gives us strength. *All* means *all*, right? So encourage the children in your life to dream big, and then follow their example.

We should all be able to believe BIG when it comes to the dreams and ambitions that God has placed within us. God wouldn't have placed them there if He weren't going to help us achieve them. So get back that childlike faith and start believing BIG.

Lord, help me to dream big and encourage others in their dreams. Amen.

God Don't Make No Junk

God created man in His own image.
Genesis 1:27 NASB

When I was a little girl growing up in the Bedford, Indiana, Free Methodist Church, I absolutely loved going to kids' church. Our two leaders, Ivan Hunter and Donna Cummings, not only taught me important Bible stories, but also taught me that Jesus loved me unconditionally. Ivan would often share his salvation testimony, telling us that if Jesus could love him, then He could love anyone. And sweet Donna took every opportunity to build us up with words of encouragement. I can still hear her saying, "You kids are wonderful. Do you know how I know that to be true? Because God don't make no junk!"

I needed to hear that.

We all need to hear that—not just during our growing-up years, but today, and every day. We need to know that we were formed by the Master, and we need to love ourselves. Not in a self-absorbed, arrogant sort of way, but rather in a grateful-to-God-for-creating-us sort of way.

Most importantly, we need to understand how much God loves us. We don't deserve it. We can't earn it. Yet He freely gives His love to us.

I challenge you to look up the following scriptures: Genesis 1:27; Psalm 139:13–16; John 3:16–17; Romans 5:8; and Romans 8:38–39.

The next time you're feeling unlovable, think on those truths and say out loud: "I am a child of the Most High King." And you might add, "I'm wonderful, because God don't make no junk."

Lord, help me to see myself through Your eyes. I love You. Amen.

YOUR FIRST LOVE

"And you shall love the Lord your God with all your heart, and with all your soul, and with all your mind, and with all your strength."
MARK 12:30 NASB

Remember when you first fell in love with your significant other? Every minute apart seemed like an eternity! You couldn't wait until the next time you could be together. You thought about him all the time. You talked about him all the time. Everything reminded you of him. Just hearing his name made you smile. Face it, you were obsessed with him, right?

Well, that's how we should feel about Jesus! After all, He is our first love, yet it's easy to lose sight of that fact in the busyness of everyday life. So if you've lost that "loving feeling" when it comes to your Lord and Savior, then it's time to fall back in love. How do you do that? Bottom line: the more time you spend with Jesus, the more time you'll want to spend with Him. Having your devotional and prayer time shouldn't feel like an obligation; rather, it should be exciting and wonderful. You should look forward to it!

Here's the best part. The God of this universe is looking forward to spending time with you! He can't wait to reveal things to you in His Word. He adores you, and He has been waiting for you.

Lord, I love You. Help me to always keep You in first place in my life. Amen.

FRIENDS ARE IMPORTANT

A friend loves at all times.
PROVERBS 17:17 NASB

I've always liked the song "Friends" by Michael W. Smith. In fact, I get a little teary-eyed when I think about the lyrics because I have friends I love and cherish. I bet you do, too. But if you're like me, keeping up with those friends can be challenging with a spouse, children, deadlines, volunteer work, and church commitments. It's difficult to schedule regular get-togethers, and I miss my gal pals.

The truth is, we need friends. They play an important role in our lives. In fact, friendship is a biblical concept. Did you know that the word "friends" is used fifty-three times in God's Word? Obviously, God knew we'd need friends. So if you've been neglecting your friends lately, maybe it's time to reconnect. Dr. Jan Yager, author of *Friendshifts: The Power of Friendship and How It Shapes Our Lives* can help.

She advises not trying to invest time in absolutely every friend on your Christmas card list. If you do, you'll start diffusing intimacy with the friends who are most important to you. Once you've determined which friendships you wish to rejuvenate, call those friends just to say hello. Send random texts to stay connected. Make a big deal out of each other's birthdays. Choose a neutral location for get-togethers (so no one has to worry about a spotless house), and be flexible (in case she has to cancel unexpectedly).

*Father, help me to be a better friend to the special people
You've placed in my life. Amen.*

WORTH THE WAIT

This vision is for a future time. . . . If it seems slow in coming,
wait patiently, for it will surely take place. It will not be delayed.
HABAKKUK 2:3 NLT

When I was pregnant with my first daughter, Abby, she tried to arrive a month before her due date. Determined to keep her inside me as long as possible, the doctor gave me medicine to stop my contractions and placed me on bed rest. I was disappointed that I left the hospital that night with a baby still in my belly, not in my arms, but Doc said we needed to keep Abby "cooking" until mid-November.

My due date came and went, and I was still preggers. Finally, a week later, Doc induced my labor and Abby Leigh made her entrance on December 3.

I've often reflected on that season. Yes, the bed rest was uncomfortable and the contractions were irritating, but those things weren't the cause of my pain. I was simply disappointed because I hadn't given birth in October. Was that immature? You betcha. But at the time, I didn't think so. I just wanted to have my baby.

Isn't that how we act with God sometimes? He puts a dream within our hearts, and then we try to give birth to it before its appointed time. Just like Abby might have encountered some health challenges if I'd had her too early, our dreams can suffer if we try to birth them before their time. It's important to wait on God and His timing.

Father, help me to be patient as I wait for Your perfect timing.
I love You. Amen.

PRAISE HIM IN THE MORNING

And each morning and evening they stood before the LORD
to sing songs of thanks and praise to him.
1 CHRONICLES 23:30 NLT

. . . .

I've never been much of a morning person. This was especially true when I was a child. However, my morning "wake-up call" began at 6:00 a.m. every weekday, courtesy of my mother, Marion Medlock, who *was* a morning person.

She didn't just knock on the door and say, "Time to get up." Oh no—she was far too joyful for that. My mother had an entire musical extravaganza worked out. She'd begin with her rendition of "This is the day that the Lord has made. We will rejoice and be glad in it." All of this singing was accompanied by very loud hand clapping, and if that didn't do the trick, she would flip the lights on and off in time with her singing.

At the time, I thought this morning ritual was pure torture, but as I grew older, I realized that I didn't have to be a morning person to praise God in the a.m. In fact, I discovered praising God in the morning was actually scriptural.

Who knew?

Psalm 59:16 (NLT) says, "Each morning I will sing with joy about your unfailing love."

So, yes, I get my praise on in the morning now. Why not join me, morning people and non-morning people alike? It doesn't matter if your voice is less than angelic or even if you're totally out of tune—God likes it.

. . . .

Father, I will praise You with my whole heart morning,
noon, and night. Amen.

WHO'S TOO OLD?

"For I know the plans I have for you," says the LORD. "They are plans for good and not for disaster, to give you a future and a hope."
JEREMIAH 29:11 NLT

. . . .

I have what I like to call a "heavenly bucket list." You know, the dreams that God has put in my heart that I've journaled about, prayed over, and treasured, but haven't yet accomplished.

As I looked over that list recently, I started to panic a little, wondering if I was too old to accomplish all of the items yet to be checked off. If we're being honest, probably all of us have dreams we haven't yet realized, but here's what God reminded me of this weekend—it's not too late! No matter your age, you're not too old to fulfill the plans that God has for your life.

Did you know that Grandma Moses didn't start painting until she was seventy-six years old? Without any special training, she painted beautiful, simple, realistic pictures of rural settings—paintings that are of historic importance.

Colonel Sanders was well over sixty when he made it big with Kentucky Fried Chicken. Prior to that, he simply operated a service station in Corbin, Kentucky.

What dream has God placed inside of you?

Spend some time today meditating on whatever dreams are still on your "un-checked-off list," and commit to pray over them every day until they are realized.

It's not too late, and God is always on time.

. . . .

Father, thank You for placing such big dreams in my heart. Amen.

Aim High

We are many parts of one body, and we all belong to each other.
Romans 12:5 nlt

Recently I helped my daughter, Allyson, put the finishing touches on her new apartment, which involved a lot of picture hanging. From photo collages to oversized mirrors to framed artwork, we measured and hammered and remeasured, used a leveler, and eyeballed every single piece of wall art. Even with all of that preparation, we still managed to hang a few pictures too high.

Apparently I'm not alone in my picture-hanging mistake. In fact, of all decorating mistakes, hanging pictures too high is one of the most common, according to Martie Spaulding, who is not only my older sister but also a gifted interior designer.

"If a picture is positioned too high on a wall, the artwork will appear disjointed from the rest of the room," explains Martie. "Instead of complementing the room, the picture becomes distracting and disconnected—serving no purpose."

Wow, so much wisdom in that one decorating tip. It started me thinking about how it's the same way in the Body of Christ. We all need to be connected. So if you don't have a church home, find one. Don't let past hurts keep you from enjoying the benefits of a church family. Find your place and serve your purpose! Need more convincing that being a Lone Ranger Christian isn't the best plan? Read 1 Corinthians 12:12–27 today and let God speak to you through His Word.

Aim high today—just not with your pictures.

Father, help me stay connected and fulfill my purpose. Amen.

UNCONDITIONAL LOVE

*"For the LORD your God is living among you. He is a mighty savior.
He will take delight in you with gladness. With his love, he will calm
all your fears. He will rejoice over you with joyful songs."*
ZEPHANIAH 3:17 NLT

Be honest. Do you have a picture of your adorable dog or cute kitty in your wallet or possibly on your smartphone? Do you find yourself telling funny stories about your darling doggy or precocious cat?

I'm guilty of this. I often post pictures of Mollie Mae, our adorable, chubby dachshund, on Facebook. I love to share funny stories about her antics, and I gravitate toward all things dachshund. I also love to buy presents for Mollie. Just last week I bought her a new blinged-out collar—purple with rhinestones. She looks so cute in it, and she knows it!

Bottom line, we love to dote on our kids—even the canine and feline ones. Well, guess what? That's exactly how God is. He is a doting parent, too. If He had a "Daddy's Brag Book," our pictures would be in it! And just like I couldn't wait to buy Mollie Mae a new collar, God loves to give His children good gifts. The Bible says, "If you then, though you are evil, know how to give good gifts to your children, how much more will your Father in heaven give the Holy Spirit to those who ask him!" (Luke 11:13 NIV).

God just flat-out loves us.

Father, thank You for loving me so much. Amen.

Fix Your Eyes on God

Let us run with endurance the race that is
set before us, fixing our eyes on Jesus.
Hebrews 12:1–2 nasb

. . . .

"Your stories are so cute," Gena, my coworker, said. "I can't wait to see them in print."

"Thanks," I answered, beaming. "I can't either."

Just then, the meeting began and my boss hurried through the items on the agenda. Finally, we were going to discuss *my* picture book manuscripts.

"Michelle, in order to give your books a better chance of selling, we have decided to put our children's minister's name on the front," my boss explained. "She already has quite a following, and her name recognition alone will guarantee sales. After all—isn't it about getting the message out? It's not really about who wrote the book."

My heart sank.

"You mean, my name isn't going to be on the books at all?" I asked, trying to remain calm. "But I wrote them!"

"Yes, but you work for us," she said sternly. "And we've decided that this is the best way to proceed."

That was a turning point in my life. I realized there was a part of me I had never given to God. All of my publishing dreams seemed too precious to hand over to Him.

I began a new career that day in 1999, working for a new Boss. Once I gave my writing to God, He has given me more than sixty book contracts in return.

What are you withholding from God today?

. . . .

Father, I trust You with every dream I have.
I know I can never outgive You. Amen.

GOD KNOWS YOU

"I knew you before I formed you in your mother's womb."
JEREMIAH 1:5 NLT

. . . .

While in Los Angeles with my daughter, Ally, I lost my wallet and all that was in it—including my Indiana driver's license.

I realized just how important that driver's license was when I tried to go through LAX airport security without a photo ID. When my turn came to show my boarding pass and ID, I handed over my boarding pass and shared my story with the airport security officer. He looked at me and said, "This could be a problem. Stand to the side while I call for my supervisor."

About fifteen minutes later, the supervisor escorted me to a different holding area. "So you don't have anything on you that identifies you? A piece of mail? Possibly a library card?"

"No, my library card was in my wallet. . . . I do have a prescription bottle with my name on it because I was fighting an ear infection before I left for this trip—will that help?"

He took the bottle from my hand and disappeared for a bit.

When he returned, he smiled at me and said the words I'd been longing to hear: "Michelle, you're cleared to fly."

I had finally proven I really was me.

Isn't it wonderful that the Creator of the world knows you by name? The Bible says that He knew you before you were even formed in your mama's belly. He knows you—really knows you—and He calls you His child. No proof needed.

. . . .

Father, I am so thankful that You know me. Amen.

Walk in Your Calling

Therefore, since we are surrounded by such a great cloud of witnesses,
let us throw off everything that hinders and the sin that so easily entangles.
And let us run with perseverance the race marked out for us.
Hebrews 12:1 NIV

What is your calling?

That's a question our pastor recently asked us. Then he said, "Just because you weren't called to be a pastor doesn't mean you won't impact the world with the love of God in your own way."

Whether you're called to be a firefighter or a teacher or a stay-at-home mom, you are important. Your life means something. God called you to fulfill that special role because He had a plan for your life from the time you were in your mother's womb. It's powerful to realize that you're doing exactly what you were born to do, and the devil knows this truth. That's why he will do everything he can to discourage you and get you to compare yourself with others and their callings, trying to convince you that your calling is not as important. Don't fall for his lies. Instead, thank God for your calling and walk in it with great enthusiasm and courage. Run your race. When you do, you'll enjoy the journey and every step toward that finish line will be purposeful.

Father, I thank You for creating me for such a time as this. Help me never
to forget the importance of my calling, and help me to fulfill my divine
destiny. I love You, Lord. In the mighty name of Jesus, amen.

ERR ON THE SIDE OF LOVE

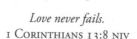

Love never fails.
1 CORINTHIANS 13:8 NIV

"Honey, I've found that if you err on the side of love, you'll never have any regrets. Let me show you something. . ."

With that, Dad turned to a page marker in his Bible and read 1 Corinthians 13—the Love Chapter—out loud.

"I read this chapter every morning," he said, peering over the top of his reading glasses. "I've been doing that for many years. It'll change your life."

Of all the wonderful words of wisdom that my father shared with me while he was still on this side of heaven, I think that piece of advice was the most monumental.

You see, I was struggling with my love walk at the time Daddy shared that with me. In fact, my love walk was more of a limp.

I started that very day reading the Love Chapter as part of my daily time with God. Sure, I've missed a day or two over the years, but I've read it so many times that I now have it memorized. And when I'm confronted with a rude salesperson or an irritable family member, I simply recite verses 4–8 until I can once again walk in love—just like my father and my heavenly Father.

Take it from my dad—it's always better to err on the side of love. Let's start living the Love Chapter in our daily lives, and let's start today.

Father, please fill me up with Your love. Amen.

RECIPE FOR DISASTER

Your word is a lamp to my feet and a light to my path.
PSALM 119:105 NASB

. . . .

Early in my marriage, I tried to make one of my mama's recipes from memory. I knew it called for two cans of mushroom soup, but I couldn't remember what kind of mushroom soup. I used two cans of golden mushroom. Problem was, the recipe actually called for two cans of cream of mushroom.

Not the same.

My husband couldn't even pretend he liked the dish. In fact, he still loves to share that culinary disaster story every chance he gets.

The obvious lesson here? Don't just *assume* you know what the recipe says. Always read it and follow it exactly.

I wonder how many Christians just assume they know what the Bible says. How many times have I neglected the Bible simply because I think I know what it says when I really just need to slow down, open the Word, and meditate on those precious promises? How many times have you done the same?

The Word of God is often referred to as spiritual food, meaning we need to eat of it every single day. In other words, we can't live on yesterday's manna. And we can't just assume we know what the Bible says and simply skim it and hit "the highlights." That's a recipe for disaster.

Trust me.

Bottom line, we all need to make time for God's Word, because He has important messages, promises, instruction, and wisdom awaiting us within its pages.

. . . .

Father, help me to fall in love with Your Word. Amen.

GOD DOESN'T SLEEP

He will not allow your foot to slip; He who keeps you will not slumber.
PSALM 121:3 NASB

I recently had lunch with a good friend who shared an amazing testimony of when God awakened her at 3:00 a.m. concerning her son—a proud U.S. soldier—who was serving his first tour in Afghanistan.

She and her husband were sound asleep when she heard what sounded like machine guns going off in her bedroom. At first she thought they had fallen asleep with the TV blaring a war movie of some kind, but when she looked up, the TV was off.

Just then, she heard that still, small voice say, "Pray for your son right now."

Immediately, she began praying Psalm 91 over her son—a passage of scripture she knew by heart. Though she thought she was praying quietly, her husband woke up and asked, "Who are you talking to?"

"I'm praying," she said. "God told me to pray for our son."

"That's so strange," he answered, "because I was sure I heard him calling, 'Dad! Dad!' a few minutes ago. It sounded like he was in this room."

The two of them joined hands and began praying a hedge of protection around their son wherever he was at that very moment.

Later they found out that their son had been in a Taliban ambush at that exact time, and though his sergeant who was standing right beside him was killed, their son was not hit.

Even while we're sleeping, God is on call. Isn't that a wonderful promise?

Father, thank You for always being on call. Amen.

Big Faith

"The LORD rewards everyone for their righteousness and faithfulness."
1 Samuel 26:23 niv

. . . .

We used to call my mom the "Big M," which seems quite fitting, looking back. Not because she was big in stature but rather because she had such big faith. She possessed the kind of faith that changed the atmosphere. She was sassy, funny, smart, classy, beautiful, and feisty all rolled into one magnificent Marion.

When she was given the grim news that her cancer was inoperable, Mom's faith never waned. She beat many odds and outlived every prognosis the medical experts gave her. It was her enormous faith that carried her through to the very end—the day she let go of my hand and took hold of the Master's.

As I stood by the casket greeting those who had come to honor my mom, I knew her spirit was no longer there. She was celebrating her new body and life in heaven, surrounded by many who had gone before her, including my dad. Still, Mom's faith filled the room. She had imparted it to us, and story after story revealed how each of our lives would never be the same because of Marion Medlock's faithfulness. She truly taught me how to live and die in faith.

As I glance down at my hands today, I see my mom's hands. I only hope that one day people will look at me and see more than just my mother's physical characteristics—I want them to see my mother's big faith. Let's carry on the legacy of faith in our families.

. . . .

Father, help me to live life with big faith. Amen.

JESUS SAVES

"For God so loved the world that he gave his one and only Son,
that whoever believes in him shall not perish but have eternal life."
JOHN 3:16 NIV

Having recently moved my daughter, Ally, from one part of LA to her new apartment in the Fashion District, we had to learn an entirely different part of the city.

While our everyday exploring was fun, neither one of us has a very good sense of direction, and at times we were a little lost. But you know what always helped us find our way back to Ally's apartment complex?

Jesus.

Well, not Jesus exactly, but a large illuminated "Jesus Saves" sign that is situated near Ally's new apartment. Whenever we found ourselves a bit turned around, we'd just look up, and immediately we knew our way home.

I couldn't help but think how much this paralleled my own life. Anytime I have lost my way, all I've had to do is look up and find Jesus. He is my compass. Whenever I need answers, I go to His Word. Whenever I need direction, I look up. Jesus has always been and will always be the One who guides me when I'm unsure which way to go; the One who loves me when I feel unlovable; the One who encourages me when I am questioning my choices; and the One who promises never to leave me or forsake me.

He is the One.

Is He the One in your life? If you've never given your life to Jesus, it's not too late. Just look up.

Lord, please be my compass. Amen.

ASK GOD FOR HELP

You do not have because you do not ask God.
JAMES 4:2 NIV

I had been on a crazy book deadline for weeks, writing twelve to fourteen hours a day. Like most writers, I have a favorite place to write in my house, equipped with a comfy chair, made especially for people with short legs. I love my writing spot. The problem is, my writing spot doesn't always love me.

After weeks of my bum being planted in the soft, comfy chair, my lower back started hurting so much that I could no longer sit anywhere. Finally I went to see a local chiropractor, and after two appointments, I still had intense pain, sleepless nights, and a book deadline that I was trying desperately to meet.

While I was icing my back, my cell phone rang. I smiled when I saw the name Cecil Stokes, always happy to hear from my über-talented writer/director/producer friend.

"Hey, how are you?" he asked.

"Well," I shared, "I'm a mess, actually," and proceeded to tell Cecil all about my back situation and everything I'd been doing to try to rectify it.

He listened without interrupting and then asked, "So I know this may be a silly question, but have you prayed about it?"

"Uh, you know, I haven't done that," I answered, completely embarrassed. "Would you pray for my back?"

"I would love to pray for your back," Cecil said, and then he did.

The Bible says, "We have not because we ask not."

So go ahead: ask for His help!

Lord, help me to turn to You first in all situations. Amen.

THE JESUS FILTER

This means that anyone who belongs to Christ has become a new person.
2 CORINTHIANS 5:17 NLT

. . . .

I love everything about beach vacations—feeling the ocean breeze, watching dolphins play in the waves, sinking my toes into the sand, walking the beach with my handsome husband at sunset, and more.

I love it all—except the bathing suit part.

Seriously, is anything more humbling than standing in front of a dressing room mirror, under those unforgiving fluorescent lights, trying on bathing suit after bathing suit?

I dread it every year. Because no matter how many miles you've logged in previous months, no matter how many crunches you've crunched, no matter how many desserts you've passed up, bathing suits show every imperfection. While you might be able to hide a few dimples underneath a nice black dress with the help of Spanx, you're not hiding anything in a swimsuit.

That's how it is with God. You might be able to fake-grin your way through church. You might be able to "play Christian" in front of your friends and family. But when you enter the throne room, it's like wearing your bathing suit before God. You can't hide any imperfections from Him. That truth used to horrify me—even more than trying on bathing suits—but not anymore.

Because now I know how God truly sees me.

Once we ask Jesus to be the Lord of our lives, God sees us through the "Jesus filter," and all He sees is perfection. Now if we could just figure out some kind of "perfection filter" for bathing suit season.

. . . .

Thank You, God, for my salvation. Amen.

Get a Spiritual Makeover

This is the verdict: Light has come into the world, but people loved
darkness instead of light because their deeds were evil.
John 3:19 niv

. . . .

Sometimes when I travel, the lighting in the hotel room isn't so great. I apply my makeup as best I can, but it's like getting ready by candlelight and when I get into the car and look at myself in the bright sunlight, I'm often horrified—I have on way too much blush and eye makeup.

Because of the dark hotel room, I had no idea I looked like Bozo the Clown. In fact, I thought I was looking pretty good until the natural light proved that was not the case. Light is a powerful thing. It reveals much about us.

This is also true in spiritual matters.

The Bible says that Jesus is the Light of the world. When we look to Him and His Word, we find that much about ourselves is revealed. You'll most likely see some flaws in yourself you didn't realize were there. (You may find that you also look like Bozo, spiritually speaking.) Don't run from Jesus and the Bible when you see your flaws. Instead, embrace the truth and ask the Lord to get rid of the flaws that He so graciously exposed, because He will! God heals what He reveals. Continue to look into the Word and allow His light to reveal areas where you need growth. As you do, you'll find that you are being transformed from Bozo to Beauty. Talk about an extreme makeover!

. . . .

Thank You, God, for giving me a spiritual makeover. Amen.

WRITE THE VISION

If people can't see what God is doing, they stumble all over themselves; but when they attend to what he reveals, they are most blessed.
PROVERBS 29:18 MSG

One of my favorite poems is this: "Ah, great it is to believe the dream / As we stand in youth by the starry stream / But a greater thing is to fight life through / And say at the end, 'The dream is true!' "

Isn't that good?

No matter where you are in life—right out of college or approaching retirement—you need to have a goal, a dream, a vision. If you don't, you'll wind up drifting on a sea of pointlessness. In fact, the Word says that where there is no vision, the people perish. So do you have a vision? If not, ask God to show you His vision. Seek His plan, and once you discover it, write it down and keep it before you. Thank Him for that vision every day. Keep the vision close to your heart.

Habakkuk 2:2 (NASB) says, "Then the LORD answered me and said, 'Record the vision and inscribe it on tablets, that the one who reads it may run.' " So I have an assignment for you. I want you to create a vision board about your dreams. Place on it pictures, quotes, scriptures, power words—basically anything that will inspire you to accomplish your dreams. Keep that vision before you. . .it's time to run with it!

Lord, help me never to lose sight of the vision You've placed in my heart. Amen.

What's Your Story?

*"They triumphed over him by the blood of the Lamb
and by the word of their testimony."*
Revelation 12:11 niv

. . . .

I've spoken at numerous churches in my travels and attended many more services than that, and in all of those services, I've never heard the definition of faith explained so simplistically, yet so profoundly, as I did earlier this month at the Bedford First Church of God in southern Indiana.

Pastor Travis Inman took us to the "Faith Chapter"—Hebrews 11—and we began reading:

> *Faith is the confidence that what we hope for will
> actually happen; it gives us assurance about things we
> cannot see. Through their faith, the people in days of old
> earned a good reputation.* (11:1–2 nlt)

Pastor Travis said, "So basically, this chapter is filled with stories of people's faith, right? So when I ask you about your faith, I'm really asking, 'Hey, what's your story?' "

How simple, yet how true. Sure, there are many theological definitions of what faith is and what faith is not, but really, what people want to know is this—how has your faith in God affected your life? In other words, what's your story?

. . . .

Lord, help me to share my story every chance I get. Amen.

PRETTY WEEDS

A perverse person stirs up conflict, and a gossip separates close friends.
PROVERBS 16:28 NIV

- -

As I was vacuuming up the last of the petrified french fries wedged under the backseat of our SUV, my then six-year-old daughter called for me.

"Mommy!" Abby said in her most excited voice. "I picked you a flower!"

I smiled and graciously accepted it, though upon further inspection, I realized it wasn't a flower at all. Abby had given me a very pretty purple weed. As I looked at the weed more closely, I thought, *This weed really is lovely. It could fool almost anybody into thinking it's a flower.*

Later that evening, I received a call from a friend at church. She began sharing some very damaging information about a person in our congregation. Even though it felt wrong to listen, I hung on every juicy detail because my friend kept interjecting, "I'm just telling you all of this so that you'll know how to pray about it."

As I hung up the receiver, I felt just awful.

I prayed, "God, I'm sorry I was a part of that. I should have identified that information as gossip."

That pretty, purple weed that fooled Abby fooled you, too, God spoke into my spirit. Not in an audible voice but deep down inside.

I knew it was God, and I knew what He meant.

Let God be the ultimate gardener in your life. As you live close to Him, you'll become more skilled at identifying the weeds in your life— even the pretty ones.

- -

Father, help me to identify the weeds in my life. Amen.

Mirror, Mirror

"But we all, with unveiled face, beholding as in a mirror the glory of the Lord, are being transformed into the same image from glory to glory."
2 Corinthians 3:18 nkjv

I was fresh out of journalism school with lots of drive and very little experience. Still, I was really hoping my hometown newspaper would hire me. I had taken the "Keys to a Successful Interview" class at Indiana University, so I was sure I would do great.

As the interview progressed, I answered each question to the best of my ability, offering big, confident grins—so pleased with my performance. After shaking hands with both editors, I walked briskly out of the office and slid into my car.

"I did it!" I said to myself, glancing at my reflection in the rearview mirror. That's when I noticed—I had lipstick all over my teeth! Every toothy grin had been plagued by Peony Pink lipstick.

I was mortified.

I should've looked in the mirror right before going into the interview.

We need mirrors so that we can see what needs to be brushed, cleaned, touched up, and readjusted. None of us would let even one day pass without inspecting ourselves in a mirror. So why do we think we can get by neglecting God's mirror—His Word? If we don't look daily into His Word and let the Holy Spirit reveal what needs to be cleaned, touched up, and readjusted, we might have ugly sin all over our teeth and never realize it.

Have you checked your reflection in God's Word lately?

Father, please give me a hunger for Your Word. Amen.

TOO GOOD TO BE TRUE?

*"For this is how God loved the world: He gave his one and only Son,
so that everyone who believes in him will not perish but have eternal life."*
JOHN 3:16 NLT

* *

I was recently shopping in a local drugstore when I passed by a display of boxes that said "The Cookie Diet."

I was hopeful this new cookie diet would allow me to eat all of the chocolate chip cookies I wanted in a day and still lose weight. Upon further investigation, I learned I would only be able to eat six cookies a day and one small meal, and I had to eat the cookies from this company.

Still, six cookies in one day seemed like a dream come true, so I bought the cookie kit. Once inside my car, I quickly unwrapped one of the cookies and sank my teeth into it. It wasn't exactly a Mrs. Fields chocolate chip cookie. It was dry and had a really strange aftertaste. I simply chalked it up to another "too good to be true" gimmick I had fallen for in the world of weight loss.

When it comes to Jesus, that old "too good to be true" adage doesn't apply. Hearing that God's precious Son died on a cross for our sins so that we might have eternal life, and that He loves us unconditionally, *sounds* too good to be true, but it's not! It is the absolute truth! He has a plan for you, and I promise, it's even better than a Mrs. Fields cookie.

* *

Father, I'm thankful Your promises aren't too good to be true. Amen.

THE BLAME GAME

"In this godless world you will continue to experience difficulties.
But take heart! I've conquered the world."
JOHN 16:33 MSG

. . . .

While I was visiting Oasis Church in Los Angeles, one of the pastors shared his testimony. Like all of us, he had gone through some adversity. Some difficulties, he admitted, were due to his own bad choices, while others were simply attacks of the enemy. But no matter the reason, those adversities had driven him to a place of desperation, hopelessness, and pain.

Sitting on the edge of his friend's futon, where he'd been sleeping since his marriage had fallen apart, this broken man prayed, "God, I know You said You would never leave me or forsake me, but why would You lead me here, to this place in my life that is filled with so much pain?"

In a still, small voice, God clearly answered him: "Son, I didn't lead you here, I followed you, never leaving your side, but now that you're ready to follow Me, I will carry you out."

I love that so much.

Too many times God gets the blame for bringing the pain, when in reality, we have caused it by our poor choices or it is simply the result of living in a world that is far from perfect.

But God is the God of the impossible, and He will make a way where there seems to be no way. He did it for that pastor on the staff of Oasis LA, He's done it for me countless times, and He will do it for you!

. . . .

Father, please lead me out of the pain today. Amen.

SPIRITUAL SPOT REDUCING

But if we confess our sins to him, he is faithful and just to forgive us
our sins and to cleanse us from all wickedness.
1 JOHN 1:9 NLT

Over the course of my life, I've been certified through Mary Mayta's
Fit For Life, the Aerobics and Fitness Association of America, and
Zumba International Network. I have taught at Fit For Life, the Indiana
University Hyper, the Bloomington, Indiana YMCA, Rick's Gym, and
Priority Fitness. I even ran my own lunchtime fitness business, "Body
Basics," in the mid-1990s while working full-time as a reporter for my
local newspaper.

In other words, I have been involved in the world of fitness for
the past twenty-six years. But in all of those years, I've never seen "spot
reducing" actually produce the promised results. You won't have that
Brazilian bum you desire if you're carrying a lot of extra weight on top
of your toned glutes. You'll have to do cardio three to four times a week
to burn that fat layer.

I've got news for you; spot reducing in the spiritual realm doesn't
work that well either. If you only work on your anger problem but
leave those six inches of unforgiveness untouched, it won't really make a
difference.

But in the spiritual realm, there is no cardio required. Just confess your
sins and ask God to forgive you. Then God will help you "spot reduce" until
your spiritual life is as fit as Jane Fonda in her leg-warmer-wearing years.
You don't have to go for the burn. You just have to go to God!

Father, help me to be spiritually fit. Amen.

GOD'S WAY

You should clothe yourselves instead with the beauty that comes from
within, the unfading beauty of a gentle and quiet spirit,
which is so precious to God.
1 PETER 3:4 NLT

Today is my twenty-fifth wedding anniversary. I'm not saying it has
been butterflies, sunshine, and bluebirds sitting on my shoulders every
day of my marriage, but it has been pretty wonderful.

We've had our seasons of "sticking it out" simply because we
promised we would. But you know when it became more wonderful?
When I finally learned what I'm about to share with you—stand by
your man.

Remember that old country song "Stand by Your Man"? (You're
singing along right now, aren't you?) Whether you're married, engaged,
or would like to have a special man in your life someday, this nugget of
truth is for you. If you'll stand by your man and let him know you're
in his corner, cheering him on, he will think you are the most beautiful
woman in the world and love you like crazy.

It doesn't matter if we don't have abs and buns of steel; our men
will only see the beauty within us. Someone once said, "People don't
remember what you said; rather, they remember how you made them
feel." Meditate on that awhile. Are your words and actions making the
man in your life feel loved, adored, appreciated, valued, and happy?
If not, decide today to start showing admiration and support for your
man, and soon you'll become absolutely irresistible to him. Your happily
ever after awaits.

Father, help me to honor and love my man the way You intended. Amen.

OUR COACH

Show me your ways, LORD, teach me your paths. Guide me in
your truth and teach me, for you are God my Savior,
and my hope is in you all day long.
PSALM 25:4–5 NIV

As any good team knows, what happens off the field is just as important as what happens on the field. Young players first learn by watching the older ones play, longing for the day when they will be old enough to get in the game. They take notes and pay attention. When it's time to suit up, they are under the teaching and authority of their coach. A good coach will demonstrate the behavior he expects from his players, then watch closely as they do the drills and learn the plays. A coach analyzes, encourages, and corrects, over and over again, until the players get it right.

Our heavenly Father does much the same for us. He is a model, coach, and cheerleader. He shows us what he wants for us through His Word. He teaches us, using pictures we can understand. When we stray, he lovingly corrects us and guides us to a better way. Good coaches win games and lead their teams on the right path. When we testify that God is our Savior, we can trust Him to teach us and guide us and never lead us astray.

Heavenly Father, thank You for being my coach, my cheerleader,
and my Savior. Thank You for going before me, showing me Your ways,
and giving me Your Holy Spirit to guide me into all truth. Amen.

The Right Tools for the Job

By his divine power, God has given us everything we need for living a godly life. We have received all of this by coming to know him, the one who called us to himself by means of his marvelous glory and excellence.
2 Peter 1:3 nlt

Have you ever tried to hang a picture without a hammer? Or make a dress without a sewing machine? Or bake a pie without an oven? Trying to do a job without the right tools can be difficult, inefficient, and even impossible. Having the right tools for the job can mean the difference between frustration and success.

As we journey through the Christian life, we may feel frustration. We may feel like we lack the patience to deal with a difficult spouse, or the forgiveness to let go of anger toward someone who has hurt us. We may become tired and discouraged, lacking the energy to continue the Lord's work. But the Bible promises us that God has already given us everything we need. From time to time the tools we need may not seem readily available, but we can hold tight to the truth that His divine power has made them available to us. The more we come to know Him, the more we realize our calling. We can be assured that He will equip us with everything we need to do His work.

Father, thank You for Your divine power and for giving me everything I need to live the Christian life. When I feel discouraged, remind me to seek to know You more so that I can experience Your great and perfect promises. Amen.

A LOVING FATHER

For the LORD corrects those he loves, just as a father
corrects a child in whom he delights.
PROVERBS 3:12 NLT

Not many people would walk up to an unruly child in the grocery store and correct or discipline him. Not only is this socially unacceptable, but really, unless you know the child and, more importantly, love the child, it is impossible to provide correction. While the child may respond, he likely would do so out of fear—fear of a stranger stepping into his world.

Children respond to correction best when it comes from a loving parent. A loving parent doesn't discipline a child because they are embarrassed about the behavior, but because they love the child and long for a better future. They want to protect their child from unnecessary pain and teach them the way they should go. Our Father corrects us because He delights in us. We can listen and respond to His correction, because we know, beyond a shadow of doubt, that everything He does springs from His deep, deep love for us.

Father, You love me and You delight in me. I can hardly believe it's true.
When You are correcting me, help me to remember this blessed truth
and receive Your correction as a beloved child. Amen.

GROWING PAINS

*Dear brothers and sisters, when troubles of any kind come your way,
consider it an opportunity for great joy. For you know that when
your faith is tested, your endurance has a chance to grow.*
JAMES 1:2–3 NLT

. . . .

The Greek philosopher Epictetus said, "Life is not what happens to
you; it's how you react to it that matters." These profound words carry
biblical truth. Yes, Jesus brings us hope and joy and peace, but He never
said there wouldn't be trouble. In fact, in John 16:33, as He says His
good byes to the disciples, Jesus guarantees that we will have trouble. So
often in life, our goal is to eliminate the problems completely. We look
for ways to avoid troubles of any kind. We see troubles as inconvenient,
a bump in the road, an obstacle preventing us from going where we
want to go.

However, the author of James offers a different perspective. What
would happen if we saw troubles—of any kind—as an opportunity
for growth, rather than a roadblock? What if we responded eagerly to
trouble, grateful for an opportunity to have our faith tested and our
endurance grown?

When troubles come your way, don't resist. Consider them joy, for
you can be sure that growth is ahead.

. . . .

*Father, it's difficult for me to thank You for my troubles, but I can say that
I'm grateful for an opportunity to grow. Help me to respond appropriately
to trouble and to squeeze every ounce of learning from it that I can. Amen.*

WHATEVER IT IS, DO IT FOR HIM

*So, my dear brothers and sisters, be strong and immovable.
Always work enthusiastically for the Lord, for you know that
nothing you do for the Lord is ever useless.*
1 CORINTHIANS 15:58 NLT

Have you ever stopped to count how many menial tasks you do each day? Laundry, dishes, bill payments, errands, meal preparation, grocery shopping. . .whether you work inside or outside the home, you work hard. But is this work really important?

It would be different if we were on the mission field, preaching the Good News to those who haven't heard it yet, or tutoring needy children, or teaching God's Word to our peers. But dishes? Laundry? Grocery shopping? It's tempting—especially when we're tired—to think of those things as useless. But God's Word tells us to be strong and immovable, working enthusiastically for the Lord. Even when our work doesn't seem important, it is never useless when we are doing it for Him. Colossians 3:17 says that whatever we do, in word or deed, we should do it for the Lord.

Father, help me to stop distinguishing between important and unimportant work. Regardless of what I do, help me to do it for You. Amen.

A Listening Friend

The purposes of a person's heart are deep waters,
but one who has insight draws them out.
Proverbs 20:5 NIV

. . . .

Diane was faced with a tough decision. She had been offered her dream job, but it involved a salary cut and a cross-country move. Her current job paid the bills, but she was not happy. She longed for change but craved security. She called her friend Lisa, who met her for coffee. As Diane talked about her dilemma, Lisa merely listened and asked questions. "How would you feel if you didn't take the job? What if the move doesn't work out and you have regrets?" Before long, Diane had made her decision. Ironically, Lisa didn't offer a word of advice, but Diane found herself extremely grateful to her good friend for helping her sort things out.

When friends come to us with problems, it's easy to give advice. We immediately think of what we would do in the situation and offer a quick solution. But this proverb offers wise words about listening. Most people can find the answers to their own problems, especially through the eyes of a friend who listens well and asks good questions. Insight is about asking the right questions, not offering up solutions. One of the best ways we can love others is to listen, draw them out, and support them as they come up with their own solutions.

. . . .

Father, thank You for friendships. Help me to be wise,
to ask good questions instead of offering my own solutions. Amen.

EMBRACING PAIN

But he said to me, "My grace is sufficient for you, for my power is made perfect in weakness." Therefore I will boast all the more gladly about my weaknesses, so that Christ's power may rest on me.
2 CORINTHIANS 12:9 NIV

Theologians have speculated on the nature of Paul's thorn in the flesh. We don't know much about it except that it must have tortured him. Paul says in Corinthians that he begged God—three times—to remove this thorn from him.

God always answers prayer, but often not in the way we want Him to. God could have healed Paul of this thorn, but He chose not to. Why? So His power could be felt profoundly—"so that Christ's power may rest on me," Paul says. Physical and emotional pain has a way of quickening our hearts toward God. When we are pain-free and trouble-free, we tend to think we can handle things on our own. We acquire a false sense of strength. On the other hand, pain gets our attention. If you are in pain, whether physical or emotional, be reminded that God hears your prayer. Our pain can be a literal reminder to trust in God's strength.

Father, I confess that I don't like pain. Like Paul, I have often begged You to remove my weakness. I long for comfort and to live a pain-free life. But I know that, as my Father, You know what's best for me. Help me to rest in Your power when I feel weak. Amen.

The Path to God's Will

*All the paths of the LORD are lovingkindness and truth to
those who keep His covenant and His testimonies.*
Psalm 25:10 NASB

It's an age-old question: What is God's will for my life? It's easy to
agonize over this question, pondering which path to take and fearfully
wondering what will happen if we take a wrong step. But God's will
is not necessarily a matter of choosing precisely the right step in each
and every situation. This verse teaches that we should focus on God's
covenant and His testimony. As we do so, the journey becomes part of
the destination.

God doesn't always give us a clear road map, but He does clearly
ask us to keep His covenant and His testimonies. When we do so, our
individual steps will become clearer, and we will find ourselves more and
more in step with His will. As He guides us closer to our destination, we
will find much joy in the journey.

*Lord, when I agonize over which way to take, help me to focus on Your
covenant and Your testimonies. Help me to trust You to lead me on
the paths You want me to take, knowing that when I follow
Your Word, I am always in Your will. Amen.*

GIVING OUT OF NEED

"Give, and you will receive. Your gift will return to you in full—pressed down, shaken together to make room for more, running over, and poured into your lap. The amount you give will determine the amount you get back."
LUKE 6:38 NLT

As usual, Jesus saw things from a different perspective. He was in the temple, watching people bring their gifts. Instead of honoring the Pharisees, with all their pomp and circumstance, Jesus points out a poor widow. "'Truly I tell you,' He said, 'this poor widow has put in more than all the others. All these people gave their gifts out of their wealth; but she out of her poverty put in all she had to live on'" (Luke 21:3–4 NIV).

While the rich gave out of their abundance, the widow gave out of her need. It's not difficult to give when we are sure all our needs are met. We just scrape a little off the top and leave it in the offering plate. Giving out of our poverty is a profound act of faith. When we lay our all on the altar, God promises to multiply it beyond our wildest imagination. What are you holding back from the Lord today? Give. God cannot wait to multiply your efforts.

Father, help me to be a giver. Teach me to give out of faith in You, not in my finances. Reveal to me where I may be holding back, waiting until my own needs for time or money are met. I long to trust You with the poor widow's faith. Amen.

An Anchor for the Soul

But when you ask him, be sure that your faith is in God alone.
Do not waver, for a person with divided loyalty is as unsettled
as a wave of the sea that is blown and tossed by the wind.
James 1:6 NLT

Imagine being on a life raft in the middle of the ocean. When the storms come, the seemingly weightless raft is picked up and tossed wherever the wind chooses to take it. There is no ability to steer, no sail to work with the wind, certainly no protection from the storm. When the storm ends, the raft's destination is really left up to chance.

James tells us that this is how unstable we become when we do not have a strong foundation. When our loyalty is divided—between serving God and pleasing others, for example—we are as unstable as a raft in a storm on the raging sea. The writer of Hebrews speaks of our hope in Jesus as "a strong and trustworthy anchor for our souls" (Hebrews 6:19 NLT). Faith in God anchors us and braces us against the raging storm. When we are firmly anchored, the winds may whip us around, but ultimately we cannot be moved. Anchor your faith and loyalty on Him.

Lord Jesus, You are the anchor for my soul. Help me to hold firmly to You,
to keep my loyalty focused on You and You alone. Thank You for the
promise that You will keep me steadfast and strong. Amen.

Redemption Is Near

"But when these things begin to take place, straighten up and lift up your heads, because your redemption is drawing near."
Luke 21:28 nasb

. . . .

Take one look at the world news, and there is no doubt. The events Jesus speaks of in Luke 21 are certainly happening. Nations are at war. Kingdoms are shattered. Every day the news tells us of earthquakes, plagues, famine, and terrors so great we can hardly speak of them. As if this isn't enough, throughout the world, followers of Christ are being persecuted. It's easy to be discouraged. Who wouldn't be? Even if you knew your favorite team was ultimately going to win the game, it would be difficult to see them take such a beating.

But Jesus exhorts us to take a posture of victory—backs straight, heads held high. His promise is clear and rings through the centuries since He first spoke these words. Redemption is near! The battle is fierce, but the war is already won. Soon, all the pain and sorrow will be a distant memory. In the light of Jesus' face, the pain will dim as we rise victorious to reign with him forever.

Stand tall. Hold tight to the promise. Jesus is near.

. . . .

Father, my heart gets discouraged. It is so difficult to hear what is happening in the world around me. I'm tired and my human self feels so defeated. Give me a posture of victory. Help me to stand tall and hold my head up high. Thank You for the promise that will soon be ours. Amen.

PRAYING FOR YOU

*With this in mind, we constantly pray for you, that our God may make
you worthy of his calling, and that by his power he may bring to fruition
your every desire for goodness and your every deed prompted by faith.*
2 THESSALONIANS 1:11 NIV

When we share prayer requests, we often pray for health and for healing,
maybe an open door for a job opportunity or safety and protection.
But throughout the books of Thessalonians, Paul shares his prayers for
the church at Thessalonica. His prayers are not for health and healing,
but that God would make them worthy of His calling. That He would
bring to fruition their hearts' good desires. This is not to say that prayers
for healing and health are not important; James 5:14 instructs us to
pray this way. However, there is more to prayer than asking for healing
or comfort. By following Paul's example in 1 and 2 Thessalonians, our
prayers can take on more substance and spiritual meaning.

Take a moment to read through the books of 1 and 2 Thessalonians,
noting the way Paul prays for his fellow believers. Deepen your prayer
life. Make a commitment to pray for others on a spiritual, rather than
superficial, level.

*Heavenly Father, thank You for my friends. Help me to pray for them
regularly and expansively. Thank You for all that You
do to show us Your presence. Amen.*

OTHERS FIRST

Do nothing from selfishness or empty conceit, but with humility of mind regard one another as more important than yourselves; do not merely look out for your own personal interests, but also for the interests of others.
PHILIPPIANS 2:3–4 NASB

It's difficult to do anything with absolutely no selfishness or vain conceit. Our human nature clamors for us to be noticed and recognized for the good things we do. If we're honest, we'll notice that selfishness creeps into just about everything we do. However, Jesus calls us to a greater way of being. Following His example of humility, we are to regard others as more important than ourselves. This doesn't mean we shouldn't consider our personal interests (Paul says we aren't "merely" to look out for our own personal interests), but instead of first asking, "How will this affect me?" we should ask, "How will this affect others?"

That isn't always an easy question to answer. Sometimes we do things for others because we want to avoid feeling bad. Sometimes we feel guilty and do things for others that we really should let them do for themselves. Before taking any action, we should examine our hearts and motives and consider how our actions affect others.

I admit it, Lord—I'm a selfish person at heart. Teach me to put my own needs on the back burner. Not to ignore them entirely, but to consider what is best for others rather than myself. Help me to trust You to take care of my needs. Amen.

HE IS MORE THAN ABLE

*Now all glory to God, who is able, through his mighty power at work
within us, to accomplish infinitely more than we might ask or think.
Glory to him in the church and in Christ Jesus through all
generations forever and ever! Amen.*
EPHESIANS 3:20–21 NLT

Did you ever hear the saying, "The more you know, the more it is you
know you don't know"? It's true. Whether it's bees or poetry or chemistry
or space, the more we learn about a subject, the more we discover how
much more there is to know. But while there is ultimately an end to man's
knowledge of earthly things, it's impossible to even begin to grasp how big
God is. We don't know even a fraction of His power. Our minds are just
not capable of fully comprehending His ability, His character, and His
love for us.

When we think of God, we tend to think about His abilities relative
to our own. We don't even consider doing great things for Him, because
we can't fathom how it could happen. Could you be unknowingly
limiting God? Whether or not we recognize it, His mighty power, the
Holy Spirit, is at work within us, doing more than we can imagine. Avail
yourself of this power—let Him do through you things that you can't
even begin to comprehend.

*Father, You are too big for me. I cannot even begin to comprehend Your
majesty. Thank You for the Holy Spirit, working in and through me,
to accomplish Your purposes through Christ and the church.
Help me to cooperate with Your Spirit's work. Amen.*

THE WORLD IS WATCHING

How great is the goodness you have stored up for those who fear you.
You lavish it on those who come to you for protection,
blessing them before the watching world.
PSALM 31:19 NLT

We humans have a tendency to focus on what we don't have. We lament not having enough money or time. We become frustrated with our physical limitations and fret about things not turning out the way we wanted them to. We're good at whining about these things. But remember, the world is watching. You may not think much of a whine here and there, but others are watching to see how we respond to this God whom we say is so loving and good.

One of the ways God demonstrates His love to a hurting world is to lavish His love upon His children. When we whine and complain about little things, we diminish God's blessing to us before a watching world. It's important for us to respond appropriately to all of God's blessings and to demonstrate how deeply our heavenly Father loves us.

Father, You have blessed me abundantly. I confess that I sometimes
miss those blessings and spend more time focusing on what is lacking
than on what You have provided. Help me to be grateful
before a watching world. Amen.

It's Not about the Rules

*For the Kingdom of God is not a matter of what we eat or drink,
but of living a life of goodness and peace and joy in the Holy Spirit.*
Romans 14:17 nlt

Rules. We love rules. Whether it's a diet, an exercise plan, a recipe, or a road map, we find a lot of comfort in knowing exactly what is expected of us. With speed limits, tax breaks, or the time-clock at work, we always want to know just how far we can push the boundaries without getting into trouble.

While there are some do's and don'ts, the Christian life is ultimately not about rules. In fact, the more rules we make for ourselves and others, the more vulnerable we are to creating our own version of the Gospel, just like the Pharisees did. We become ensnared in a legalistic way of life, bound to a man-made version of what not to do that leads us a long way from the abundant life God has planned for us. The rules are secondary to living the Christian life, which is about goodness, peace, and joy, available only through the Holy Spirit.

Holy Spirit, help me not to focus on rules. Instead, draw me to living a life of goodness, peace, and joy, gifts I can only receive through You. Amen.

SET APART

May God himself, the God of peace, sanctify you through and through.
May your whole spirit, soul and body be kept blameless at the coming of
our Lord Jesus Christ. The one who calls you is faithful, and he will do it.
1 THESSALONIANS 5:23–24 NIV

Sanctification is a big word that means "to be set apart" for a specific purpose. The Bible teaches that as Christians we are sanctified, or set apart, for God's purposes. This act is initiated by God. There is nothing we can do to set ourselves apart. But if you have ever tried to change the diaper of a squirming baby, you know how important cooperation is for a person to be changed.

God has already done the work. He has made your spirit, soul, and body blameless through the death and resurrection of Jesus Christ. This work is done. Paul expresses to the Thessalonians the importance of being kept blameless. This is the work of cooperation—our need to trust and obey God in every situation. We can cooperate with his setting-apart work in our lives by reading and studying His Word, by praying to Him, and by sharing our knowledge with other believers.

How have you been set apart for God? He has called you. He is faithful. He *will* do it.

Father, thank You for Your sanctifying work through Jesus on the cross.
Thank You for choosing me and setting me apart for righteousness.
Help me to trust and obey this work You are doing in my life. Amen.

The Old, Old Story

I have inherited Your testimonies forever,
for they are the joy of my heart.
Psalm 119:111 NASB

Aren't family stories the best? No family reunion would be complete without them. For the hundredth time, Grandma tells of the day she and Grandpa met, Grandpa tells what it was like to storm the gates of Normandy, and everyone laughs about the day when Susie sold the neighbor's dog for a quarter. These family stories provide us with a sense of connection and identity. They link us with family members who died before we were born and give us common ground. In a sense, we inherit the stories of our families. We don't have to experience the event to relish the details as if we were there.

And so it is with the testimony of God. No, we weren't there when He parted the Red Sea and carried the Israelites out of captivity. We weren't with Moses when he received the Ten Commandments, nor were we with young David when he killed the giant. But as God's children, we have inherited these testimonies. These stories are a part of our legacy and give us a common connection with believers throughout the centuries—our brothers and sisters in Christ. Relish the stories of God; they are the joy of your heart.

Father, thank You for the testimony in scripture. I praise You for my
family legacy—thank You for sharing these sweet stories with me.
I want to pass them down to my loved ones and experience the joy of
family togetherness with all the believers throughout the ages. Amen.

NO WORRIES

*"So don't worry about tomorrow, for tomorrow will bring
its own worries. Today's trouble is enough for today."*
MATTHEW 6:34 NLT

. . . .

It has been said that today is the tomorrow you worried about yesterday.
Isn't it true? How many of the things you worry about actually happen?
Worry is a thief. It robs us of the joy of the moment and plants us
firmly in the future, where we have absolutely no control. Instead of
focusing on the problems that this day brings, we propel ourselves into
an unknown tomorrow. In living this way, we miss out on all the little
moments that make life precious.

The antidote to worry is to focus on today—this hour, this moment
in time. What is happening now? Experience it with all five of your
senses. Allow the wonder of today to touch your heart and settle it down.
Sure, there is trouble today, and there are problems to solve, but Jesus is
right here with us. We have the gift of the Holy Spirit who can counsel
and comfort us and help us get through any and every situation. There
is nothing you can't face without Jesus by your side. When you focus on
what He can do instead of what you can't do, you will experience a deep
and abiding peace that comes only from Him.

. . . .

*Lord, worry is such a part of who I am! When I'm not worried,
I worry that I'm missing something. Please help me not to worry about
tomorrow. Help me to focus on today, on what is happening now,
and to let You take care of all my troubles. Amen.*

A Good Word

*Anxiety in the heart of man causes depression,
but a good word makes it glad.*
Proverbs 12:25 NKJV

As most of us know, anxiety and depression are two sides of the same coin. According to this verse, keeping anxiety in our hearts causes depression. We are anxious about what might happen and we become depressed about what didn't. Anxiety and depression create a vicious cycle, keeping us bound to the past and paralyzed about the future.

But this proverb reminds us that "a good word makes [the heart] glad." Where can you get a good word? Philippians 4:8 (NLT) tells us to "fix [our] thoughts on what is true, and honorable, and right, and pure, and lovely, and admirable. Think about things that are excellent and worthy of praise." This is a good word! We know it to be true experientially, and studies prove that reading the Bible, singing praise songs, and hearing encouraging words from friends can literally change our brain's chemistry and lift a dark mood. These good words replace the anxiety and depression in our hearts with joy and peace in the Holy Spirit.

Father, my heart is sometimes weighed down by anxiety. I know what it feels like to be depressed. Thank You for Your Word and the reminder that I don't have to settle for these feelings. Thank You that I can trust You to bring joy back to my soul. Amen.

WHAT DO I NEED?

*What is causing the quarrels and fights among you? Don't they come
from the evil desires at war within you? You want what you don't have,
so you scheme and kill to get it. You are jealous of what others have,
but you can't get it, so you fight and wage war to take it away from them.
Yet you don't have what you want because you don't ask God for it.*
JAMES 4:1–2 NLT

You have probably never schemed to kill anyone, and it's doubtful you
have ever declared war. Fighting and quarreling are probably a little
more familiar to you. Whether metaphorically or literally, we all have
schemed to get what we want, have felt jealous of what others have, and
have even waged war against God because of our evil desires.

It has been said that jealousy is wanting what others have, while envy
is wanting what others have to be taken away from them. When we focus
on the things we don't have, we become bitter and quarrelsome. We may
start feeling sorry for ourselves, comparing ourselves to others and wishing
we could have what they have. But our energy is focused in the wrong
place. Whatever it is you want, ask God. He may not always give you
what you ask for, but He will always give you what you need.

*Father, when I feel jealous or envious of others, return my focus to You.
Help me to trust You to give me everything I need. Amen.*

JESUS' EYES

*"Your eye is a lamp that provides light for your body.
When your eye is good, your whole body is filled with light."*
MATTHEW 6:22 NLT

. . . .

The day after an award show is terribly exciting for the entertainment industry. Soon after celebrities have walked the red carpet, their clothes, jewelry, and companions are scrutinized. *She wore what designer? The jewelry cost how much? I can't believe they're not together anymore!*

It is so easy to look at these famous people and become enamored by the things of this world. When we look at others through human eyes, we see their stuff, their money, and their failures. This can be a dark and depressing viewpoint. It causes us to judge and evaluate them on superficial criteria. It may cause us to be dissatisfied with our own lives and long for fame and worldly possessions.

But what do you suppose Jesus sees when He looks at those same celebrities? Instead of a powerful, rich, or popular star, He merely sees a child in need of a Father. He sees a broken and needy human being, with faults and problems just like the rest of us. He feels compassion and love for this person and cares deeply about every moment of their life. When we look at others through the eyes of Jesus, we can be filled with hope and light and a longing to share the good news of the Gospel.

. . . .

Jesus, help me to look at others through Your eyes. Help me to have Your perspective, so that I might see the heart instead of superficial things. Amen.

THE SPIRIT OF TRUTH

"If you love me, keep my commands. And I will ask the Father, and he will give you another advocate to help you and be with you forever—the Spirit of truth. The world cannot accept him, because it neither sees him nor knows him. But you know him, for he lives with you and will be in you."
JOHN 14:15–17 NIV

Turn the other cheek. Love your enemies. Do good to those who hurt you. Give generously, Don't be anxious. Store up treasures in heaven. In the Sermon on the Mount (Matthew 5–6), Jesus presents a perspective on living that must have confused many of His listeners.

For those who don't know or recognize the Holy Spirit, Jesus' teachings don't make any sense. They are countercultural and go against the grain of natural instinct. When Christians forgive those who have hurt them, give generously, or refuse to follow the latest trends and fashions, the world gets confused. To those who don't have the Holy Spirit, these seemingly extraordinary actions must seem unreal, impossible even. Knowing the Holy Spirit makes all the difference. When the Holy Spirit lives in us, we can finally see truth. We have the advocacy and the help we need to follow Jesus' commands—and they make all the sense in the world.

Jesus, thank You for the gift of the Holy Spirit. My life would be so meaningless and confusing without this precious Comforter, Advocate, and Friend. Help me to follow Your commands and shine Your light to a watching world. Amen.

NEW EVERY MORNING

*This I recall to my mind, therefore I have hope. Through the LORD's
mercies we are not consumed, because His compassions fail not.
They are new every morning; great is Your faithfulness.*
LAMENTATIONS 3:21–23 NKJV

For many people, one of the most difficult times of the day is nighttime.
We fall into bed physically exhausted, grateful to finally be done with
the activity of the day. Suddenly our brains are awake and alert with
swirling thoughts. Thoughts of today lead to thoughts of yesterday and
ten years back. We think of things we should have said but didn't, and
things we shouldn't have said but did. We rehearse bad decisions and
mistakes and worry anxiously about the future. The thoughts that keep
us awake some nights can be daunting, to say the least. These thoughts
can consume us with worry, fear, and regret, robbing us of peace and
sleep. We feel hopeless and exhausted.

But God's Word says we don't have to be consumed by regrets from
the past or fears of the future. Every morning with the rising of the sun
comes a new measure of His mercy, compassion, and faithfulness. So
let your worrisome thoughts go and replace them with hope. His mercy
and compassion will never fail.

*Father, when I can't sleep, bring Your mercy and compassion to my mind.
Give me hope in Your faithfulness. Thank You for the promise of the
new morning, and help me to rest in You. Amen.*

TRUTH IN LOVE

Instead, we will speak the truth in love, growing in every way more and more like Christ, who is the head of his body, the church.
EPHESIANS 4:15 NLT

· ·

Sometimes it's difficult to say just the right thing at just the right time. Especially when we are hurt, confused, or angry, we tend to go to one extreme or the other. Either we blurt out whatever comes to mind, hurting others in the process, or we nurse our pain and keep silent, fearing how others might respond. Neither of these extremes is effective—or truthful. Instead, we can follow the example of Jesus, who demonstrated the perfect balance of speaking the truth in love. He was not afraid to confront others when they needed to hear the truth, but at the same time, He did so in gentleness and love. Jesus was hard in the right places and soft in the right places.

Keeping this balance requires maturity and work. We won't always get it right, but speaking the truth in love will become more natural as we grow more like Christ. Becoming more Christlike means staying connected to His Body, the Church, and working through communication and conflict with a heart of love.

· ·

Jesus, sometimes it's hard for me to speak up, while others times I blurt out the wrong thing at the wrong time. Teach me to be more like You and to speak Your truth in love. Amen.

HIS RIGHTEOUS RIGHT HAND

"Do not fear, for I am with you; do not anxiously look about you,
for I am your God. I will strengthen you, surely I will help you,
surely I will uphold you with My righteous right hand."
ISAIAH 41:10 NASB

It was first discovered in animals, but humans have it, too. When we sense danger, our bodies and brains are flooded with stress chemicals that cause us to either fight or flee. These chemicals turn off rational thought and focus on physical strength. It's the stuff that allows mothers to lift cars off children or carry a loved one from a burning building. The moment the danger has passed, these chemicals subside and allow us to return to our regular activities.

Unfortunately, because of sin in the world, these chemicals can be activated even when we are not in immediate danger. We can become fearful—fighting the feeling that something horrible is about to happen. This is called anxiety. Anxiety can be crippling and cause us to look around fearfully, waiting for a crisis. When we are plagued by anxiety we feel week, like we could fall. With God as our Father, we never have to fear. Anxiety is completely unnecessary because He promises to strengthen us and uphold us with His righteous right hand.

Lord Jesus, I confess that I get anxious. I'm sometimes afraid
and distracted by worrisome thoughts. Help me to rest in
Your strength. Take my hand and help me. Amen.

PLANTED BY THE WATER

"But blessed are those who trust in the LORD and have made the LORD their hope and confidence. They are like trees planted along a riverbank, with roots that reach deep into the water. Such trees are not bothered by the heat or worried by long months of drought. Their leaves stay green, and they never stop producing fruit."
JEREMIAH 17:7–8 NLT

While trees don't get to choose where they're planted, the ones growing by the riverbank have it made. Their roots are free to reach deep in the water. They never have to worry about drought or blistering hot days. They are in the ideal position for growth.

This familiar analogy, also found in Psalm 1, paints a beautiful picture of what it means to stand steadfastly with the Lord. Trees don't get to choose where they're planted, but we do, and we must choose carefully. For maximum growth, we must plant ourselves near a source of living water. . .close to the Body of Christ. We must immerse ourselves in prayer, feed ourselves with God's Word, and be fertilized and challenged by the companionship of other believers. When we do this, we can be assured that we will stay healthy and never stop producing fruit.

Father, Your Word paints such beautiful pictures. Thank You for the image of a tree by the riverbank and for the peace it gives me to imagine being planted so close to You. Help my roots to grow deep as I learn more and more to depend on You. Amen.

SHINING LIGHTS

*No one lights a lamp and then puts it under a basket. Instead,
a lamp is placed on a stand, where it gives light to everyone
in the house. In the same way, let your good deeds shine out
for all to see, so that everyone will praise your heavenly Father.*
MATTHEW 5:15–16 NLT

In 1990 on a weekend retreat, students from a youth group in Burleson, Texas, were led to go to their schools at night and pray. This small act birthed a grassroots prayer movement that is now held on the fourth Wednesday of the month of September at school flagpoles across the world. Students initiate, organize, and lead these prayer gatherings, and God has used this time to transform the lives of countless students who simply begin their Wednesday morning in corporate prayer.

Despite being misunderstood and sometimes even mocked by their classmates, the prayers of these courageous students shine like a beacon of light through their dark and hurting schools. These prayers open the door for them to share the reason for the hope they have. Sure, these prayer meetings could take place in the safety and quiet of a church or even a classroom. But the prayers shining from a flagpole give hope and light to all who see.

*Father, thank You for the students who obediently responded to Your call
so many years ago and committed their Wednesday morning to prayer.
I pray for the students who gather this morning, that they would be
a light to their teachers and classmates and that You would
continue to use them to transform the world. Amen.*

No Shame

Those who look to him for help will be radiant with joy;
no shadow of shame will darken their faces.
PSALM 34:5 NLT

Adam and Eve had the perfect home—a beautiful garden. Every plant, tree, and animal was theirs. Their perfect Father met every one of their needs. His rules were clear. All the garden belonged to them—except the fruit of the one tree. Adam was told plainly by God: Eat the fruit of this tree, and you will surely die (Genesis 2:16–17).

Of course, the one thing they couldn't have was the one thing that captured their attention. When the serpent presented an opportunity, Adam and Eve took the bait. What followed was a feeling known to all of us thereafter—shame. They hid their faces and their bodies from God, covered with the profound awareness that they had failed Him. In the cool of the garden, Adam tried to avoid God and hide from Him further. Yes, the consequences were severe, but God demanded Adam and Eve look to Him so He could remove their shame.

No matter how we disappoint God, we never have to hide from Him or cover our faces in shame. All we need to do is turn to Him and ask for His forgiveness, mercy, and grace. One look at the Father and our faces can be radiant with joy.

Father, when I have disappointed You, the last thing I want is to look
to You for help. I know it's because I can't comprehend Your
mercy and Your love for me. Thank You for freedom
from the shadow of shame. Amen.

Sheep Need a Shepherd

*All of us, like sheep, have strayed away. We have left God's paths
to follow our own. Yet the LORD laid on him the sins of us all.*
Isaiah 53:6 NLT

Because of their tendency to follow the crowd and simultaneously wander away, sheep have the reputation of being dumb. However, studies show sheep may be a little smarter than they've been given credit for. They can learn certain skills, they can be trained, they demonstrate the ability to recognize and remember faces, and they can even make their way through a maze. Sheep seem to be able to make friends, and exist best in communities. Thus, they can easily be led astray by anything that catches their eye—especially a wandering friend.

Sheep may not be stupid, but they are dependent. Without a shepherd, they would lead one another into all kinds of trouble. To survive, they must rely on the shepherd, who protects them and guides them through the darkest valleys. Without a shepherd, they would surely perish.

We, like sheep, go astray. We are easily distracted and vulnerable to our enemies. We are dependent on our Shepherd to lead the way. We can be grateful to our Good Shepherd for always staying close beside us, leading us on His righteous paths.

*Jesus, my Good Shepherd, thank You for leading me and for staying
close beside me. Thank You for Your faithfulness and protection,
no matter how dark the way. Amen.*

NEW BEGINNINGS

*"Unless a kernel of wheat falls to the ground and dies, it remains only
a single seed. But if it dies, it produces many seeds."*
JOHN 12:24 NIV

In most parts of the United States, October ushers in a change of
seasons. The heat, harvest, and holiday of summer end, and preparations
for winter begin. One season goes and another comes. Then after a time
of dormancy or death, new growth breaks through. When roots push
out seeking nourishment, new life sprouts.

Jesus used this illustration to teach His followers two things: First,
that He Himself would die and lie in the earth for a time, but His death
and resurrection would provide eternal life. Second, that we Christians
who desire to follow Him should die to our self-seeking ways and live
for Him, which will produce fruit for eternity. "Anyone who loves their
life will lose it, while anyone who hates their life in this world will keep
it for eternal life. Whoever serves me must follow me. . . . My Father
will honor the one who serves me" (John 12:25–26 NIV). God will
reward His children who serve Him faithfully.

Are you in a dark or dormant season? Nourish your mind with
the Word of God and with Christian music. Dwell on God's goodness
and stay close to Him in prayer. Think of someone you can serve in a
meaningful and self-giving way, dying to your own needs for a time.
Soon your heart will bloom with a springtime of hopefulness.

*Lord of the dark, when I dread changes and fear the future,
help me to immerse myself in seeking You and in serving others.*

Community and Service

*And let us consider how we may spur one another on toward love
and good deeds, not giving up meeting together, as some are in
the habit of doing, but encouraging one another.*
Hebrews 10:24–25 NIV

"I don't need to attend church to be spiritual. My relationship with God is personal, and I can worship Him anywhere. Besides, on Sundays I need time for myself to catch up on loose ends at home." Lone Ranger Christians often express this justification for not connecting with a local church.

Yes, we can worship God anywhere and everywhere, but church involves more than worship. Church is about community (considering one another) and encouragement (spurring each other to love and goodness). We Christians need each other. As members of the Body of Christ, we have spiritual gifts that God expects us to use "for the common good" (1 Corinthians 12:7 NIV). He has gifted us the way He wants (12:18). We cannot say we don't need each other (12:21) because what concerns one concerns all (12:25). We share each other's sufferings and successes (12:26).

Therefore, when we make the sacrifice of time to meet together weekly, we are fulfilling God's purpose for us. Isn't that more important than getting our chores done or having "me" time? Our membership in Christ's Body includes benefits and responsibilities. Like coals in a fire, we keep each other warm and glowing as long as we're connected.

*Lord Jesus, I confess that I often want to be served or to serve only when
convenient. Make me willing to minister to fellow Christians
and fulfill the function You have given me.*

My Morning Prayer

*Let me hear Your lovingkindness in the morning; for I trust in You;
teach me the way in which I should walk; for to You I lift up my soul.*
Psalm 143:8 nasb

Mornings can excite or depress us. Do you say "Good morning, Lord!"
or "Good Lord, it's morning!"? When David wrote Psalm 143, he
probably dreaded the sun coming up because that meant his enemies
could continue pursuing him and persecuting his soul. "The enemy. . .has
crushed my life to the ground" (verse 3 nasb). "My spirit is overwhelmed
within me; my heart is appalled" (verse 4 nasb).

What did David do when he didn't know which way to turn? He
turned to the Lord. He stayed in prayer contact with God and meditated
on God's faithfulness and righteousness (verse 1), God's past work in his
life (verse 5), and His loyal love (verses 8, 12). He also took refuge in God
(verse 9) and continued serving Him (verse 12).

No matter what our day holds, we can face it confidently by practicing verse 8. Let's look for God's loving-kindness and keep trusting
Him no matter what. Ask Him to teach and lead us in the way He
wants us to go. We have the privilege of offering up our souls (thoughts,
emotions, and will) to Him anew each morning. Have a good day.

*Good morning, Lord. You are my loving Father, secure Refuge,
and trustworthy God. Deliver me from my enemies and show me Your
loving heart as I trust in You. Help me to please You today in my
decisions and goals, in my attitudes toward circumstances,
and in the way I respond to people around me.*

Cure for Discontent

*Always giving thanks for all things in the name of
our Lord Jesus Christ to God, even the Father.*
Ephesians 5:20 NASB

Do you struggle with being satisfied with your current situation in life? Discontent is a heart disease that manifests in comparing, coveting, and complaining. What is the cure? The habit of gratitude. Thanking God for everything—the good and the bad—means we accept it as His will, even if we don't like it.

Sometimes we receive birthday or Christmas gifts we have no desire for, but we still thank the giver. God is the good giver of every perfect gift (James 1:17). Failing to thank Him is rebellion against His wisdom and ways. If we expect Him to do things the way we want or to give us more, we forget that God owes us nothing.

When God commands thanksgiving, He is not mandating our feelings but rather our submission. However, because thankfulness changes our attitude and outlook, it does affect our feelings. Discontent and resentment cannot coexist with humble acceptance of what happens to us. Therefore, thanking God must become our lifelong habit. When we turn out the light every night, we can review our day and thank God for each event—good and bad—because He allowed it, and He is good. We can be satisfied with that.

*Bountiful Father, I'm sorry I often rebel against Your sovereign plan for me.
Thank You for doing all things well. Your essence is love, and every mark
You make in my life is a love mark, conforming me to Christ.
I accept Your will and Your ways.*

EVE SYNDROME—WANTING MORE

*So when the woman saw that the tree was good for food,
that it was pleasant to the eyes, and a tree desirable
to make one wise, she took of its fruit and ate.*
GENESIS 3:6 NKJV

God created our bodies with the ability to lust and desire. If we did not desire food and water, we would die. Craving intimacy and sexual arousal propagates civilization. The desire for survival keeps us alive through fight or flight. Our lusts can also be dangerous and cause us to sin (James 1:14–15). "All that is in the world—the lust of the flesh, the lust of the eyes, and the pride of life—is not of the Father but is of the world" (1 John 2:16 NKJV).

Eve gave in to her physical appetites when the serpent convinced her to ignore God's generous bounty, which included every tree in the garden except one. Her longing for the immediate because of what she heard, saw, felt, and craved brought sin upon the entire human race.

While men usually find sexual sins the hardest to resist, women struggle with covetousness—comparing with others and wanting what they have. Acquiring material things and cluttering our homes can result from this desire gone awry. How can we know if our craving for more is healthy or harmful? Make Jesus your shopping buddy. Would He approve your purchases? Hebrews 13:5–6 tells us to be content with what we have because we have God Himself, our ever-present Helper.

*Gracious God, You have given me everything I need for life and godliness.
Help me to discipline my desires and to be content with You.*

Lasting Treasure

"Sell your possessions and give to those in need.
This will store up treasure for you in heaven!"
Luke 12:33 nlt

In Luke 12, a rich man wanted bigger barns. Jesus told this parable to warn "against every kind of greed" (12:15 nlt). He said we are foolish to store up earthly wealth but not have a rich relationship with God (12:21). Greed is an obscure sin, but it causes many perils:

- We can become more focused on storing (12:18) than on sharing (12:33).
- The greater our wealth, the greater our worry (12:25–26).
- When our possessions possess us, we start to trust in our finances instead of depending on God (12:29–31).

The rich man was preparing for the wrong thing. Like him, we can spend our income acquiring more instead of spending our lives laying up heavenly treasure by being generous (12:33). When we give of our finances and sacrifice ourselves to help others, we invest in eternity. Treasure in heaven never loses value or disappears, and it keeps our hearts rich toward God (12:34). Loving physical treasure can lead to spiritual poverty. Loving what God loves makes us eternally rich.

Father, I must not measure my life by how much I own.
It all belongs to You anyhow. Who can I invest in today?

WORKING FOR US

*Even though our outward man is perishing, yet the inward man is being
renewed day by day. For our light affliction, which is but for a moment,
is working for us a far more exceeding and eternal weight of glory,
while we do not look at the things which are seen,
but at the things which are not seen.*
2 CORINTHIANS 4:16–18 NKJV

"A moment of pain is worth a lifetime of glory," Pete Zamperini told
his brother Louis in the movie *Unbroken*. He wanted Louis to focus
on the big picture. If he could endure the physical pain of training and
punishing himself as a runner, he could enjoy Olympic glory the rest of
his life.

Scripture has a similar idea: a lifetime of affliction is worth an
eternity of glory. Not to minimize our trials—they are painful and often
progressive because our physical bodies are perishing. But compared
to eternity, our troubles are light and momentary. And extremely
beneficial. Somehow God allows them to work for us to produce
exceeding glory in eternity. The passage tells us to look at the big
picture, at the unseen spiritual things. As we focus beyond this life and
fellowship with Christ through His Word and prayer every day, we will
be renewed on the inside.

A gospel song says, "It will be worth it all when we see Jesus." We
Christians can endure suffering in this life knowing it works for us in
the next.

*Dear Jesus, You are the originator and finisher of my salvation.
Help me to fix my eyes on You and run my earthly race with endurance.*

Glorifying God

*Do you not know that your body is the temple of the Holy Spirit. . .
and you are not your own? For you were bought at a price;
therefore glorify God in your body.*
1 Corinthians 6:19–20 NKJV

Godly Christians desire to glorify God with their lives. We imagine this will involve significant accomplishments and praiseworthy acts of service. But we also glorify God through less desirable means. Paul's earnest expectation and hope was to magnify Christ in his body, even by dying (Philippians 1:20).

Jesus told Peter he would "glorify God" by a death he did not want and could not control (John 21:18–19). He was actually crucified as a martyr. Why did Jesus tell him he would die a horrible death? Perhaps to assure him that he would never again deny knowing Christ. He would be faithful unto death, thus glorifying God.

The way we suffer also brings God glory. Jesus said a man was blind from birth so that "the works of God should be revealed in him" (John 9:3 NKJV). First Peter 4:16 tells us to glorify God when we suffer as a Christian.

Also, we glorify God in our bodies when we resist sexual immorality (1 Corinthian 6:18–20). Because the Holy Spirit dwells in our bodies, they belong to God, not to ourselves. We magnify God by how we treat our bodies.

The way we face death, endure trials, resist sin, and keep God's temple pure—these all glorify God as much as bearing fruit does.

*Holy Father, may my life and my death, my successes and sufferings,
and my choices regarding holiness all bring You honor and glory.*

ALL-PURPOSE CLEANER

*Then Peter. . .asked, "Lord, how often should I forgive
someone who sins against me? Seven times?"
"No, not seven times," Jesus replied,
"but seventy times seven!"*
MATTHEW 18:21–22 NLT

Feelings of resentment, anger, jealousy, and revenge can be cleansed
away by one solution—forgiving those who offend us. When Jesus told
Peter to forgive 490 times, He meant an unlimited amount. Forgive as
often as it takes. It's not easy, but it works. Here's how:

1. Ask God for help. Forgiveness is a spiritual matter, requiring
   God's power and enablement.
2. Read God's words about forgiveness: Matthew 6:12–15;
   Mark 11:25–26; Ephesians 4:32; Colossians 3:13.
3. Read God's words about the evils of vengeance: Romans
   12:17–21; 1 Peter 3:8–12.
4. Verbalize forgiveness. Tell God, "I forgive [the offender] for
   [the offense]. Ask God to forgive the offender, too.

Even though we cannot forget what happened, that's okay. When
it shoves back into our thinking, we must substitute this thought
instead—*I have forgiven this person because I am a sinner too, and God
has graciously forgiven me.*

*Forgiving Father, thank You for wiping me clean. Help me to forget
the past and look forward to what lies ahead—the heavenly prize,
when because of Christ, I will enjoy Your presence forever.*

WORTH THE RISK

All these died in faith, without receiving the promises. . .having confessed
that they were strangers and exiles on the earth. For those who say
such things make it clear that they are seeking a country
of their own. . .that is, a heavenly one.
HEBREWS 11:13–16 NASB

On October 12, 1492, a sailor on the *Pinta* spotted land. Christopher
Columbus named it San Salvador, meaning Holy Savior, to honor the
One who answered their prayers. By sailing to an unknown destination,
Columbus braved the ocean with no assurance that he would ever
return home. He risked everything, trusting in Providence.

Several Bible people did likewise, as Hebrews 11 points out.
We can imitate their faith and risk our earthly lives for God and His
promises. Like Sarah, who considered God faithful (verse 11). Or
Moses, who considered "the reproach of Christ [to be] greater riches
than the treasures of Egypt" (verse 26 NASB).

Columbus's mission was also a journey of faith. Toward the end, the
needle on his compass had started pointing northwest instead of to the
North Star. His pilots grew fearful and anxious. Allegedly they threatened
to sail back to Spain, but Columbus convinced them to press on.

In our spiritual voyage, we too are prone to fear. When the
circumstances we see make us anxious, we must push on, "as seeing
Him who is unseen" (verse 27). Someday we will land on heavenly
shores and know our hardships and hazards were worthwhile.

Faithful Father, You promise to reward those who diligently seek You.
May I be one whose faith pleases You and who endures to the end.

RESCUED

"Sirs, what must I do to be saved?" So they said,
"Believe on the Lord Jesus Christ, and you will be saved."
ACTS 16:30–31 NKJV

. . . .

Many people think that we have to qualify for heaven, that gaining eternal life is like being in a deep ditch with slippery sides. We scramble up as much as we can. God reaches down and does the rest.

This misconception has two problems. First, God does not need our help! Jesus paid the penalty for our sins when He died in our place and said, "It is finished," meaning: "Paid in full!" Second, the Bible says that eternal life is a free gift. We can do nothing to earn it, deserve it, or pay God back. We receive it by faith, not by works. "For by grace you have been saved through faith, and that not of yourselves; it is the gift of God, not of works" (Ephesians 2:8–9 NKJV).

A better analogy for eternal life pictures us drowning in sin. We cannot save ourselves. The nail-pierced hand of Jesus reaches out to us. If our response is, "Lord, save me!" He does. Whoever believes in Him will "not perish but have everlasting life" (John 3:16 NKJV).

Where are you spiritually? Still in the slippery ditch, trying in vain to claw your way up to God? Or have you trusted in Christ alone to rescue you from sin and save you forever?

. . . .

Lord Jesus, I am a sinner who deserves the punishment of spiritual death.
Thank You for dying in my place and guaranteeing me eternal
life because I have put my faith in You and nothing else.

CARNAL CHRISTIANS

*But put on the Lord Jesus Christ, and make no
provision for the flesh in regard to its lusts.*
ROMANS 13:14 NASB

. . . .

Some people believe that a person who stops living like a Christian
wasn't one in the first place. But the Bible tells about a prodigal son
(who was still a son), men who turned away or strayed from the truth
(2 Timothy), disciples who forsook Jesus or denied knowing Him, and
carnal believers (1 Corinthians 3). Not to mention the Old Testament
saints who messed up big-time.

When we believe in Jesus, we become a child of God (John 1:18),
and a child can never undo her parentage. She may legally change her
name and never contact her parents again, but that does not cancel her
DNA. Even when we act and feel like an unbeliever, that does not negate
God's promise of eternal life to everyone who believes. Jesus' death and
resurrection paid for our sins so we can have the gift of eternal life and
never perish (John 3:16). His promise is as good as His word.

When Christians continue making provisions for the flesh and
persist in sinful lifestyles, it does have consequences. If we deny Christ,
He will deny us spiritual blessings and the reward of reigning with Him
(2 Timothy 2:12–13). We also lose out on fellowship with Him, but we
never lose Him. A Christian may turn her back on God, but God will
never reject her.

. . . .

*Lord Jesus, help me to wear You like a garment, surrounding myself
with Your life and power so I will be a good and faithful servant.*

KNOWING CHRIST MEANS OBEYING HIM

We know that we have come to know him if we keep his commands.
1 JOHN 2:3 NIV

· ·

When we trust in Jesus as our Savior from sin, we believe in Him for eternal life. This decision guarantees that we will live forever with Him in eternity (John 3:14–17). Our assurance is based on God's promise (John 5:24), not on our behavior. However, God wants His children to live for Him during their time on earth. Paul's life goal was to magnify Christ with his life (Philippians 1:20–21). He called it "knowing Christ" and knowing the power of His resurrection, participating in His sufferings, and becoming like Him in His death (Philippians 3:10).

How do Christians *know* Christ? By obeying His Word and living as He did (1 John 2:5–6). How do Christians *obey* Christ? By loving. Jesus said all the commands hang on these two: "Love the Lord your God with all your heart and with all your soul and with all your mind" and "Love your neighbor as yourself" (Matthew 22:37–40). God knows that life works best when we obey, and that means loving God and people.

Christ's resurrection power enables us to obey. "Becoming like Him in His death" means living the self-denying life of the cross—death to being selfish, to indulging sinful passions, and to demanding our own way.

· ·

Father in heaven, thank You for bringing me to the cross of Christ, where all my sins were forgiven and I received Your gift of new life because I believed. As Your child, I want to live for You by being obedient. It's the least I can do in gratitude for Your salvation.

GRAD COURSES

"Take my yoke upon you and learn from me."
MATTHEW 11:29 NIV

. . . .

Considering God's training process, Jesus does seem like a hard task-master occasionally. He may appear to ignore our sacrifices or let us get knocked down when we are serving Him best. Sometimes He denies us what He freely gives to others. This reminds us that we work for Him, not for ourselves, not for the people we're trying to help, and not for God's gifts and blessings.

Rather than being hard, He is our wise and loving coach. He disciplines us, putting us through rigorous training to develop our spiritual muscles. Like a doctor who hurts in order to help his patients, God gives us what we need. It may be that our suffering will glorify Him best.

First Corinthians 10:13 says we will not be tempted beyond our endurance because we can always escape [by saying no]; however, 2 Corinthians 1:8–9 (NIV) indicates that we can be tested "far beyond our ability to endure," even despairing of life. This happens so that "we might not rely on ourselves but on God."

When God's curriculum and tests overwhelm us and we feel like dropping out, we can look forward to our glorious future. At "commencement," we will be forever with the Lord.

. . . .

Lord Jesus, when I face more than I can bear, remind me that I am yoked with You, and Your yoke is easy when I submit to it. I give up my self-reliance and surrender to Your ways. You promise me rest when I come to You with my burdens. Thank You for carrying my load today.

IT'S ALIVE!

But if you look carefully into the perfect law that sets you free,
and if you do what it says. . .God will bless you for doing it.
JAMES 1:25 NLT

Reading God's Word has many benefits. First, the Bible reveals God's heart like a "love letter," nurturing our fellowship with Him. His love is not a mere feeling—it's a fact that gives us confidence to keep trusting Him. Therefore, as we grow in our knowledge about God, we love Him more.

Second, the Bible explains how to live God's way. When we obey God, we will avoid sinful habits, along with the guilt and regrets they cause.

Third, God's Word has power to transform us. Mysteriously, it is "alive and powerful" (Hebrews 4:12) and works effectively in us (1 Thessalonians 2:13). Jesus said, "Blessed are all who hear the word of God and put it into practice" (Luke 11:28 NLT).

Want to field-test this? What is currently your greatest need or concern? Find verses that deal with that issue and write them out. Choose one to memorize. Every time that problem pesters you, wield your sword (quote your verse) and ask God for help. Romans 10:13 promises that when we call on the name of the Lord, we will be delivered (saved or rescued).

In a few weeks you will find the problem or temptation diminishing. When we keep responding to the seed of God's Word and using it in our lives, it grows and bears fruit even when we don't realize it.

Dear Lord, thank You for being the Lover of my soul
and for speaking to me through Your written word.

USE IT OR LOSE IT

"Therefore consider carefully how you listen."
LUKE 8:18 NIV

Doing God's Word, not merely hearing it, was one of Jesus' repeated themes. His parable of the sower illustrated four different responses we can have whenever the seed of the Word of God hits our thinking. With a hard heart, we will have no response and the truth will disappear as if *stolen*. A rocky heart *starves* the seed, not allowing it to take root. If our heart is cluttered with weeds of worldly cares, the seed gets *strangled*. But with a positive response to truth, we *sustain* it and let it change us, producing fruit in our lives.

Jesus concluded by saying that the more truth we learn and practice, the more God will reveal. But if we stop using what we learn, we will lose even what we thought we had (Matthew 13:12; Mark 4:24–25; Luke 8:18). If we do nothing with the seed, it can do nothing for us.

This principle reminds me to evaluate what I do with truth from God. When I read His Word or hear a sermon, do I respond to Him obediently? Does it correct my behavior, shape my worldview, and get all the way to my fingers and feet? Like panning for gold, the more I seek, the more I will discover. James 1:25 says that continuing in God's Word—not forgetting what we hear, but doing it—makes us blessed in what we do.

Perfect Father, every time I encounter Your Word, help me to respond positively and use it so that Your truth will grow and bear fruit in me.

God Sees and Hears

*"You shall call his name Ishmael, because the LORD has heard
your affliction." Then she called the name of the LORD
who spoke to her, You-Are-the-God-Who-Sees.*
Genesis 16:11, 13 NKJV

. . . .

Scripture gives the account of a woman who was marginalized, who had
no voice, who was used sexually and treated harshly. Yet God met her
in the wilderness. He spoke to her and let her speak. Then He told her
what to do and she obeyed. Who was it? Hagar—a maid servant, an
Egyptian, not a Hebrew, a woman of no social status, and yet she was
the first person in scripture to whom the Angel of the Lord appeared. He
sent her back to the place of her suffering but gave her promises regarding
her unborn son: he would become a great nation; he would be free and
independent, hold his own in conflict, and live in the presence of his
brethren. Believing what God said and knowing that Ishmael would not
be a servant like she was gave her courage to face her conflicts back home.

She obeyed because of who God was. He was the *Ishmael*—God-
who-hears—and the *El Roi*—God-who-sees. Other Bible people named
the place where God encountered them; Hagar alone gave God Himself
a new name.

When we are stuck in undesirable circumstances and wish we could
run away, we can endure suffering if that's what God wants because He
has promised never to leave us or forsake us.

. . . .

*My ever-present God, in my wilderness places, thank You for
seeing all my needs and hearing all my pleas.*

SARAH'S CHOICE

Then the LORD said to Abraham, "Why did Sarah laugh?
Why did she say, 'Can an old woman like me have a baby?'
Is anything too hard for the LORD?"
GENESIS 18:13–14 NLT

Every time Sarah called her son's name, it reminded her of laughter—Isaac means "laughter." Sarah had a choice. She could recall her embarrassment at doubting God's promise or remember the joy of its fulfillment.

We cannot blame this postmenopausal woman for thinking that having her first baby at the age of ninety was funny, but then she tried to cover her tracks by denying she laughed. But the Lord said, "No, you did laugh" (18:15 NLT). Sarah must have regretted how she acted and what she said that day.

"Is anything too hard for the LORD?" does not mean we should expect God to do the impossible for us. It means that what God had promised Abraham, He would do, no matter how impossible it seemed. Sarah learned this firsthand when her skepticism turned to joy. God redeemed her barrenness, and Sarah got the joke! She said, "God has brought me laughter. All who hear about this will laugh with me. Who would have said to Abraham that Sarah would nurse a baby?" (Genesis 21:6–7).

Like Sarah, we all regret some of our past actions and words, but we must not let them control us. We can choose to rejoice in God's forgiveness rather than ruminate about what we should have done.

Promise-keeping God, thank You for doing the impossible—forgiving
my past, giving me strength for today, and guaranteeing
my future with You forever.

GUILT REMOVAL

*If we confess our sins, He is faithful and just to forgive us our sins
and to cleanse us from all unrighteousness.*
1 JOHN 1:9 NKJV

Sometimes we don't feel forgiven. Even though we have believed that
Christ's death and resurrection paid the penalty for all our sins and we
now have eternal life, we still sin. First John 1:9 tells us believers to
confess our sins to God, and He cleanses us. What if we still feel guilty?
Some people say we should forgive ourselves. This is not a biblical
concept, but it probably means accepting God's forgiveness. If feelings
of guilt return every time we recall what we have done, perhaps we are
still grieving the losses a particular sin has caused. Sin can be forgiven
and restitution can be made, but most consequences are permanent.
Something broke like an egg when we sinned, and it cannot be fixed
in this life. Yet God can redeem it for good. Failures can keep us
dependent on Him and give us empathy for others.

Two things will help us "feel" forgiven. (1) Thanking God for His
promise that we are cleansed "from all unrighteousness." The promise is
as sure as God is. And (2) Meditating on Galatians 5:1 (NKJV): "Stand
fast therefore in the liberty by which Christ has made us free, and do
not be entangled again with a yoke of bondage." Stand victorious in the
truth that Christ has freed us from our sin and guilt. It cannot enslave
us again unless we let it.

*Dear Lord, although I don't deserve Your mercy and grace,
I gratefully accept Your complete forgiveness.*

REGRETFULLY YOURS

By the mercies of God. . .present your bodies a living and holy sacrifice,
acceptable to God, which is your spiritual service of worship. And do not
be conformed to this world, but be transformed by the renewing of
your mind, so that you may prove what the will of God is,
that which is good and acceptable and perfect.
ROMANS 12:1–2 NASB

Regrettably, no one gets through life without regrets. Some nag us occasionally; others confront us daily. Even Jesus had regrets. Not from His own decisions, but from the unbelief and attacks of the people around Him. He responded with weeping at times, and by saying, "Father, forgive them."

Often we likewise regret how others have hurt us. And we deal with relationship conflicts, accidents, age and health issues, crime and corruption, along with burdens others impose on us. For situations beyond our control, Romans 12:1–2 offers the best way of handling hurts and regrets. Based on God's mercy, we can offer our lives and circumstances as a sacrifice to Him. We may struggle in doing this, but trusting God is the only safe option. Saying, "Your will be done," is a worshipful response that can become our mind-set for facing all of life's difficulties. We also need God's Word transforming our thinking. A renewed mind prevents us from conforming to the world's philosophies and temptations.

What will result? We will discover that God's will is good and acceptable and perfect for us. Knowing this truth nullifies regrets.

Merciful God, thank You for accepting what I offer up to You.
Please take me—body, mind, and will. I surrender all.

Dealing with Depression

"My grace is all you need. My power works best in weakness."
2 Corinthians 12:9 NLT

. . . .

A grief response to loss feels a lot like depression. Having been widowed twice, Elisabeth Elliot knew that feeling well. A poem that helped her is called "Do the Next Thing." We may feel like we can't go to work or carry out our responsibilities, but we should do them anyway. There is power in obeying. Before God parted the Jordan River, the priests had to step into the water (Joshua 3). God gives strength when we take the first step. He has promised to exchange His power for our weakness.

As a missionary, Elisabeth Elliot served the tribal people of Ecuador, including those who martyred her first husband. Her work as a speaker and author of more than twenty books is timeless. Schooling herself in the poetry of Amy Carmichael, Elisabeth often quoted Amy's poem "In Acceptance Lieth Peace." We may seek solace in denial, busyness, withdrawal, or defeatist attitudes (martyrdom), but God's peace comes from accepting the "breaking sorrow, which God tomorrow will to His [child] explain."

Often when we feel depressed, we want to hibernate and brood, but that does nothing to change our condition. Telling God we accept His will and timing pacifies internal chaos. Then, choosing to move—to do something useful—will improve our mood.

. . . .

Gracious Father, I know You are wise and loving and good even when I don't feel that could possibly be true. Although I cannot see You with my limited understanding, I want to trust You and do the right things. Help me, Lord.

IT ALL BELONGS TO HIM

*He does as he pleases with the powers of heaven and the peoples
of the earth. No one can hold back his hand
or say to him: "What have you done?"*
DANIEL 4:35 NIV

Elisabeth Elliot wrote about her first years on the mission field in her book *These Strange Ashes*. She went to Ecuador to help break down the Quichua language. God sent her a national Christian helper who knew both Spanish and Quichua, which helped greatly. After only a few weeks, however, shots rang out—the Christian helper had been murdered. Elisabeth had to continue as best she could on her own.

After two years, she accomplished her mission of developing an alphabet system. By that time, Jim Elliot had asked her to marry him, so she put all her linguistics work into a suitcase and gave it to a coworker. The suitcase was stolen, never to be found. Elisabeth decided it was God's work, not hers, and He could do whatever He wanted with it. The servant has no right to advise or question her Master.

Often God's ways bewilder us. However, figuring Him out is not our responsibility—trusting Him is. Nebuchadnezzar learned that lesson after seven years of insanity. Job learned it after losing everything except his embittered wife. God knows what He's doing in our lives, and that means we don't have to.

*Oh Lord, You are merciful. You don't give me what I deserve or I would
be miserable and hopeless. You are gracious in giving me what
I need, even if it pains me at times. I submit to You.*

ENJOY YOUR ROLE

*The head of every man is Christ, and the head of the woman
is man, and the head of Christ is God.*
1 CORINTHIANS 11:3 NIV

In the 1960s American society began to commend "doing your own thing." People called it freedom because it broke established limits. While segregation boundaries needed to be eliminated, society's moral values did not. The book of Judges portrays the downward spiral that results from everyone doing what is right in their own eyes. Being a law unto ourselves will never work in society, in schools, in churches, or in families. Why are companies called organizations? Because things run properly when order is followed.

The Bible tells us to submit to government authorities (Romans 13:1–7), to spiritual leaders in our local churches (Hebrews 13:17), and to our husbands (Ephesians 5:22–24). One of the results of being filled with the Spirit is submitting to one another (Ephesians 5:21). The Greek word for "submitting" does not mean being controlled by another, but placing oneself under someone's authority. Will our leaders and husbands always be right? No, but they are responsible, before God, for us. The husband's role is to lead lovingly; the wife's role is to follow respectfully. This in no way implies inferiority. In God's eyes, all men and women are equal in importance and value, but we have different responsibilities. Everyone's role is necessary for harmonious function.

*Lord, with Your help, I want to resist having a rebellious attitude toward
those who are in authority over me. Help me to respect and support
them and to do things their way when I should.*

Time Management Tips

*He who tills his land will have plenty of food, but he who
follows empty pursuits will have poverty in plenty.*
Proverbs 28:19 NASB

. . . .

The tension between what we want to do and what we need to do is a
daily battle. Running a household requires a certain amount of structure
and self-discipline. A wise mother of six mentored me by offering five
simple principles to help everything run more smoothly:

1. Plan ahead. Decide at breakfast what to have for dinner.
2. Practice finishing. A chore is done when all materials are
   put away. Wake up to a clean kitchen by tidying the night
   before.
3. Reward positive results. Make chore charts for yourself and
   family members. Use screen time and hobbies as incentives.
4. Restrain impulsiveness. Keep a list of errands to do, rather
   than running out each time you need something.
5. Stop collecting. Everything we possess needs stored, dusted,
   or maintained. Is that how I want to spend my time?

I developed good habits through practicing one of these suggestions
for a month. The next month I worked on another one. It kept chaos to a
minimum while I was raising and training my own six children.

. . . .

*Father, show me where I need to restrain my tendency toward
self-indulgence and retrain myself to use time wisely.*

MOSES CHOSE ETERNAL REWARDS

Choosing rather to suffer affliction with the people of God than to enjoy the passing pleasures of sin, esteeming the reproach of Christ greater riches than the treasures in Egypt; for he looked to the reward.
HEBREWS 11:25–26 NKJV

How could affliction and reproach be a greater goal than ruling a country and owning fabulous wealth? Human thinking would see Moses as accomplishing great things for God by becoming Pharaoh and freeing the Hebrew slaves. But then Moses would get the credit, and no one would witness the power of the one true God. Even though Moses experienced failure, exile, and a forty-year-long wait, God could only use a humble servant. Moses chose to lay up treasure in heaven, even if it meant giving up the fortune he deserved on earth.

This eternal perspective kept Moses from enjoying sin's temporary pleasures. Instead of looking at the benefits of being the son of Pharaoh's daughter (Hebrews 11:24), he focused on spiritual things, choosing "the reproach of Christ" and enduring "as seeing Him who is invisible" (11:26–27 NKJV). Moses lived for eternal, not earthly, rewards.

As Christians, we get to choose our focus and the goals we devote our lives to. While eternal life is a free gift, not a reward, to everyone who believes in Christ, the Bible also teaches that believers will receive rewards in heaven for being "good and faithful servants."

Lord, I want to remember that my life here is a temporary one so that my choices will glorify You. Make me willing to give up human pleasures in exchange for future joys at Your right hand forever.

Spiritual CPR

How long, O Lord? Will You forget me forever?
How long will You hide Your face from me?
Psalm 13:1 nasb

. . . .

Our feelings do not determine our relationship with God. Since euphoria is not necessarily spiritual joy, feeling numb is not a sign of unspirituality—it's a grief emotion. Nevertheless, Psalm 13 gives a formula for times when we feel like God is gone—two verses each for Complaints, Petition, and Resolve (CPR!).

While we should not question God as if He goofed, it is okay to ask God questions. He may not answer, but He can handle our complaints. The writer asks God how long his suffering will continue. He feels like God is absent, his heart is filled with sorrow every day, and his enemies are winning.

So he petitions God to hear and answer, to put light back into his eyes, or else he will continue to feel dead, and his enemies will gloat over him. He *complains*, he *prays*, and then he *resolves* to trust God now as he has in the past. By remembering God's loving-kindness and rejoicing in the way God will deliver him, he can count on God's bountiful nature.

Two exercises will help us when afflicted—rejoicing in the Lord and singing to the Lord (Psalm 13:5–6). List things you are thankful for or think about God's attributes A to Z. Choose a praise song to play or sing throughout the day.

Suffering can cause doubt and fear to attack our hearts, but performing CPR will revive our weak faith.

. . . .

Oh Lord, I cast all my cares upon You, because You care for me.

Undeserved Suffering

Rise up, be our help, and redeem us for the sake of Your lovingkindness.
Psalm 44:26 nasb

. . . .

God's loyal love is based on His character, not on our conduct. He doesn't always reward our righteousness in this life, and at times He inexplicably seems to mistreat us despite our faithfulness. He gives victory and allows defeat, but He is merciful. Psalm 44 expresses this well.

Attributed to the Sons of Korah, Psalm 44 has a literary structure that forms a step pyramid (ziggurat). Ten lines (verses 1–8) comprise the bottom step and recount God's *past deliverance* of Israel. The next step up has eight lines (verses 9–16) describing their *present defeat* and disgrace. Then six lines (verses 17–22) present the *people's defense*: they had done nothing wrong. The last four lines (verses 23–26) express their *perplexing dilemma*: God seems to be asleep, hidden, and forgetful.

What is the answer? The psalm gives no solution. The answer is— God does not have to give answers. We can ask God for deliverance, but it's up to Him. His discipline process often chastises our sin, but mostly it trains our character.

The structure of the psalm draws the reader's attention upward to the point at the top of the pyramid. In Hebrew, the last word of the psalm is "loving-kindness." We must trust God's loyal love despite what we are going through. Our circumstances can never negate His faithfulness.

. . . .

Loving Father, though You may cause grief, You show compassion. Because of Your mercies, we are not consumed. Your loving-kindnesses never cease. They are new every morning. Great is Your faithfulness.

Three Good Things

*Concerning this thing I pleaded with the Lord
three times that it might depart from me.*
2 Corinthians 12:8 nkjv

. . . .

When bad things happen to us, we often ask God to show us why. God is not obliged to reveal His reasons this side of heaven. We trust His character even when we don't understand His ways. It may be that He wants us to rest in Him, not figure Him out. When we cannot know *why* (Psalm 44), we can still know *who* (Psalm 46).

Afflictions have benefits when we accept them as what God wants. They prune us, develop our character, and help us relate to fellow-sufferers. Tears teach lessons we could not learn any other way. Sometimes we get dependence on God, not deliverance by God.

When Paul wrestled with his thorn in the flesh, he eventually stopped asking God to remove it. He realized a "messenger of Satan to buffet" him resulted in at least three good things. Because of how God was using him and giving him revelations, he would be tempted to exalt himself, but this piercing barb extinguished pride (12:7). He experienced God's sufficient grace (12:9), and it made him exchange his weakness for God's strength (12:10). Therefore, Paul delighted in his infirmities (12:10). Instead of hindering his ministry for God, somehow they enhanced what God accomplished through him.

It might be a good spiritual discipline to think of three good things for each of the irreversible circumstances and physical ailments we experience.

. . . .

*Wise and sovereign Father, help me to stop wrestling and to realize
benefits that can result from my flaws and frailties.*

"BE STILL" MEANS STOP STRIVING

God is our refuge and strength, an ever-present help in trouble.
PSALM 46:1 NIV

News broadcasts distress us daily. We may be living in the time of "wars and rumors of wars" that Jesus predicted in Matthew 24:6. He added, "See to it that you are not alarmed. Such things must happen, but the end is still to come" (NIV). Because God is our refuge (fortress) and strength, we need not fear. Even when natural disasters strike (Psalm 46:2–3). Even during national conflicts (46:6). Note the refrain in verses 7 and 11 (NLT): "The Lord of Heaven's Armies is here among us." *Who could defend us better?* "The God of Israel [our personal God] is our fortress." *What better protection could we have?* God is also working to end all wars (46:8–9). He will win and be exalted in the end (46:10), which is sure to come.

In light of this, how should we respond? When verse 10 tells the nations to be still and know He is God, it means they should stop striving, lay down their arms. God will do the fighting and will eventually end all conflicts. Isaiah 2 is a parallel passage that describes the latter days when metal will be used for farming and fishing tools, not for weapons.

We can personalize this psalm by remembering to let God fight our battles. Stop striving and know that He is God, our refuge and strength.

Almighty God, I run to You for refuge. I depend on You for strength. Help me to stop fighting for my rights and let You be God! I rest in You.

Everything We Need

I want you to remember what the holy prophets said long ago
and what our Lord and Savior commanded through your apostles.
2 Peter 3:2 NLT

. . . .

If you want a word from God, read God's Word. That's how God
speaks today. Usually what we think of as God's voice is really our own
minds telling us something. It happens to believers and unbelievers, to
people in false religions, to atheists, to everyone—not only to Christians
indwelt by the Holy Spirit. But when we Christians get a great idea
or feel inspired, we claim God spoke to us in a special way. Isn't that
prideful?

Peter witnessed Jesus' life, even seeing His glory and hearing God's
audible voice during the Transfiguration, but he told his readers to
grow in their knowledge of God and Jesus by observing "the message
proclaimed by the prophets" (2 Peter 1:19 NLT). "Everything we need
for living a godly life" comes from "great and precious promises," not
from supernatural experiences (2 Peter 1:3–4 NLT).

Scripture never tells us to seek a special word from God. We can
ask for wisdom during trials (James 1:2–5), but for us who have the
Bible in our own languages, that is sufficient. We live by faith in the
facts, found in God's written revelation, not by our feelings.

. . . .

Lord, I often desire for You to bless me in special ways. Instead, help me to
grow in grace and wisdom through learning and doing Your Word every day.

TRICKED AND MISTREATED

*Then when lust has conceived, it gives birth to sin; and when sin
is accomplished, it brings forth death. Do not be
deceived, my beloved brethren.*
JAMES 1:15–16 NASB

Why does Halloween focus on death and abound with satanic symbols?
Possibly because Satan is the ultimate trickster. He counterfeits God's
methods, and his modus operandi is deception and death. By mixing
truth with lies, he deceives us into thinking little sins don't count; no
one will ever know; I'll only try this once; how can something that feels
so good be bad?

We forget that unconfessed sin escalates into habits and eventually
addictions. Sometimes consequences are irreversible. That's why we
must deal quickly and drastically with sin. Small weeds are easily pulled
out, but those that take root and grow require stronger measures.

God has promised that our temptations will not be more than we
can bear (1 Corinthians 10:13). Why? Because He has provided "the
way of escape"—just say no! Sin's sources are the world, our own flesh,
and the devil. We must flee from sin (1 Corinthians 6:18; 1 Timothy
6:11; 2 Timothy 2:22), but we can make Satan flee from us by resisting
him (James 4:7; 1 Peter 5:9). When we access the full armor of God, we
will "stand firm against the schemes of the devil" (Ephesians 6:11 NASB).

*Most Holy One, help me to grieve over what grieves You. Sin's pleasures can
trick me into forgetting the consequences. Give me strength and wisdom
to extinguish Satan's fiery darts as well as my evil desires,
before they kindle destructive fires that I will regret.*

CLOTHED

She is clothed with strength and dignity;
she can laugh at the days to come.
PROVERBS 31:25 NIV

You, as a daughter of the Most High, are clothed with strength and dignity. In those moments when you feel particularly vulnerable and naked, just remember—you are clothed with the strength that God gives you and with the dignity of being His image bearer.

No matter the circumstance, you are valued because you are one of God's children. Just like a child who looks so much like his father that it's obvious they're family, you bear your heavenly Father's image. You clearly belong to Him and are loved by Him as part of His family. The value and dignity that God places on you are more significant than whatever the society or anyone else tells you your value is.

Even when you feel totally beaten down and think there is no way you can continue, all you need to do is ask for God's strength. He will clothe you in it to cover up all your vulnerability and brokenness.

No wonder the woman in this verse could laugh at the future. She knew that in God she had limitless strength and a dignity that no one could take away. Nothing in her future, or yours, could change that.

Lord, thank You that I am clothed with strength and dignity.
Nothing on this earth can take away the dignity I have as
Your daughter or break the strength that You offer me.

DO NOT FEAR

*"Do not fear, for I am with you; do not anxiously look about you,
for I am your God. I will strengthen you, surely I will help you,
surely I will uphold you with My righteous right hand."*
ISAIAH 41:10 NASB

Fear can seep into our lives so easily. We fear the unknowns of the
future. We fear we didn't handle a certain situation as well as we should
have. We fear we are too inadequate, or too busy, or too unmotivated to
handle the things being thrown at us in the present.

In this verse, God tells you not to fear. This isn't just an idle, "don't
worry, you'll be okay" kind of statement. In fact, He *commands* you not
to fear. How can He be so confident that you are completely safe so that
He can command you not to fear? Because He is with you. The God
who created, sustains, and governs this entire world is with you. With
that perspective, what is there to fear?

Stop looking anxiously around you at all the burdens, worries,
and fears of your life. Instead, focus on your God. He promises to
strengthen and help you. Nothing in this world is so overwhelming that
you cannot overcome it with the almighty God's strength. Even when
you feel that you have fallen with no strength to get up, He promises to
hold you up with His hand.

*Lord, help me to fully understand that You are with me,
strengthening me, helping me, and holding me in Your hands.*

DAUGHTER

And He said to her, "Daughter, your faith has made you well;
go in peace and be healed of your affliction."
MARK 5:34 NASB

. . . .

The woman in this passage had suffered greatly from an affliction that made her ceremonially unclean; she was an outcast, not able to participate in society. In an act of desperation, she pushed through the thick crowd to Jesus and touched His garments. When Jesus turned around and asked who had touched Him, she fell in fear and trembling at His feet and told her whole story. This woman had probably been in shameful hiding for many years and now, in front of a large crowd, recounted her humiliating story. Probably some of the spectators were repulsed by her story, and yet Jesus, in front of the whole crowd, called her "daughter." Can you imagine how it must have felt to this rejected and shamed woman to hear herself called "daughter"—a term of belonging and love?

You also have been adopted and called a daughter of God. Don't hide your shame and struggles from Him. In circumstances where you can hardly stand up under the weight of your burden, fall at His feet as this woman did. You will not be rejected or shamed by Him. He calls you daughter. He loves you and is able to heal you.

. . . .

Lord, may I have the same faith that this woman had.
Thank You for making me Your daughter.

Trust and Lean

*Trust in the LORD with all your heart and do not lean
on your own understanding.*
Proverbs 3:5 NASB

This verse contains two commands—trust in the Lord and don't rely on your own understanding.

Do you trust in God? You can rely on God because He is truly trustworthy—He has the strength to sustain, help, and protect you and an incomprehensible love for you that cannot be broken or grow stale. You are not bringing your prayers before someone who is powerful but fickle, or one who is loving and good, but weak. You pray to a God who is all-powerful, but also good and loving. Therefore, you can be confident that your life is placed firmly in His hands and His control and that He considers it precious.

How often do you lean on your own understanding and strength instead of God's? You are remarkably less capable of controlling your life than God is. Instead of trusting yourself, someone who doesn't know the future and certainly can't control it, lean on the all-powerful God who knows each step you will take. Relinquish all your anxious thoughts over to His control. Trusting God with your future is far more productive than worrying about it. So lean on Him and trust Him with *everything* in your heart. He will sustain you.

*Lord, forgive me for not trusting You as I should. Forgive me for leaning
on my own understanding instead of relying on Your infinite wisdom
and strength. Thank You that these commands You
give me are for my greatest benefit.*

Acknowledge God

In all your ways acknowledge Him,
and He will make your paths straight.
Proverbs 3:6 nasb

. . . .

When do you acknowledge God? Do you acknowledge Him when things are going well by thanking Him for the blessings in your life? Or maybe when things aren't going well, you realize that you need His help.

This verse commands you to acknowledge God in *all* your ways. When things are going well, praise Him, because everything good comes from His hand. Have a grateful heart and look for ways to bless others with the bounty that God has given you.

When things are not going well, pray to Him; pour out your heart to Him (Psalm 68:2). He loves you in ways that you cannot even comprehend. He wants you to come before Him. Even in the deepest grief, still praise Him—He has loved you enough to die on your behalf, securing your salvation so you can spend eternity with Him. That is something that no circumstance can take away.

When life feels mundane and meaningless, acknowledge that He has put you where you are for a reason and that He will not waste your time or your talents. Worship Him while you wait for the next step in life.

God promises that when you acknowledge Him in all your ways, He will make your paths straight. What a comfort that He will guide you and lead you on the path you should take.

. . . .

Lord, I acknowledge that You are sovereign and loving in the circumstance
that I am in right now. Continue to lead me down a straight path.

Dust

Just as a father has compassion on his children, so the Lord has compassion on those who fear Him. For He Himself knows our frame;
He is mindful that we are but dust.
Psalm 103:13–14 nasb

Do you ever feel weak or inconsequential, like the slightest wind of difficulty could just blow you away? These verses tell you that you are but dust and that God is aware of that. That doesn't sound very encouraging, does it? But in actuality, great strength can be gleaned from this truth.

The Lord knows your frame. He knows that at times you are prone to weakness and worry and lack the strength to continue. So if you are harboring guilt that you have not lived up to some heavenly standard that you feel God has placed on you, release that guilt. He is mindful of what you are capable of and doesn't ask that you be some kind of superwoman. This is not an excuse for complacency or laziness, but an encouragement that your efforts are recognized and smiled on by God.

Even though you are but a speck of dust in the history of the universe, God has compassion on you and knows you as a father knows his child. How stunning! It doesn't matter that you sometimes feel weak and inconsequential—the Most High God knows and loves you. In that truth resides all the strength and value you need.

Lord, thank You that You know my frame. Please grant me
the strength and value that I long for.

LOVE IN THE DARK

This I recall to my mind, therefore I have hope. The LORD's loving-kindnesses indeed never cease, for His compassions never fail. They are new every morning; great is Your faithfulness.
LAMENTATIONS 3:21–23 NASB

. . . .

This is a familiar and beautiful passage. The Lord will always show you loving-kindness. He will never cease to have compassion on you. He is forever faithful. And yet, if you are going through a time when God's love seems farther away than it's ever been, you may think these sentiments are only for those who are experiencing good things in their lives.

Though these verses are familiar, they are almost always taken out of context. These verses are a small island of hope in an otherwise desolate chapter. The author of these verses is suffering deeply. He is greatly afflicted and nearly without hope. Even in the deepest pit of despair, he has the experience to back up his claims that God's love has never ceased from his life. When you go through a dark period in your life, be encouraged by the testimony of this fellow child of God. God is not a fair-weather God who abandons you when the going gets rough. His love will find you and carry you through the darkest and most soul-wrenching of trials. You can have the same faith and unwavering confidence in His compassion that you have in the fact that the sun will rise in the morning. There is hope even in the darkest place.

. . . .

Lord, may I experience Your compassion in amazing ways so that I too can have faith in Your love in the midst of trials.

BLAMELESS

Now to Him who is able to keep you from stumbling, and to make you stand in the presence of His glory blameless with great joy, to the only God our Savior, through Jesus Christ our Lord, be glory, majesty, dominion and authority, before all time and now and forever. Amen.
JUDE 1:24–25 NASB

The Lord is able to keep you from stumbling. What an encouragement this is. You no longer have to fear the pitfalls and road bumps in life. Christ took the fall for you when He was separated from His Father on the cross to take away your every sin. Because He was forsaken, you never will be.

Thinking about standing in the presence of God, the ultimate Judge, can be terrifying. But this verse promises that those who are in Christ can stand completely blameless in the overwhelming glory and holiness of God. Your sins are no match for Christ's sacrifice; therefore, they have been washed completely away and totally obliterated. You can come into the presence of God with great joy. What a beautiful thing to know that no matter what happens in this life, you have an eternity of time to spend with God in unspeakable joy as a blameless and loved child.

The Lord holds all glory, majesty, dominion, and authority from eternity past, present, and future. He is the God who protects and cares for you—of course He can keep you from stumbling.

Lord, thank You for the beautiful promise that I can look forward to standing in Your presence with great joy, totally blameless and loved.

HOPE

Now may the God of hope fill you with all joy and peace in believing,
so that you will abound in hope by the power of the Holy Spirit.
ROMANS 15:13 NASB

. . . .

Hope is something that can easily be marred and destroyed. It seems almost like a childlike, naïve concept. In the harsh world we live in, we quickly learn to not hope for things so that we won't end up disappointed.

This verse is a prayer that you would *abound* in hope. What an interesting concept, to abound in hope—to be surrounded by, filled up with, and buoyed by hope. The biblical concept of hope is a steadfast confidence that something *will* happen in the future. So what can you possibly hope for that you can be confident will come to pass?

You can hope for an eternity spent illumined by the light of your heavenly Father. You can hope for the time when God will wipe every tear from your eye. You can hope for the time when you will be reunited with all God's children who have gone before you. You can hope in a God who will never leave you and never forsake you through life on this earth and even through death. You can hope in a joyful welcome home at the end of this life. You can hope in the fact that God works everything according to His will for the good of His children. God truly is the God of hope.

. . . .

Lord, fill me with the joy and peace that come with putting my hope in You.

No Condemnation

Therefore there is now no condemnation for those who are in Christ Jesus.
ROMANS 8:1 NASB

. . . .

There is no condemnation for those who are in Christ Jesus. This means there is no room for guilt or blame in your life. Even when you do things that make you feel like you have failed God, yourself, or others, your standing before God does not change. When you are in Christ, you are clothed in the clean, holy robes of God's Son. When God looks at you, He doesn't see the sins you've committed or the things you haven't done; He sees His holy, blameless Son.

How is this possible? It's possible because Christ died in your place. The sins that would have condemned you in God's holy court were placed on Christ's shoulders and buried with Him. They have no hold over you anymore. So let go of your guilt and regret. Acknowledge that Christ's work on the cross was enough to cleanse and purify you before a holy God. Live in the freedom of the knowledge that no one and nothing can condemn you. Christ has stood in your place so that you can come boldly before the Father in the clean robes that have been washed in the blood of the Lamb. Ask for His forgiveness and claim His forgiveness in your life.

. . . .

Lord, thank You that I am not and cannot be condemned because I am in Christ. Help me to more fully understand what Christ did for me on the cross so that I can let go of the guilt and blame I so often carry.

DRAW NEAR WITH CONFIDENCE

Therefore let us draw near with confidence to the throne of grace,
so that we may receive mercy and find grace to help in time of need.
HEBREWS 4:16 NASB

In this verse you are told that you can approach God's throne with confidence. Why do you approach the throne? So that you can receive mercy and find grace to help in time of need. Why would you need to receive mercy? Those who need mercy are those who have done something wrong and are therefore not in right standing with whomever they are asking mercy from. Inevitably you come before the throne of God with the baggage of your sin. Yet you are told to come with confidence before the throne of a holy God who hates sin. You don't need to be perfect or have your act together to come before God with confidence. You only need to be covered in Christ's blood. This confidence with which you approach God's throne is not a self-confidence, but a God-confidence. It's a confidence that assures you that God is for you, that He loves you, and that He sees Christ in you. Your standing before God depends completely on His view of you and not on your own merit. He sees you as His beloved child. So go boldly to the foot of His throne, knowing that you will receive mercy and grace.

Lord, thank You that I don't need to be perfect before I can come
before You. I come before You now with my confidence
placed in You, not in my own merit.

CAST YOUR BURDEN

Cast your burden upon the LORD and He will sustain you;
He will never allow the righteous to be shaken.
PSALM 55:22 NASB

This verse assumes and acknowledges that you have a burden. Everyone has burdens. It's okay to admit that you are carrying around concerns, responsibilities, and emotional baggage that is heavy and often overwhelming. You especially should admit this to God. There is no reason to hide from God the strength-depleting and sometimes crushing burden that you are carrying. He knows all about it anyway. There is *every* reason to come to Him with it.

He asks you to give Him your burden. Just think about it. Wouldn't you be thrilled if someone came along and asked you to let go of whatever it is you're carrying and hand it over to them so that you can stand upright and use your energy in other ways, free from the heaviness of your burden? This is exactly what God is asking of you. But He is perfectly capable of carrying it. In fact, He's more capable than you are of dealing with whatever hardships you're facing. You can trust Him with your burden.

When you cast your burden on God, He will sustain you and not allow you to be shaken. What an awesome God you serve, that He would desire to come alongside you, carry your heavy load, and walk with you through life to strengthen and protect you.

Lord, I give You my heaviest burden now. Release me from its hold
and sustain me with Your hand.

TRUST IN HIS LOVING-KINDNESS

*But I have trusted in Your loving kindness; my heart shall
rejoice in Your salvation. I will sing to the LORD,
because He has dealt bountifully with me.*
PSALM 13:5–6 NASB

. . . .

How do you trust in God's loving-kindness? First, you have to believe
that He loves you, right now, as you are. Do you really believe that? Or
are you still trying to earn God's love by attempting to do enough good
things to merit His favor? Maybe you're convinced that God is merely
putting up with you and your daily failures to be perfect. Because
you have received Christ, you must believe that God loves you fully,
perfectly, and unconditionally, despite what you have or haven't done.
Isn't this the kind of love we all long for? So accept it, be humbled by it,
and be eternally grateful for it.

Because you know that God *loves* you and is *for* you, you can trust
that He will take care of you and work out everything in your life for
your good and His glory. It may be hard to comprehend how a certain
circumstance could possibly be worked out for good. But the all-powerful,
sovereign God is on your side. You can trust fully in His loving-kindness.

So praise God and rejoice in the love He has for you. He loves you
and has set you aside as one of His own. There will not be one moment
in this life, in death, or in eternity when He will not be with you. He
has indeed dealt bountifully with you!

. . . .

Lord, may I trust in Your loving-kindness more every day.

WATCH EXPECTANTLY

*But as for me, I will watch expectantly for the LORD; I will wait
for the God of my salvation. My God will hear me.*
MICAH 7:7 NASB

In this verse, Micah has prayed to God and is now waiting expectantly for what He will do. How often do you pray without really thinking that God hears or cares? Maybe you think your prayers are just too big (or too small) to matter to Him.

You pray to the sovereign and all-powerful God who loves you. This means you can pray big and often and you can expect God to act. Obviously, we don't know how God will answer a prayer, because His ways are far above our ways. So watch expectantly to see how He will act in ways beyond your imaginings.

Wait for God. Too often we become impatient after we pray, wanting a quick fix or an obvious and direct answer. In this verse we find that Micah was willing to wait for God to answer. While you wait, praise Him for what He is already doing in your life.

Your God will hear you. Be confident in this. God does not turn away from His children. He hears you and desires to give you good things. Next time you pray, be confident that the Most High God is listening.

*Lord, thank You that You hear every one of my prayers.
I wait expectantly to see in what ways You will answer me.*

God's Love

For I am convinced that neither death, nor life, nor angels,
nor principalities, nor things present, nor things to come, nor powers,
nor height, nor depth, nor any other created thing, will be able to
separate us from the love of God, which is in Christ Jesus our Lord.
Romans 8:38–39 NASB

In this life we often feel we need to work for love. Love can grow stale or be lost altogether or given to another. The promise of love can be used as a weapon against us. But in this verse, an eternal, genuine love is promised you. This promise can be trusted because the love of God has been secured through the sacrifice and death of Christ. This is no promise made on a whim or as a manipulation but one made in blood by the perfect Lamb.

No natural or supernatural power can separate you from God's love. Nothing that is currently happening in your life will separate you from God's love. No matter how scary or uncertain the future seems, it will not separate you from God's love. No height of success or depth of depression and despair will separate you from God's love. Nothing that this life and those in it can throw at you and nothing that you do will separate you from God's love. Not even death, which separates us from everything else we know, will separate you from God's love.

Therefore, go forward in peace and boldness, knowing that you are eternally secure and eternally loved.

Lord, I can't comprehend this kind of everlasting love, but I thank You
that I can rest in the promise that You will always love me.

PEACE

Let the peace of Christ rule in your hearts, to which indeed
you were called in one body; and be thankful.
COLOSSIANS 3:15 NASB

You are to let the peace of Christ rule in your heart. What kind of peace does Christ offer? The peace that you can find in Christ hinges on the fact that He died in your place, that you are redeemed, blameless, and inseparable from God's love and salvation. Nothing in this world can snatch you out of the loving care of your heavenly Father. Your life is watched over and cared for by the almighty God. You can come to Him with all of your cares and concerns and He will listen. He is for you and loves you in a way that can't be comprehended. How different would your life be if you were truly convinced of and dwelled often on these facts? You would have a true and lasting peace. It would rule and sway every decision you make. It would assuage the pain and suffering you endure in this world. It would give you the courage and perseverance you need to face even the most daunting and fearful of circumstances.

Let these truths wash over you. Rest in them and let them take authority in your heart and mind. Be thankful for the immense gift that Christ has offered you—to live a life free from the anxiety, fear, and restlessness of the world.

Lord, may I be grounded in Your peace. I ask now that You would
dethrone anything else that has taken authority in my life
so that You can rule unchallenged.

Desire God

*Whom have I in heaven but You? And besides You, I desire nothing
on earth. My flesh and my heart may fail, but God is the
strength of my heart and my portion forever.*
Psalm 73:25–26 nasb

Do you ever look forward to meeting God in heaven? He is waiting
for you there to welcome you home once your pilgrimage on earth is
done. You can look forward to that extraordinary meeting. But God
is not a distant Being who is looking down on you from the sky, aloof
and unreachable until the next life. He is present and active in your
life now and offers you a relationship with Him. The psalmist who
wrote these verses says that apart from God, there is *nothing* on earth
that he desires. What an amazing perspective and remarkable passion.
Do you have that same desire for God—believing that nothing on this
earth could please you if it is devoid of Him? God will be your focus
and all-consuming passion in heaven, so start on the trail of eternity
now by putting Him first in your life and committing to spend time
with Him and in His Word.

Even when your heart, body, and emotions fail you, God is your
strength and will be for eternity. He is the only One in whom you can
have a rock-solid faith and who will never fail you even through death.

Lord, grant me an all-consuming desire to know You here on this earth.

Known and Loved

*I am the good shepherd, and I know My own and My own know Me,
even as the Father knows Me and I know the Father;
and I lay down My life for the sheep.*
John 10:14–15 NASB

. . . .

Do you fear being known and rejected? Do you feel that if someone
truly knew you they couldn't possibly love you? In these verses, Christ
asserts that He knows you. He doesn't just know you as a casual
acquaintance or even an intimate friend. His knowledge runs deeper
than that. He knows you in the same way that He knows the Father.
In the Trinity, Christ and the Father are one. So He is saying that He
knows you in the same way that He knows Himself. There could not be
a deeper or more intimate knowledge. He knows all the things that you
hide from everyone else—He knows the temptations, the frustrations,
the lost hopes, the rejections, the insecurities, and the deep desires that
you may hardly acknowledge to yourself.

Even though Christ knows the darkest and most secret parts of you,
He still loves you. He doesn't love you because He can gain something
from it. He doesn't love you on a surface, nonchalant level. He *laid
down His life* for you. There is no greater love. He knows you better
than anyone else does, and yet He loves you with a deeper, purer love
than anyone else can give you. You are deeply known and deeply loved.

. . . .

*Lord, I can't comprehend that You would love me in spite of all my faults.
Thank You for bestowing on me a love I don't deserve.*

Good Gifts

*Every good thing given and every perfect gift is from above,
coming down from the Father of lights, with whom there
is no variation or shifting shadow.*
James 1:17 nasb

Take a moment to thank God for the good things and blessings in your life. At times it's easy to get in the pattern of only requesting things *of* God as though He were your divine servant, without recognizing all the beautiful and bountiful blessings He has already lavished on you. This verse says that *every* good thing is from God. Think through all the good things in your life—each one is from God. They are tokens to remind you of His care and love for you. Don't take them for granted. Be grateful for the perfect gifts that He loves to give His children.

God is described as the Father of lights in this verse. Since He is a source of light, there is no shadow or variation with Him. He does not manipulate. He does not change. He doesn't try to hide behind something He is not. He doesn't give gifts to you to try to earn your allegiance or love. He gives to you purely out of His love. There is no guile in Him. He expects nothing in return. So accept His gifts freely and with a thankful and humbled heart.

*Lord, thank You for all the good things in my life. Thank You that
You know how to give perfect gifts. Keep me from taking
anything You've given me for granted.*

LOVE AND ASSURANCE

Little children, let us not love with word or with tongue, but in deed and truth. We will know by this that we are of the truth, and will assure our heart before Him in whatever our heart condemns us; for God is greater than our heart and knows all things.
1 JOHN 3:18–20 NASB

. . . .

These verses start out with an admonition—you ought to show your love in what you do. Love is not well expressed by superficial, noncommittal statements. Rather, a true, earnest love will drive you to action. Think about those around you to whom you can express love, not just by telling them, but by showing your love to them in your deeds. Don't allow laziness or excuses to keep you from reaching out to those who need love.

These verses end with a wonderful assurance for those of us who struggle with guilt and fear. When you are in Christ, be encouraged that nothing can take away your salvation. Your heart may condemn you when you fall into the same pattern of sin again or when you fail to do what you promised yourself and God you would do. But be encouraged—you are not in charge of your standing before God. God is. He is greater than any guilt-ridden and self-abasing heart. Once you are one of His children, you will always have that status. He knows all things, including the fact that your name is written, irrevocably, in the book of life.

. . . .

Lord, help me to show love not only in what I say, but even more so in what I do. Thank You that You are greater than the fears of my heart.

EARTHEN VESSELS

*But we have this treasure in earthen vessels, so that the surpassing
greatness of the power will be of God and not from ourselves.*
2 CORINTHIANS 4:7 NASB

You know those times when you feel especially weak and vulnerable and
you think you couldn't possibly be of any use to God or to those around
you? Oddly enough, that propensity to weakness is by design. God
could have created beings with immense power and perseverance, with
the ability to resist all temptation. Instead He created "earthen vessels."
Earthen vessels are weak, easily broken pieces of pottery. A piece of
pottery will only let light through if it has cracks and fissures. In the
same way, God's power and glory shine all the more brightly through
your weakness and brokenness. As this verse says, because you are
vulnerable and lack infinite strength, it is obvious that the power that
God manifests through you is of Him and not yourself.

Maybe you balk at the thought of being weak. After all, self-
sufficiency is a highly regarded trait in our world. But we all experience
various times of weakness and brokenness. Instead of being ashamed
of this, ask God to use it for His glory. Don't be afraid to admit your
vulnerability to Him and ask Him to shine through it.

Carry the treasure He has bestowed on you with joy, rejoicing that
He would choose you as a vessel through which to shine His glory.

*Lord, may I see my weaknesses not as something to be ashamed of but as
something to be thankful for as they display Your glory all the more clearly.*

ETERNAL PERSPECTIVE

*Therefore we do not lose heart, but though our outer man is decaying,
yet our inner man is being renewed day by day. For momentary,
light affliction is producing for us an eternal weight of glory far beyond
all comparison, while we look not at the things which are seen,
but at the things which are not seen; for the things which are seen
are temporal, but the things which are not seen are eternal.*
2 CORINTHIANS 4:16–18 NASB

This passage is such a good reminder about the eternal perspective
we should have. It's a fact of life that our bodies will slowly go into
decline as we get older. But as a believer, you have hope that even as
your body wears out, your heart and soul are being renewed and made
stronger each day. Your inner being is what will last into eternity. Take
time nourishing your soul each day through prayer, Bible reading, and
scripture meditation.

The difficulties you face here on earth are nothing compared to the
glory awaiting you in heaven. Take courage and find strength in that
truth as you encounter various trials.

It's easy to let your focus get distracted by the myriad issues
confronting you on a daily basis. This verse encourages you to look
less at the things that are seen and more at the eternal things that are
unseen. Commit to strengthening your relationship with God—that
is what will last into eternity. When you have the right perspective, the
difficulties of this world will truly seem momentary and light.

Lord, give me an eternal perspective. Focus my attention on eternal matters.

Let Your Thankfulness Show

In everything give thanks; for this is God's will for you in Christ Jesus.
1 Thessalonians 5:18 nasb

. . . .

You were probably taught from a young age to say "thank you" when someone does something for you. Being thankful doesn't seem like a big deal. But in this verse, Paul asserts that being thankful is God's will for you. All of a sudden, thankfulness sounds like an essential part of our walk with God.

Those who are in Christ have abundant reason to be thankful. You were owned by and enslaved to the horrible master of sin. You were bought from him with a price that could never be repaid—the blood of a flawless Lamb. Not only were you rescued from a life of separation from God, but you were adopted into His family. You have been lavished with grace and love. The Lord has provided for you, brought you into a relationship with Him, and promised you an eternity with Him. He did all this, not because you could do something for Him, but because He decided to place His love on you. It makes perfect sense that Paul would say your life should be characterized by thankfulness.

In a world where people exhibit an increasing sense of entitlement and self-centeredness, think of how much a thankful spirit will stand out to those around you. Everyone *is* entitled—to death and an eternity away from God. Be thankful, for God's will for you is infinitely better than anything you could deserve.

. . . .

*Lord, may I grasp more fully what You have done for me
so that my life is characterized by thankfulness.*

GIVE THANKS

I will give thanks to the LORD with all my heart;
I will tell of all Your wonders.
PSALM 9:1 NASB

Today is a day that is set aside nationally as a day to give thanks. Sometimes the stress and chaos of Thanksgiving Day can impede thoughts of thankfulness. Maybe you're stressed about hosting family and friends. Maybe you have to travel and are nervous about the logistics or weather conditions and the interactions that will take place once you get there. Or maybe you're spending Thanksgiving Day by yourself and feel discouraged. No matter what the circumstance, take a moment now to give thanks to God with all your heart. Consider the wonderful things He has done for you and the love and blessings He has bestowed on you. Remind yourself now of all His wonders. Reminisce about the work He has done in your life and the lives around you in the past year. Ground your mind now in an attitude of thanksgiving that will saturate the rest of your day.

Lord, thank You for choosing and adopting me as one of Your children.
Thank You for all the material blessings You have freely given me.
Thank You for the people You have placed in my life to encourage me
and stand by me. Thank You that I live in a country where I can openly
give You thanks and speak of Your wonders. Thank You for Your faithfulness
through my life. Thank You for lavishing on me a love that is beyond
comprehension. Thank You that I have a steadfast hope in my salvation and
an eternity with You. Thank You that You will never leave or forsake me.

Rooted and Grounded

*And that you, being rooted and grounded in love, may be able to
comprehend with all the saints what is the breadth and length and height
and depth, and to know the love of Christ which surpasses knowledge,
that you may be filled up to all the fullness of God.*
Ephesians 3:17–19 nasb

Pray these verses over yourself. Pray that God's love would ground you
and make you secure. Pray that the roots of His love would reach deeper
and deeper into your heart, leaving no room for fear, guilt, or sin. To
be rooted and grounded in His love is to fully understand that He is for
you and that He desires you to walk more closely with Him.

Pray that you would be able to comprehend the love of Christ that
surpasses knowledge. What an interesting oxymoron to think that you
could understand something that surpasses understanding. His love
for you is so overwhelming that you *can't even imagine* its breadth and
length and height and depth. Pray to comprehend even a fraction of His
love for you so that it will transform your life.

Pray that you would be filled up to all the fullness of God. Being
filled up to the fullness of God leaves no room for anything else. That
God would desire to condescend to fill us up with Himself is awe-
inspiring. Ask Him to do just that.

*Lord, ground me in Your love. Help me to comprehend Your
overwhelming love for me. Fill me up to overflowing with Your Spirit.*

PROMISES

*Let us hold fast the confession of our hope without
wavering, for He who promised is faithful.*
HEBREWS 10:23 NASB

In this life, you can have endurance and hope because your God is
faithful to keep His promises. The Christian life would be hopeless if
God were not faithful and trustworthy. He will absolutely keep His
promises. You can (and do) bet your life on that.

God has promised to complete and perfect the good work He has
started in you (Philippians 1:6). He will never leave you or forsake you
(Hebrews 13:5). He has promised that He will wipe away every tear
from your eyes and that in heaven there will no longer be any mourning
or crying or pain (Revelation 21:4). He will never allow you to be
separated from His love (Romans 8:38–39). He promises that He will
come again and that you will be with Him forever (1 Thessalonians
4:16–17). He assures you that no one can take you from His hand
(John 10:29).

These are just some of the promises God has made. These aren't just
nice sentiments. These are things that God will, without question, bring
to pass. He does not break His promises—He will do what He has said
He will do. You can put your hope in these promises, knowing that you
won't be disappointed.

*Lord, in a world where promises are so often broken, thank You that
I can trust that You will keep Yours. What beautiful promises You
have made. I put my hope firmly in their fulfillment.*

Citizenship

*For our citizenship is in heaven, from which also we eagerly
wait for a Savior, the Lord Jesus Christ.*
Philippians 3:20 nasb

. . . .

Your citizenship is in heaven; you are just passing through this world.
This is not your home, your country of origin, or your final destination.
You were created by God and will one day return home to Him.

If you ever feel like you don't belong here, like the world is too
confusing and frightening for you, it's because deep down you know
that this is not your home. God has placed you here for a purpose. He
has sent you as His ambassador. Strive to do His will and to glorify
Him on this earth. Make the most of this pilgrimage you're on. Just
as someone from another country loves to talk about and teach others
about their home country, so we ought to tell others about heaven and
the One who is enthroned there. Always be aware that something better
awaits you. That the very city in which God dwells is your home.

Keep your eyes focused on your Savior. Wait for Him with eager
anticipation. He will come again and you will be with Him forever.
What a beautiful life you have to look forward to. Don't lose sight of it.

. . . .

*Lord, thank You that my home is with You in heaven and that I can look
forward to spending my eternity there. Come quickly, Lord Jesus.*

PERFECTION

*For I am confident of this very thing, that He who began a good work
in you will perfect it until the day of Christ Jesus.*
PHILIPPIANS 1:6 NASB

. . . .

The Lord is working in you—you are a work in progress! He has started
a good work in you that has not yet been completed. Take this truth to
heart and don't be overly discouraged when you fall into the same sin
patterns—God is working in you. If you ever feel that you must not be
saved because you're struggling with things that you shouldn't struggle
with as a Christian, be encouraged that no matter how it feels to you,
from the moment you were saved God started working in you. On the
days when it doesn't feel like God is working at all, remind yourself of
Philippians 1:6.

God will perfect the work He has started in you. Even if there are
road bumps along the way, He *will* complete and perfect His work in
you. He won't abandon you if you don't perform up to some standard.
He perfects the good work in you because He desires that you be more
like Him and that you walk in closer relationship with Him. So be
encouraged and try to recognize the areas in which God has already
been perfecting His work in your life. You are on a good and perfect
trajectory.

. . . .

*Lord, thank You for working in me even when I don't feel it.
Thank You for not abandoning the work that You have started in me.*

Never Alone

❦

For He Himself has said, "I will never desert you,
nor will I ever forsake you."
Hebrews 13:5 NASB

. . . .

Life is full of disappointments, broken promises, failed relationships, and loneliness. It may seem like you are the only person you can really trust. But the Lord will never desert you or forsake you. He promises to be with you through this life and the next. When all else feels hopeless, know that He remains steadfast.

For those who have trusted people in the past but have been let down, this may be a hard concept to accept. But this is no idle promise based on the feeling of a moment. When Christ hung on the cross, He was forsaken by God. The sin that was laid on Him was so horrific and abhorrent that the Father, who was one with Jesus, could not look at Him. In the most heart-wrenching act of history, the holy Father turned His face away from His once blameless Son. Because Christ was willing to be forsaken and utterly alone, you never will be. God won't ever have to turn away from you—you now bear the pure innocence of Christ. Christ took your sins upon Himself so you would never have to experience what it's like to be completely alone and forsaken by God.

. . . .

Lord, I can't possibly be grateful enough for what You have done
for me. I humbly praise You for promising never to desert or
forsake me. Thank You that I will never be alone.

SIN NO MORE

He. . .said to them, "He who is without sin among you, let him be the first to throw a stone at her.". . . When they heard it, they began to go out one by one. . .and He was left alone, and the woman, where she was, in the center of the court. Straightening up, Jesus said to her, "Woman, where are they? Did no one condemn you?" She said, "No one, Lord." And Jesus said, "I do not condemn you, either. Go. From now on sin no more."
JOHN 8:7, 9–11 NASB

This beautiful passage illustrates Jesus' countercultural treatment of women and His treatment of sinners. The male leaders of the time forcefully brought this adulterous woman into court to degradingly use her as a tool to catch Jesus in a wrong statement. They then planned to brutally stone her. Imagine the fear this woman must have been experiencing, surrounded by a crowd of onlookers in front of a notable teacher of the law.

Instead of condemning her, Jesus poignantly pointed out the sin and hypocrisy of the supposedly pious people who had dragged her to Him. He put this woman, who was worthless in the eyes of the culture, on a level playing field with the leaders of the society. He didn't condone the sin, but rather condemned all sin and loved this broken, scared sinner. He then told her to go and sin no more. This woman, standing alone with Jesus, faced not her condemner, but her Savior.

Christ came not to condemn, but to save. As His daughter, confess your sin; then go and sin no more.

Lord, thank You for coming to save me and free me from sin.

Let Your Fire Burn

Our God is a consuming fire.
Hebrews 12:29 nkjv

The Holy Spirit is often referred to as a fire. Each believer's heart carries that flaming light of God. Just as heat boils out the impurities in elements such as gold, so the Spirit burns in our hearts both to refine and to fuel the work He has called us to do.

Paul admonishes believers not to quench the fire (1 Thessalonians 5:19), but many restrict it from growing so there is barely a glow in the coals of their bellies. They fear that the flames might actually spread and purify their hearts, compelling them to give up their darling sins—the ones that aren't hurting anyone, the ones that stay hidden.

So when the heart is convicted of sin or called to mission work or challenged to change, it's easier to smother the Spirit with logic and justification and keep the coal neither hot nor cold, but comfortably lukewarm.

Henry Blackaby wrote, "If the Spirit speaks to you about God's will for you, and if you refuse to take action, a time will come when the Spirit's voice will be muted in your life."

Is it time to remove the bushel that has hidden your light so long and trust the winds of God's Spirit to fan the flames? Fuel the fire with prayer, obedience, and meditation, and watch in amazement as God transforms you into what He's always wanted you to be.

Father, let the fire of the Holy Spirit blaze and spread among Your people so that we burn with passion for Your Word and the coming of Your kingdom.

A Contrast of Two Lives

"Behold, I am laying in Zion a stone, a tested stone, a costly cornerstone for the foundation, firmly placed. He who believes in it will not be disturbed."
Isaiah 28:16 NASB

. . . .

Kelly called herself a Christian. She attended church on holidays and thought of herself as a good person. When her husband died of cancer, the pain and suffering she felt awakened her, and she questioned her faith. Then a thought crossed her mind—had she ever really known God?

Soon Kelly was attending church and studying the Bible and devotionals. Even though she struggled through grief, her newfound relationship with Christ gave her hope.

Renee was another young widow struggling through grief. Unlike Kelly, Renee was considered a strong Christian. Until her husband died, she was highly involved in Bible studies and church leadership.

Like most, she also questioned her faith, but instead of seeking purpose, she shut down, wanting more than anything to die and join her husband. It wasn't long before Renee took her own life.

Both women loved their husbands deeply, and their tears fell long and hard. When tragedy struck, Kelly found purpose and beauty in her suffering because Christ became the cornerstone of her life. Renee followed her sorrow into despair because the foundation of her life was her husband.

How sturdy is your foundation? Continually test the strength of your spiritual footing so you can be prepared when tragedy comes.

. . . .

God, give my faith a firm foundation to withstand the winds and storms of life. Give me a love for Your Word and a relentless thirst for spending time with You in prayer.

YOUR CHILD'S SALVATION

*"Ask, and it will be given to you; seek, and you will find; knock,
and it will be opened to you. For everyone who asks receives,
and he who seeks finds, and to him who knocks it will be opened."*
MATTHEW 7:7–8 NKJV

When John Spurgeon returned home from a ministry trip, he found the house quiet except the voice of his wife from behind the bedroom door. She was pleading for the salvation of all their children, but especially their strong-willed firstborn son. The young man she carried such a burden for later became one of the greatest preachers and evangelists of all time, Charles Spurgeon.

We spend so much time disciplining our children for social behavior, and so little time in prayer for their souls. A relationship with God can't be earned by good works or a sweet disposition. It can't be passed down through bloodlines or learned like a language. Salvation is a gift from God.

Jesus said in Matthew 21:22 (NIV), "If you believe, you will receive whatever you ask for in prayer." So we must ask the Giver to grace our children with His endowment of salvation. Don't take it for granted that because kids are raised in a godly home or go to a Christian school they will have a personal relationship with Christ. Instead, sincerely, humbly, and relentlessly pray to God, who is generous in His gifts and waits for a people who are desperate for His work in their lives.

*Dear Lord, fill my children with Your Holy Spirit. Give them the desire
to love You, serve You, and honor You all the days of their lives.*

DO NOT BE CONFORMED

Do not be surprised. . .if the world hates you.
1 JOHN 3:13 NIV

History shows that those who live in stark contrast to the status quo accomplish great things.

In 1876 President Rutherford B. Hayes brought strength of mind and character to the White House. He also brought his unapologetically Christian wife, Lucy. The couple began each day with prayer and devotions. Sunday evenings they sang hymns with the staff. Men in office and their wives were irritated when Lucy banned alcohol calling her "Lemonade Lucy." Despite this, she was also well known for her care toward soldiers and compassion for slaves. She carried herself with confidence and kindness, and many called her "Mother Lucy."

The Bible encourages us not to be conformed to this world. We are called to stand out by our behavior like "aliens and strangers." "Live such good lives among the pagans," Peter wrote, "that, though they accuse you of doing wrong, they may see your good deeds and glorify God on the day he visits us" (1 Peter 2:12 NIV).

The world needs Christians who will practice the convictions of their faith, despite public criticism. Yes, the world will think you're strange. Yes, you will be mocked. But there will be others who find you inspiring.

Dear Lord, let my faith convictions strengthen despite strange looks and judgmental attitudes from others. Let the goal of my actions always be Your glory.

Waiting on God

Let us not become weary in doing good, for at the proper time
we will reap a harvest if we do not give up.
Galatians 6:9 NIV

Theologian John Owen wrote, "For the most part we [Christians] live upon successes, not promises—unless we see and feel the print of victories, we will not believe."

The Christian walk is about faith. Hebrews 11:1 (NKJV) describes it as "the substance of things hoped for, the evidence of things not seen." Faith is trusting God to keep His promises, even while we wait.

It's easy to depend on God when all is well, but hard times may cause us to doubt whether God really is good. However, if you cling to God's promises, you will experience tremendous growth. Grapes don't grow overnight. They slowly ripen, attached to the vine for sustenance. Likewise, Jesus said, "I am the vine; you are the branches. If you remain in me and I in you, you will bear much fruit" (John 15:5 NIV).

In the Old Testament, God called David to the throne, but King Saul refused to abdicate and attempted to kill his successor. David had many opportunities to kill Saul, but spared him because he trusted God. David wrote, "Indeed, none of those who wait for You will be ashamed" (Psalm 25:3 NASB).

No matter what you're facing, sustain yourself in the Word and in prayer. Trust that God will bring you through this season, and don't give up. In God's time, He will deliver you.

God, give me wisdom as I wait for You to carry out Your will,
and peace knowing that You will work it out for my good.

Woman versus the Devil

Resist the devil, and he will flee from you.
James 4:7 nlt

Satan is often depicted as a dark creature with spiny ears and a pointy tail. But the Bible describes Lucifer as a beautiful angel, his mind full of wisdom and his brightness captivating. He is portrayed as an alluring work of art, not a monster. That's what makes him dangerous.

Like the ring in Tolkien's Lord of the Rings trilogy, the offerings of Satan are attractive and appeal to the sense of power. Arthur Jackson wrote, "[Satan] conceals [his] hook in a godly bait, and like a skillful angler, he knows how to use the temptation best suited to our palate."

The devil is so subtle we often don't recognize the attack. He whispers thoughts and follows up with their justification. He includes emotional and biblical "proof," just as Satan said to Eve, "Has God not said. . . ," and used the same tactic to tempt Christ, saying, "It is written. . ."

Temptation can come in the form of begrudging your spouse, criticizing others, envying other women, or allowing bitterness to take root in your heart. These aren't just innocent flaws. These are satanic tools to hold you back from the abundant life and your full potential in kingdom work.

Ephesians 6:11 (nkjv) says, "Put on the whole armor of God, that you may be able to stand against the wiles of the devil." No matter what logical fallacies Satan whispers, be steadfast in prayer and Bible study. Seek the truth and you will find it.

Lord, help me discern between the voices of deception and the truth.
Give me strength to stand even when lies tempt me.

Freedom from the Past

*"[Christ] gave himself for us to redeem us from all wickedness
and to purify for himself a people that are his very own,
eager to do what is good."*
Titus 2:14 NIV

Jim listened to the preacher's call to be saved. As much as his soul cried out, Jim felt too dirty. There were too many terrible things in his past. He wasn't good enough for God, he thought. Finally, the pastor told Jim that God would wash him clean. "Though your sins are as scarlet, they will be as white as snow" (Isaiah 1:18 NASB).

Today, Jim is a deacon and a member of the Gideons. He counsels others who carry similar shame, recounting how God redeemed his life.

Satan uses our mistakes to whisper condemnation: "Look at what you've done! You're not fit for God." But Romans 8:1 (NLT) says, "Now there is no condemnation for those who belong to Christ Jesus."

God redeems your sinful life to use it for His kingdom. Your imperfect past is what gives you compassion for others who struggle. Your teen abortion can help you at crisis pregnancy centers. Your failed marriage can give you a ministry to blended families.

2 Corinthians 1:4 (NLT) says, "He comforts us in all our troubles so that we can comfort others. When they are troubled, we will be able to give them the same comfort God has given us." No past is too terrible. No sin is too great to be used by the redeeming God.

Father, help me to accept the freedom I have in Christ, and show me the purposes for my past mistakes for the sake of others and Your glory.

YOUR HUSBAND IS FIRST YOUR BROTHER

Those who love God must also love their fellow believers.
1 JOHN 4:21 NLT

We hear the word *love* so often in our culture that it has lost the richness it is meant to convey. Jesus said, "By this everyone will know that you are my disciples, if you love one another" (John 13:35 NIV). Yet in the church as a whole, the greatest of all love institutions—marriage—is often lacking the unconditional love to which God calls us.

The care we show for the homeless, mentally handicapped, foster children, cancer survivors is the same love the Bible admonishes us to show our spouses. It is no less a witness of God's unconditional love as the others, perhaps even more.

G. K. Chesterton once wrote, "Love means loving the unlovable—or it is no virtue at all." Perhaps the reason we can love strangers better than spouses is because we aren't faced with a stranger's sins every day. We can give money or a hug or an afternoon and move on. But a wife must live with her husband's financial irresponsibility, workaholism, or critical tongue every single day.

Until we learn to love our spouses with the same unconditional love we proclaim to have for others, we will damage our witness for Christ. In the words of John Piper, "Staying married. . .is not mainly about staying in love. It is about keeping covenant. . .the same kind Jesus made with His bride when He died for her."

Lord, help me to love my husband most on the days he doesn't deserve it, and remind me how much I need grace and unconditional love, too.

Keeping Up with the Christian Joneses

*"Come to Me, all you who labor and are heavy laden,
and I will give you rest."*
Matthew 11:28 nkjv

. . . .

Christians have a lot to do. There are so many needs in the world, from spreading the Gospel and feeding the poor to teaching children the Bible and remaining in prayer.

Somehow our practice of the faith has morphed into a jam-packed schedule of women's meetings, Christian sporting events, and committees. It's almost an unwritten rule that good Christian people must load their schedules with good Christian stuff to do, especially during the holidays.

John Wesley said, "I have no time to be in a hurry." He has a point. With all the hurrying around, the precious limited time we have each day isn't allocated toward the actual works of God. It's taken up with busyness. Consequently, our families are strangers, our hearts are unfulfilled, our minds are stressed, and our Bible reading and prayer life are shallow.

God isn't impressed with a clean house or schedules marked with every church event for the next six months. He wants our hearts, minds, and souls, and He wants us to be obedient to share His love with all people throughout our lives. It's not complicated.

If you find yourself unable to keep up with the fast-paced Christian life, then be at peace and say no sometimes. What matters is the condition of our hearts, not the number of Christian acquaintances we have or the number of Bible studies we attend.

. . . .

*Lord, help me see the difference between the life of a Christian and
the heart of a Christian, and help me discern when my life is misaligned.*

IT ONLY TAKES A MOMENT

"Jesus wept."
JOHN 11:35 NASB

In the words of Barnaby from *Hello, Dolly!*: "It only takes a moment to be loved your whole life long." Americans are intrigued by the idea of love at first sight, but there is another kind of love that can happen in a moment that is deeper than romance.

Susan was having trouble finding a friend's grave site when an older woman at the cemetery helped her locate it. On the way out, Susan saw the woman standing at her son's grave and brought her some leftover flowers. As Susan explained, tears welled up in the woman's eyes. Soon they were crying in each other's arms. "I probably won't ever see her again," Susan said, "but I think about her a lot. It's not often you share a fragile moment like that with a stranger."

Romans 12:15 (NASB) says, "Rejoice with those who rejoice, and weep with those who weep." You never know when you are going to be called by God to reach out to a stranger. You never know when a soft word of a kind act of compassion will touch someone's life forever.

Jesus experienced this kind of empathy from Simeon, a stranger in the crowd, who literally felt Jesus' pain when he was summoned to carry the cross for a while. Like Simeon, may every Christian be prepared at any time to bear another's burden and relieve their suffering if only for a little while.

Dear Lord, give me eyes of compassion to see those who are hurting.
Give me a sensitive spirit that is compelled to comfort wounded souls.

Make Someone Happy

"Anyone who wants to be first must be the very last,
and the servant of all."
Mark 9:35 niv

The Christian life requires a servant attitude, even at home. It's easy to say, but difficult in practice. Like the young boy who vowed, "I have resolved this year not to fight my sister. . .unless she fights me first or makes me mad or I feel like it," we might say, "I have resolved to serve my husband unless he doesn't deserve it or makes me mad or I don't feel like it."

Katherine von Bora was a living example of servant love. She and Martin Luther shared a love that was sincere and expressive, but he was poor and often sickly. Katherine took care of the home and farm and even slaughtered the animals herself. Katie (as he called her) frequently nursed Luther through gout, hemorrhoids, and the like, all while raising six children.

"My Katie is in all things so obliging and pleasing to me," he wrote, "that I would not exchange my poverty for the riches of Croesus."

James 4:6 (nkjv) says, "God resists the proud, but gives grace to the humble." Jesus was the perfect example of servanthood, and He calls us to follow Him. An attitude of service and humility pleases God, and that includes during home life.

How glad we should be, how eager to follow Him, knowing that Christ didn't stop serving, even to the point of death for a people who didn't deserve it.

Lord, soften my heart to serve my family with a good attitude,
and bathe me in Your grace when I fail.

THE MIND—SATAN'S BATTLE GROUND

Blessed are those who find wisdom, those who gain understanding.
PROVERBS 3:13 NIV

. . . .

Charles Stanley said, "The mind is the devil's battleground." Satan has been using mind games to twist the truth since the beginning of time, and nothing has changed.

Have you ever had a thought like this: *John left his clothes all over the floor again! Who does he think I am? His maid? He never has had any respect for me and all the work I do around here. He doesn't love me. He probably never has!*

Suddenly, just because your messy husband left clothes around, in your mind, he has never loved you. In many cases, a few more convincing fallacies like these will add up and eventually lead you to divorce.

2 Corinthians 10:5 (NIV) says, "Take captive every thought to make it obedient to Christ." Satan has the ability to make anything sound like the truth, so capture each thought and test it against scripture. This holds true for what we think of others, ourselves, and God.

Romans 12:2 (NKJV) says, "Do not be conformed to this world, but be transformed by the renewing of your mind." Keep a sharp eye for these trains of logical thought that can take you to the wrong conclusions, and continually study the Word of God so that you may know the truth even when it defies the logic of this world.

. . . .

*Lord, there are times when my thoughts take me to dark places,
even when I know they're not true. Make me aware when these
battles rage, and help me win the battle with Your truth.*

WHAT YOU *CAN* CONTROL

Seek the LORD and His strength; Seek His face continually.
1 CHRONICLES 16:11 NASB

. . . .

Many women struggle with control. Often intentions of loving concern result in overbearing anxiety rooted in fear. Max Lucado wrote, "[Fear] turns us into control freaks. . . . When life spins wildly, we grab for a component of life we can manage: our diet, the tidiness of our home, the armrest of a plane, or, in many cases, people."

Fear in parenting takes many forms—guilt, worry, manipulation. Fear imagines every terrible future possibility, but God is Jehovah-Raphe, the Healer. Many things will happen out of your control, but these may be the circumstances God uses to make your children strong, faith-filled adults, prepared for good works.

Concerned moms have not been rendered helpless, however. There are two things we can do that will result in fruit.

First, plant seeds of God's Word. Use scriptures in your décor and in lunch box notes. Read Bible stories and sing scripture-rich songs.

Second, pray. Jesus said we should pray like a man who bangs on the door of a reluctant friend. "Because of your shameless audacity he will surely get up and give you as much as you need" (Luke 11:8 NIV). Be a prayer warrior for your children. Pray for their salvation and their callings.

Through prayer and the Word, you will go from living in fear to resting in God's sovereignty, from anxiety to thanksgiving.

. . . .

*Dear Lord, You have promised to answer my prayers, and I know
I can trust You. Thank You for listening to me and for
the comfort of Your sovereign will.*

WHO AM I IN CHRIST?

For whatever is born of God overcomes the world.
1 JOHN 5:4 NASB

. . . .

G. K. Chesterton wrote, "The Christian ideal has not been tried and found wanting; it has been found difficult and left untried."

There is a belief today that doing our best to please God is futile, and therefore unreasonable. We've even labeled the lack of trying a virtue called "just being me."

Imagine if you applied this philosophy to marriage. A husband stays on the couch, never works, and reasons that he isn't good enough to achieve success, so he isn't going to try. How much more pleased would his wife be if he worked and failed but relentlessly tried anyway?

It is the same in our relationship with Christ. James 1:4 (NASB) admonishes us, "Let endurance have its perfect result, so that you may be perfect and complete, lacking in nothing."

The self on its own can never please God. It will never be more than a sinful personality, and even if that's a relatively "good person," it will always be tainted with a tendency to push pet sins to their limits.

So the real question is not "Who am I?" but rather "Who am I in Christ?"

In Christ you are free; you are an overcomer; you are created for a purpose. You are no longer trapped by the confines of your own abilities because the Holy Spirit empowers you to be so much more.

. . . .

Dear God, thank You for saving me through Your grace, and thank You for giving me the strength to live the Christian life beyond my abilities.

With All Your Soul

"Be zealous. . ."
Revelation 3:19 NASB

Tasha's son was saved at youth group and shared the Gospel with her. She was so amazed at this news she couldn't wait to hear more. She eagerly entered the church with great expectation.

The music moved her. The message challenged her. The excitement was all over her face. She looked around at the Christians who sat stoically around her and asked herself, "Am I missing something? Is this how Christians are supposed to act?"

Why is it that Christians have no problem screaming for their favorite football team or dancing at a pop concert, but in the church with the greatest news on earth, the majority of us sit complacent and unmoved?

Jesus said we should worship God with all our heart, soul, mind, and strength (Luke 10:27). But for some reason many have cut out the soul in worship. They will worship God with their minds and mean it with all their hearts. But the emotional expressions that start in the depths of the soul are suppressed.

Every Christian should have the experience of seeing the congregation from the choir loft. The blank stares and emotionless participation are glaring. As Puritan Samuel Ward wrote, "Christian zeal is a spiritual heat wrought in the heart of a man by the Holy Ghost." Perhaps if the fire of zeal were practiced, it would spread and bring revival.

Dear Lord, let zeal for Your Word and Your glory well up in me beyond all other loves in my life. Bring conviction to my heart no matter who's watching. Burn a fire in my soul.

YOUR GREATEST DELIGHT

His delight is in the law of the LORD,
and in His law he meditates day and night.
PSALM 1:2 NKJV

. . . .

What are your heart's desires? To be happy? To find purpose? To be loved? There is a way to satisfy those longings without fail. Psalm 37:4 (NASB) says, "Delight yourself in the LORD; and He will give you the desires of your heart."

Many Christians expect God to provide their desires, but they don't want to delight in Him. They treat their relationship with God as a duty, a desperate plea for help, a religious luck-charm, or a daily dependence, but a delight? That requires far too much time and energy.

A relationship without delight is like a marriage with no passion or friendship. Yes, you can perform the duties of married life, but it will become a prison. Nehemiah 8:10 (NASB) says, "Do not be grieved [by the words of the Law], for the joy of the LORD is your strength." We should love and serve God, not to avoid His wrath, but rather out of gratitude and awe.

When you live this way, you will find the delights of your heart, just as Albert Schweitzer wrote: "Your life is something opaque, not transparent, as long as you look at it in ordinary human ways. But if you hold it up against the light of God's goodness, it shines and turns transparent, radiant, and bright. And then you ask yourself in amazement: Is this really my own life I see before me?"

. . . .

Lord, let our relationship be one of pure delight. Even though I'm grateful for Your works, I'm most grateful for You.

LIFE ISN'T FAIR. . .THANK GOD

Walk in the way of love, just as Christ loved us.
EPHESIANS 5:2 NIV

. . . .

Dartanyon Crockett and Leroy Sutton were high school teammates. A legally blind Crockett was often seen carrying Sutton, a double leg amputee, on his back.

ESPN's Lisa Penn reported their story, but wanted to help. She raised donations and coordinated events, helping Crockett win a bronze medal in the Paralympics and Sutton to become his family's first college graduate.

Leroy once asked, "Why did you stay?" Lisa responded, "I stayed because. . .we don't truly live [life] until we give it away. . . . I stayed because I love you."

Dartanyon and Leroy didn't deserve Lisa's love. She knew they could never repay her, but it wasn't fairness she wanted. Jesus said, "There is no greater love than to lay down one's life for one's friends" (John 15:13 NLT).

It's easy being on the receiving end of grace, but much harder to be the sacrificial lamb. In the face of tragedy, will you shake your fist at God, crying, "That's not fair!" or will you react like the martyr Polycarp? When given the option to reproach Christ or burn at the stake, he said, "Eighty-six years I have served him, and He never once wronged me. How then shall I blaspheme my King who has saved me?"

There will be times when God calls upon us to sacrifice, but Jesus gave up His throne, His glory, and His life for you. No, life isn't fair, and aren't you glad?

. . . .

Lord, I don't deserve any of Your free gifts.
Help me to give as generously as You've given to me.

BE THE SPARK

"As surely as I live. . .I take no pleasure in the death of wicked people.
I only want them to turn from their wicked ways so they can live."
EZEKIEL 33:11 NLT

. . . .

The Great Awakening was triggered by the evangelist George Whitefield, who spent "whole days and even weeks. . .prostrate on the ground in silent or vocal prayer." He said, "[Prayer] is the very breath of the new creature, the fan of the divine life, whereby the spark of holy fire, kindled in the soul by God, is not only kept in, but raised into a flame."

How many believers say they will pray for a situation when all they really do is think about it? Could it be that when we say, "I'll pray for you," we really mean, "I will hope for your sake that things get better"?

God said, "If My people who are called by My name will humble themselves, and pray and seek My face, and turn from their wicked ways, then I will hear from heaven, and will forgive their sin and heal their land" (2 Chronicles 7:14 NKJV).

Prayer for revival should be a daily activity for every Christian. It takes no special talent, no magic words. Prayer doesn't require strength, youth, health, or wealth. You can maintain an attitude of prayer during car trips, meals, or whenever the thought crosses your mind. It is a contrite heart that God loves, and He's waiting for the day His people cry out to Him in desperation. Today, be the spark that starts the fire.

. . . .

Lord, pour out Your Spirit on Your people,
and bring revival to our land.

A WOMAN'S AROMA

*We are a fragrance of Christ to God among those who are
being saved and among those who are perishing.*
2 CORINTHIANS 2:15 NASB

A person's smell can shape your opinion, even making him or her attractive or repugnant. The same is true of the spiritual life. Our lives leave an aroma that can be either a pleasing fragrance to God and others or a stench.

In the Old Testament, burnt offerings and incense were used in the temple as a pleasing aroma to God. When King Saul sinned, Samuel chastised him, saying, "Does the LORD delight in burnt offerings and sacrifices as much as in obeying the LORD? To obey is better than sacrifice" (1 Samuel 15:22 NIV).

Just as perfume lingers, you leave behind an aroma of the soul everywhere you go—home, church, work, and public places. Let it be a fragrance people want to keep around.

Here are some ways to leave a pleasing aroma:

- Speak kindly to others.
- Don't criticize too sharply.
- Speak often about God and His Word.
- Pray continually.

Life is short. We only have so much time to influence others with our lives. What aroma do you want to leave behind?

*Lord, I want my life to be a pleasing aroma to You—the fragrance of a
broken and contrite heart. Show me the ways I can grow in this area.*

CHRISTMAS TRIMMING CHALLENGE

*"Seek first the kingdom of God and his righteousness,
and all these things shall be added to you."*
MATTHEW 6:33 NKJV

. . . .

According to *Business Insider Magazine*, Americans will spend approximately six billion dollars on Christmas decorations this year—that's not counting gifts. We're talking just tinsel, lights, ornaments, and the like.

What's the purpose of all that spending? A neighborhood contest? An external experience? It echoes of Jesus at the temple, turning over tables and saying, "You have made [my Father's house] a 'den of thieves' " (Matthew 21:13 NKJV).

Think of how many orphans could be helped with six billion dollars. One website claims that homelessness could be eliminated with that amount. These numbers should challenge the way we use our budgets and make us question why we have the urge to buy another cute snowman or rustic cinnamon-scented kitsch.

On the other hand, decorations play an important role in setting Christmas Day apart. As the day we celebrate the birthday of our Savior, it should be generously festive. In the Old Testament, God often told His people to stack stones of remembrance at places where God performed great miracles so they wouldn't forget His faithfulness.

There is something to be said for surrounding yourself with reminders of the great gifts of God. But let us check the motive of each purchase. Perhaps Christians should reduce the amount spent on décor and use the savings to give more to the poor.

. . . .

*God, I love to celebrate the birth of Your Son. Teach me to discern
the balance between spending on the outward appearance
and meeting the needs of others.*

GIFTING WORDS OF LIFE

Encourage each other and build each other up.
1 THESSALONIANS 5:11 NLT

. . . .

Nearly every American revolutionary read Thomas Paine's pamphlet "Common Sense." Thomas Jefferson encouraged Paine, "Go on then in doing with your pen what in other times was done with the sword: show that reformation is more practicable by operating on the mind than on the body of man."

What an example of the way words inspire and encourage! The Bible clearly warns us of the influence of words in Proverbs 18:21 (NLT): "The tongue can bring death or life." Your words have power, either to tear down or to build up.

This holiday season, consider gifting encouragement through the written word. Write a tribute to someone who has positively influenced your life. It could be a teacher, pastor, good friend, or parent. You don't have to be an eloquent writer; simply speak your heart and recount specific memories and quotes that have meant a lot to you.

Ephesians 4:29 (NLT) says, "Let everything you say be good and helpful, so that your words will be an encouragement to those who hear them." The gratitude we have toward these loved ones is a cause for praise and glory to God. How much more fruitful is that gratefulness when the thanksgiving is sown as seeds in their lives. They gave so much to you, and now you can give them something they will treasure for a lifetime.

. . . .

Lord, give me the words to write a tribute to the person I love so much.
Help me overcome my fear and lethargy, and inspire me with
a message that expresses my appreciation clearly.

It Is More Blessed to Give

*Keep your lives free from the love of money
and be content with what you have.*
Hebrews 13:5 niv

. . . .

Jennifer noticed that her children, ages three and five, were developing an attitude of greed, even as young as they were. On their routine visits to relatives, she consistently overheard them say things like, "I wonder what we'll get! What will they give us?"

Jennifer's family is fairly wealthy, so the children are showered with gifts all throughout the year. Christmas was becoming just a way to hoard toys, and the meaning of the holiday was getting lost in all the material goods.

So when Christmas came around the following year, Jennifer and her husband, Sean, decided the kids would get only three gifts. "Jesus only received three gifts," she said.

In addition, Jennifer made each child pick out three toys of their own to donate to a local orphanage. She hopes this practice will teach them the value of giving and at the same time teach them to appreciate what they have.

Jesus said, "It is more blessed to give than to receive" (Acts 20:35). How can we say we are honoring Him at Christmas when we are teaching our children just the opposite? Whether you use Jennifer's method or another, do something this year to cut back the attitude of entitlement that permeates our society today.

. . . .

Lord, I want my children to understand that money and possessions come under the jurisdiction of Your glory and Your will. Help me find ways to emphasize this truth to my kids, in their lives and my own.

THE HIDDEN BLESSINGS OF GRIEF

Truly, O God of Israel, our Savior, you work in mysterious ways.
ISAIAH 45:15 NLT

The 2013 Morgan Fire was sparked by target shooting, an innocent accident that destroyed 3,111 acres on Mount Diablo, California. But the following spring rare "fire followers" burst with color, covering the mountain. The last time they were seen was half a century ago. For botanists and naturalists, viewing this phenomenon was a once-in-a-lifetime opportunity.

The death of a loved one can be like a wildfire. You don't know what parts of your life will turn to ashes and what parts will survive. Many may feel everything is lost, but just like the fire flowers, God brings beautiful things from ashes.

Grief can be difficult during the holidays. The pain of loss has a way of resurfacing when the temperatures cool and the days get shorter.

Philippians 3:14 (NASB) says, "Forgetting what lies behind and reaching forward to what lies ahead, I press on toward the goal for the prize of the upward call of God in Christ Jesus." We will never forget the significance of those lost, but we can press forward to see how God will use the influence of their lives and deaths to make us stronger believers.

Take some time this season to reflect on the unexpected treasures you have found through grief. God has brought you through this trial for your good and His glory. Don't let the sadness blind you to the beautiful display of flowers on your mountain.

Father, the grief in my heart is still tender, but I trust You to work everything together for my good. Open my eyes to see my own personal fire flowers.

HAVE YOURSELF A HOLY LITTLE CHRISTMAS

*Be completely humble and gentle; be patient,
bearing with one another in love.*
EPHESIANS 4:2 NIV

Jesus' birth happened under the humblest of circumstances. The God of heaven and earth, as the carol sings, "laid His glory by." Thomas Watson expounded, "He was born in an inn, and a manger was His cradle, the cobwebs His curtains, the beasts His companions."

Yet as modest as Jesus' birth was, kings came in worship and the heavens sang. It wasn't the pomp and ceremony they admired, but the heart of a God who emptied Himself (Philippians 2:7).

The typical American Christmas has lost that spirit. Rather than a holiday of humble circumstances with a heart of gold, it appears to be more like what Jesus said about the Pharisees—a holiday of whitewashed tombs, beautiful on the outside but full of dead men's bones (Matthew 23:27). What is the point of all the lovely decorations and expensive gifts when they are done out of stress, pressure, and resentment?

This year, let's discipline ourselves to have more than just a merry Christmas, but a holy Christmas. Let's concentrate on the true spirit of Christmas—humility and grace.

Have patience with others as you hurry through the shops. Resolve conflicts graciously and quickly. Be swift to forgive and faithful to admit fault. In all the busyness, don't give the devil a foothold. Continue to pray and meditate on the humiliation Christ endured to save such sinners as us.

*God, in the bustle of this busy season, help me shine the light of Christ
through my actions of patience and humility.*

Mary's Blessing

Count it all joy when you fall into various trials.
James 1:2 nkjv

Amanda tried several times to have a son. One baby boy miscarried; another was stillborn. Finally, after three sisters, a happy, healthy boy arrived. Five years later, he died in a car accident. "Why did God give him to me," Amanda cried, "just to take him away?"

Another young woman named Mary also suffered the death of her son. She was a simple Jewish girl, yet the angel called her "favored by God." Her cousin Elizabeth, filled with the Spirit, declared Mary "blessed among women." At the child's birth, visitors came to worship, and "Mary treasured all these things, pondering them in her heart" (Luke 2:19 nasb). Yet another prophecy was coming. At the temple, while Simeon prophesied over Jesus, he added, "A sword will pierce your own soul" (Luke 2:35 niv).

Mary was blessed among women, favored of God, and yet predestined to suffer. When she witnessed the agony of the crucifixion, did she remember those treasures she had pondered in her heart? Did she question God, crying for relief?

Every biblical hero suffered. The apostle Paul asked God three times to remove his "thorn in the flesh," but God replied, "My grace is sufficient for you, for power is perfected in weakness." Paul concluded, "Therefore I am well content with. . .difficulties, for Christ's sake; for when I am weak, then I am strong" (2 Corinthians 12:9–10 nasb). Perhaps the greatest blessings can only be found on the other side of suffering.

Father, strengthen my faith in the purpose of my sufferings.
Even though my trials are difficult, I will trust You
to work them out for my good.

A WORK IN PROGRESS

*I am confident of this very thing, that He who began
a good work in you will perfect it.*
PHILIPPIANS 1:6 NASB

With each turn in life, whether it's a job change, a new baby, an empty nest, or a major move, you may be asking, "Who am I now?" We all feel disjointed or lost sometimes, but somehow in our desire for calm, we forget that the answer to that question is an ever-changing one.

The words to the old Sunday school song sum it up: "He's still working on me to make me what I ought to be. It took Him just a week to make the moon and the stars, the sun and the earth and Jupiter and Mars. How loving and patient He must be. He's still working on me."

God is not finished defining who you are. Like a child asking, "Are we there yet?" at each new mile, trying to rush the journey is futile. You won't fully know who God created you to be until the end. As John so beautifully expressed, "Beloved, now we are children of God; and it has not yet been revealed what we shall be, but we know that when He is revealed, we shall be like Him, for we shall see Him as He is" (1 John 3:2 NKJV).

So the real question is not "Who am I?" but rather "How is this new stage in my life making me the woman God is calling me to become?"

*Father, help me find beauty in each stage of my life,
knowing that each one is part of Your ultimate plan.*

The Art of Self-Control

But the fruit of the Spirit is. . .self-control.
Galatians 5:22–23 NKJV

The 1960s said, "If it feels good, do it." This generation has added, "Do what you want when you want. Be true to yourself." This belief system has exacerbated our lack of self-control. Look at the data: $240 billion in annual health care costs from obesity, $880.3 billion in credit card debt, a rise in acts of violence.

Paul tells us there is a war between the spirit and the flesh of Christians. "They are in conflict with each other, so that you are not to do whatever you want" (Galatians 5:17 NIV). Each of us is born with a bent to a particular sin. It may be greed, gossip, violence, lust, same-sex sexual activity. . . Denial of those sins is part of the Christian journey. It's not "being fake" or "wearing a mask" to suppress your desires. Denial of sin and self is an authentic method for spiritual growth.

Sam Allberry, a British Anglican minister, openly shared his struggle with same-sex attraction and the benefits of self-denial. "Struggling with sexuality has been an opportunity to experience more of God's grace rather than less," he said. "[What I have learned is] what we give up for Jesus does not compare to what He gives back. . . . But greater than [that] is the opportunity to learn the all-sufficiency of Christ."

In order for a tree to grow and produce more fruit, it must be pruned. What are the areas of struggle where you need to practice self-control?

Dear Lord, show me the areas where I need to set boundaries in my life, and give me the strength to overcome temptation.

GOD IS NOT A "PRIORITY"

Whatever you do or say, do it as a representative of the Lord Jesus.
COLOSSIANS 3:17 NLT

. . . .

If most Christians listed their priorities, they would probably put God at the top, followed by family and friends and then other significant areas. Is that really where God belongs—at the top of a list to be compartmentalized and checked off?

Our relationship with God shouldn't be treated as a priority, but rather as the essence of everything. God should be the center of marriage, parenting, business practices, thought life, television viewing—everything.

Acts 17:28 (NKJV) says, "For in Him we live and move and have our being." Even something as mundane as meal time should be done for God's glory (1 Corinthians 10:31).

When the patriarch Jacob awoke from his dream about angels descending on a ladder, he declared, "Surely the LORD is in this place, and I did not know it" (Genesis 28:16 NKJV). A. W. Tozer commented, "Jacob had never been for one small division of a moment outside of the circle of that all-pervading Presence. But he knew it not. That was his trouble, and it is ours. Men do not know God is here. What a difference it would make if they knew."

God's presence is with you when you buy groceries, drive your car, put your children to sleep. What are you doing to honor Him through these mundane tasks? The time for God is not first thing each morning; it's every minute of every day.

. . . .

Lord, I want everything in my life to be saturated with Your character and Your Word. Teach me to consider You in all my ways.

No Regrets

*Be diligent to present yourself approved to God
as a workman who does not need to be ashamed.*
2 Timothy 2:15 NASB

Bonnie Ware nursed patients in the last twelve weeks of their lives. She recorded their dying epiphanies and compiled this top five list:

1. I wish I'd had the courage to live a life true to myself, not what was expected of me.
2. I wish I hadn't worked so hard.
3. I wish I'd had the courage to express my feelings.
4. I wish I had stayed in touch with my friends.
5. I wish that I had let myself be happier.

God has given us a great gift—life. Some use it well and others waste it.

William Borden was a college freshman when he started a prayer group with three young men. It grew to thirteen hundred by his senior year. He cared for widows, orphans, and drunks, and sought hard souls who needed the Gospel. He later pursued missions to Chinese Muslims, but Borden contracted spinal meningitis and died at age twenty-five. Inside his Bible, he had written: "No reserves. No retreats. No regrets."

In the parable of the sower, the master referred to the one who buried his money as a "wicked servant." But to the one who invested, he said, "Well done." Consider the investment of your life. If today was your last, would you be able to say, "No reserve. No retreats. No regrets"?

*Lord, I want to live my life to its fullest potential in the kingdom
so that when my time comes, I'm ready. Show me how
best to use the time You've given me.*

LESSONS FROM THE PAST

"While I was fainting away, I remembered the LORD."
JONAH 2:7 NASB

. . . .

Corrie Ten Boom once said, "Memories are not the key to the past. They are the key to the future."

This year may have been filled with beautiful nostalgia, or you may have come face-to-face with tragedy. Don't block out the bad memories and avoid the pain; rather, make an assessment of where you are. Consider the devastation of your dreams and seek the parts of you that are still alive.

Just as the farmer's land must be turned over and fertilized to make ready for a new crop, God is using each event in your life to make your heart ready to bear spiritual fruit.

Give thanks for all the blessings—and for suffering. Pray and believe in faith for what God has planned in your future.

For those who have hurt you, consider how you may return a blessing for Christ's sake. For those who have abused their power, pray for them. For those you have offended, seek the best way to make peace and find forgiveness.

Romans 8:28 (NLT) says, "God causes everything to work together for the good of those who love God and are called according to his purpose for them."

When we reflect on our lives, it isn't for the sake of self-pity or shame but to exercise our faith. You will be amazed as you watch God unfold His promises.

. . . .

Father, never let me forget the blessings You have given to me and my family, and bless me with the grace to move beyond the pain that lingers in my past.

RESOLVED: A DECLARATION FOR LIFE

Teach us to realize the brevity of life, so that we may grow in wisdom.
PSALM 90:12 NLT

. . . .

In 2005, the Higher Education Research Institute revealed what was "essential" to college freshmen. Eighty-five percent said their main goal was to get rich, up 43 percent from 1967. Only 45 percent thought developing a meaningful philosophy in life was valuable. That's a 29 percent drop. Now, more than ten years later, those freshmen are teachers, politicians, and media voices.

Jonathan Edwards was the age of a college freshman when he listed sixty-nine resolutions for life, beginning with: "Resolved, that I will do whatever I think to be most to God's glory. . . to do whatever I think to be my duty and most for the good and advantage of mankind in general. . ."

Edwards entered college by age thirteen, graduating as valedictorian. His sermons were essential in the Great Awakening, and he went on to found Princeton College. He lived a full life before he died at age fifty-four.

How have you resolved to live? This New Year's Eve, list out the philosophies you want to guide you. The apostle Paul shared his resolve in Philippians 3:12–14 (NKJV), "Not that I have already attained, or am already perfected; but I press on. . . . I press toward the goal for the prize of the upward call of God in Christ Jesus." This is the kind of resolution that brings everything else into perspective and creates a life well lived.

. . . .

*Lord, I lay my life at Your feet and give You all that I have.
I am resolved to begin this new year with You in the center. Amen.*

Contributor Index

Contributors

Michelle Medlock Adams is an award-winning journalist and bestselling author who lives in Indiana. Her readings can be found in the month of August.

Joanna Bloss is a personal trainer, writer, and student living in the Midwest. She is a coauthor of *Grit for the Oyster: 250 Pearls of Wisdom for Aspiring Authors.* Her readings can be found in the month of September.

Patricia Grau, a Washington resident, is a retired engineer who spends her winters in Florida. Pat's husband, George, went to be with our Lord in 2012. She has four children and ten grandchildren. Her readings can be found in the month of February.

Anita Higman, an award-winning author from Texas, enjoys hiking with her family, visiting caves, and cooking brunch for her friends. Her readings can be found in the month of March.

Marcia Hornok, managing editor of *CHERA Magazine* for widows/ers, raised six children in Salt Lake City, where her husband pastored Midvalley Bible Church. She has numerous publishing credits in periodicals, devotional books, and online. Her readings can be found in the month of October.

Jennifer Vander Klipp, a California native transplanted to the Midwest, navigates the tweens and teens with stepchildren and high-needs kids. She has 15 years experience in publishing, most recently as a managing editor at Zondervan. Her readings can be found in the month of May.

Kristen Larson—In Kristen Larson's own words: "I love my husband, puppies, and most of all, my Lord. He meets me in my honest quest for truth. Published with Barbour. Contributor for Faith Radio Network." Her readings can be found in the month of July.

Emily Marsh lives in Virginia with her husband, Seth, and their various pit bull foster puppies. She works at a downtown real estate firm as a client care coordinator and also teaches ballet in her spare time. Her readings can be found in the month of November.

Sabrina McDonald is the author of *Open the Windows of Heaven* and *The Blessings of Loneliness*, and she is a featured writer for FamilyLife. com. You can follow her blog at www.sabrinamcdonald.com. Her readings can be found in the month of December.

Vickie Phelps lives in East Texas with her husband, Sonny, and their schnauzer, Dobber. She divides her time between family, writing, and church activities. Her readings can be found in the onth of January.

Valorie Quesenberry is a pastor's wife, mother, musician, editor of a Christian women's magazine, and writer. She periodically contributes devotionals to a Christian literature provider. Her first book released with Wesleyan Publishing House in April 2010. Her readings can be found in the month of April.

Jo Russell is a Christian speaker, blogger, long-time author of articles, anthology contributions including several for *Chicken Soup for the Soul*, and award-winning *Which Button Do You Push to Get God to Come Out? A Humorous Devotional for Women*. Her website, www.button-to-god. com features a weekly humorous blog. She lives in northeast Arizona with her husband, Ed. Her readings can be found in the month of June.

SCRIPTURE INDEX